SOCIALIST REALISM
in
LITERATURE
and
ART

A Collection of Articles

PROGRESS PUBLISHERS
Moscow

*Translated from the Russian by C. V. James, Senior Fellow
in Language Studies, University of Sussex*

Designed by O. I. Spiridonova

«СОЦИАЛИСТИЧЕСКИЙ РЕАЛИЗМ В ЛИТЕРАТУРЕ
И ИСКУССТВЕ»

Сборник статей

Составители: Михаил Пархоменко, Александр Мясников

На английском языке

First printing 1971

Printed in the Union of Soviet Socialist Republics

CONTENTS

FOREWORD

In contemporary debates concerning the lines of development of world literature and art a major place is occupied by the question of the inherent logic of the formative processes of socialist art, and the position and role in these processes of the creative method of socialist realism. There was a time when certain critics flatly rejected socialist realism as, allegedly, an artificial product of the personality cult, as a code of laws imposed on art and intrinsically alien to it.

The studies of the half-century history of Soviet literature, art and aesthetics provide a convincing repudiation of such prejudices. Those who have still not completely overcome them might do well to recall what Mikhail Sholokhov once said:

"Whoever wishes to understand what socialist realism is should pay careful attention to the enormous experience Soviet literature has accumulated over almost half a century of its existence. The history of this literature *is* socialist realism, embodied in vivid images of its heroes and in the visual representations of the popular struggle." (Speech at the opening session of the Second Congress of Writers of the RSFSR, March 3, 1965.)

Indeed, a literature whose history is adorned by the names of Maxim Gorky and Vladimir Mayakovsky, Alexei Tolstoi and Mukhtar Auezov, Alexander Fadeyev, Nikolai Ostrovsky and Konstantin Paustovsky and is now represented by Mikhail Sholokhov and Leonid Leonov, Alexander Tvardovsky, Andrei Voznesensky and Eduardas Mieželaitis,

Konstantin Simonov, Valentin Katayev, Chenghiz Aitmatov, Rasul Gamzatov, Kaisyn Kuliyev, Yevgeny Yevtushenko and many other writers and poets known throughout the world—such a literature has no need of condescension: it merits in its own right an acknowledgement of its role in the artistic development of mankind. And to acknowledge this role means to acknowledge that the creative method this literature employs is fruitful.

Nevertheless, numerous attempts are still being made to represent socialist realism as an isolated phenomenon, a trend in the development of world art restricted to the USSR. However, a study of literature and art in countries building socialism, and of progressive trends in literature and art in capitalist countries is gradually dispelling and will undoubtedly dispel this type of delusion and prejudice, be it conscious or unconscious.

And although in each country socialist art develops and will develop in its own specific national way, the universal significance of Soviet experience (the evolution of the new socialist art) is growing and will grow as international cultural relations become broader and ensure deeper mutual enrichment of the national literatures and art of all continents.

The present volume is an attempt to acquaint the foreign reader with articles and opinions of outstanding Soviet writers and literary and art critics concerning socialist realism as an artistic method and its significance in the development of socialist art and literature.

The articles included in this collection present in a sense a history of this creative method; some of them are important steps in its theoretical formulation (articles and pronouncements of Lenin, Gorky, Lunacharsky and Fadeyev) and others contain information about the emergence of socialist realism in literature and other spheres of art—painting, the theatre and the cinema (Kagan, Freilikh, and others). The final section of the volume contains articles characterising socialist realism as a logical stage in the development of world literature and art.

The compilers were guided by a desire to give the reader as varied a picture as possible of socialist realism as an innovatory creative method, adopted by contemporary art and showing it the path to follow.

* * *

The twentieth century is the age of the struggle for socialism and the assertion of socialism. It is the century of social and scientific and technological revolutions. Writers reflecting faithfully the complicated evolution of the new era and, at the same time, aspiring to take part in the moulding of the new man, have been faced with unheard-of problems.

By the end of the nineteenth century socialism had already forcefully compelled the attention of major authors. Zola, France, Romain Rolland and many others responded to this call of history, sometimes completely unexpected by the writer himself. Remarkable in this connection is Henrik Ibsen's confession: "I simply expressed my own astonishment," he said as early as 1890, "that having taken as my life's work the task of portraying the character and fate of men, I came—in the process of working out certain problems—quite unconsciously and unintentionally to precisely the same conclusions as social-democratic moralist philosophers had reached by scientific research."[1] And it was not only Ibsen who was affected by that process. To some degree all great realists in literature and art reflected the progress of mankind towards gigantic social transformations. Many artists, while pondering over the further development of art, found themselves confronted with questions whose solution demanded basic changes in their creative methods and which, as time was to tell, could be solved only by socialist realism.

In the early years following the Great October Socialist Revolution, Lenin—the mighty architect of the new society —used to say that the land of Soviets must produce a truly new, great, communist art that would create a form corresponding to its content. In the half-century of its history, Soviet art has justified this prediction.

The search for new aesthetic principles of revolutionary art began immediately after the October Revolution. This search was most intensive and fruitful in literature, which at first was undoubtedly ahead of other forms of art in accumulating experience.

What should be the nature of the new literature and its attitude to the traditions of pre-October literature? This was

---

[1] Henrik Ibsen, *Collected Works*, Iskusstvo Publishers, Vol. 4, 1958, p. 727 (Russian translation).

the first question posed to the writers by the October Revolution.

The first steps of Russian literature after October, the first years of its development, were characterised by an intense search for new aesthetic principles, by contradictory processes of formation of a new creative method and by the appearance of its new features. This all took place in conditions of a tense and bitter ideological struggle, which further complicated the aesthetic quests of the writers, literary groups and trends of the time. The new was born in torment, and the newly emerging world had not yet taken shape. It was hardly surprising that it took the writer quite a time to free himself from the bonds of the past, to accept the new, and make up his mind to serve it actively by artistic means.

However, it must be said that the new art (including literature) based on aesthetic principles illuminated by the ideals of revolution and socialism was created not so much by "old" writers shaking off the burden of the past and breaking with the ideology of the old world as by new forces, awakened and summoned to creative work by the revolution itself.

But "old" and young writers alike felt that literature could not remain as it had been on the eve of October. "We must speak of the new in words that are new," affirmed Mayakovsky. "We need a new form in art."[1] But what was this to be? How and what should they write? The answers to these questions had still to be found.

At first many believed that a new art could arise only on the ruins of the old, only as the antithesis and antipode of the pre-revolutionary art which must be destroyed with the same decisiveness and uncompromising finality with which the revolution had destroyed the old social order and demolished the machinery of government.

The most zealous advocates of the complete destruction of pre-revolutionary art announced in one of their declarations: "It is obvious that a new, proletarian art is possible only on the ruins of the old, bourgeois art."[2] In accord with

---

[1] *Iskusstvo kommuny* (The Art of the Commune), a newspaper, 1918, No. 4.
[2] *Semafor u maibutne* (Semaphore to the Future), a collection, Kharkov, 1922.

such a programme they published an anthology *The Catafalque of Art* (Kharkov, 1922). The proponents of the destruction of "bourgeois" art were uncompromising in their rejection of all its traditions. "If anyone is worried," they wrote, "that proletarian writers make no attempt to fill the gap between the new art and the old, we may say to them— so much the better; we have no need of succession."[1]

But the Party and the Soviet Government viewed differently the problem of cultural succession. On one occasion Lenin formulated this viewpoint thus: "We shall be unable to solve this problem [the creation of a proletarian culture— *Ed.*] unless we clearly realise that only a precise knowledge and transformation of the culture created by the entire development of mankind will enable us to create a proletarian culture."[2] Lenin ridiculed various "abolishers" and said that artists should not "turn away from the really beautiful ... simply because it is 'old' ", but take it as "a point of departure for further development".

The attitudes of literary workers developed along this line, and the "destructive" ideas soon lost their popularity.

But it would be an oversimplification of the historical literary process to think that realism was immediately selected as the method of the new, revolutionary art from all the multitude of creative methods and literary tendencies. Far from it: not only the extravagantly inclined representatives of modernist tendencies, but even theoreticians remarkable for an almost academic respectability at first gave preference to other methods. Thus in one of the early post-revolutionary manifestos one could read: "We consider Impressionism and Futurism to be the most outstanding forms of contemporary art, the former for the presentation of the psychological-subjective, the latter of the objective-collective in art."[3] As for realism, one critic wrote, "In the arena of the new art it looks like an old, worn-out boot, accidentally left by some slovenly decorator against the background of a glowing sky at sunrise."[4]

Such declarations were usually supported by the practical

---

[1] *Gryadushcheye* (The Future), a journal, Petrograd, 1918, No. 3, p. 3.
[2] Lenin, *Collected Works*, Vol. 31, p. 287.
[3] "The Grono Manifesto", Grono, Kharkov, 1920.
[4] *Shlyakhi mistetstva* (Paths of Art), Kharkov, 1921, No. 1, p. 35.

work of writers and even some literary organisations united under the slogan of "the struggle for the art of the revolution".

The discordant modernist clamour, however, could not drown realism in literature, because many writers who had entered the new era from pre-revolutionary times remained faithful to realism, and above all because it became more and more apparent that realism was best able to give the fullest expression to the ideas of revolution and socialism in art. Although the first reactions to the October Revolution (and these include Alexander Blok's poem *The Twelve*) were predominantly romantic in character, it was proclaimed as early as 1918 that the future course of literature would be that of realism.[1] Critical works of the twenties gave increasing numbers of definitions of the basic style (an expression used to signify what is now referred to as creative method) which unfailingly stressed the realistic roots of Soviet revolutionary literature—"heroic realism", "proletarian artistic realism", "romantic realism", "the new realistic school", "monumental realism".

All this was not simply declarations or quests of theoreticians but a reflection of the basic tendency of literary development. Realism asserted itself in works of art. In 1924 Anatoly Lunacharsky was already able to say: "What we were waiting for, what we called upon you to produce, has come about—an all-embracing realist literature." "Our new realist school," he remarked a year later, "is scaling new heights."[2]

It is quite natural that the realist line should have become the main line of development of Soviet literature after the revolution. An explanation for this should be sought in literary traditions of realism and, more important still, in its conformity to the ideas of the socialist revolution and the needs of the working classes liberated by it.

Long before the revolution, socialist ideas had already enriched realism. But in the conditions following the October Revolution, when the working people had begun to build a socialist society, the ideas of socialism found absolutely new expression in the aesthetic ideal of literature, and this in

---

[1] *Proletarsky Sbornik* (Proletarian Collection), Book 1, Moscow, 1918, p. 3.
[2] A. Lunacharsky, Introduction to the collection *Styk* (Link), Moscow, 1925, p. 5.

turn, could not but change the principles of the realistic method itself.

In pre-revolutionary conditions the realist proletarian art showed its socialist nature in a new artistic vision of the world, which reflected the struggle of the working class for socialist ideals. But the novelty of socialist art and the fundamental changes in the principles of the realistic method were to become fully visible only after the revolution, when the ideal became the object of practical realisation and the aim and result of the daily creative activity of society. Realism was enriched by new methods of modelling, in artistic images, of the socio-historical process viewed as a realisation of the ideal in social life and in the consciousness of the builders of socialism and communism.[1] In that period the new qualities of art became well defined. They were formulated most clearly by Gorky, when he remarked on the great role of the life-asserting principle of socialist realism in literature (whose other task is that of criticising all that opposes the ideas of socialism or hinders their realisation), when he postulated the very possibility of the appearance of the new creative method as depending on the very "fact of socialist experience of the proletariat" and, finally, when by defining some of the principles of socialist realism, he was able to pinpoint the most important, if not all, aspects of the new creative method.[2]

The emergence of art of socialist realism on the basis of the revolutionary ideals and the struggle of the proletariat was as logical a development as the adoption by Soviet art of the socialist realist method as its leading method after the victory of the socialist revolution. The logic of this has been confirmed by the experience and successes of Soviet literature.

But this logical development, which found concrete expression in the works of new revolutionary writers and of those representatives of the critical school and other artistic movements who adopted socialist realism, did not come about at once. Konstantin Fedin spoke about this a short while ago: "The principles of the artist's approach to

---

[1] For further details see Moisei Kagan's article "The Formation and Development of Socialist Art", included in this volume.

[2] See Gorky's article "On Socialist Realism" and his other articles in this collection.

the presentation of reality in works of art have taken years to mature. Literary experience and the achievements of talented writers have provided the material for the building of the Soviet artistic world. Marxism and the revolutionary genius of Lenin have inspired the theoreticians and critics, expecting them to generalise ideologically the new phenomena of Soviet art and determine what they have in common with the artistic heritage and what makes them quite specific. In this way the foundation of the ideological and artistic outlook—the method of socialist realism—was laid down in literature."[1]

Socialist realism is a complicated and many-sided phenomenon. Obviously at the root of every artistic method lies a definite concept of mankind, a concept of reality and the attitude of art towards reality. In socialist realism such a concept is basically new.

Some writers in the bourgeois world regard history as a fearful chaos of struggle between unknowable forces. They work under the feeling of alienation, fear, and sometimes mystical terror. For them the historical process is a movement of strange forces hostile to people, a fatal process which they are powerless to influence.

However, one of the most remarkable outcomes of Marxism-Leninism is the fact that it has changed the ordinary man's view of history and the present. The classics of Marxism-Leninism showed that there are definite historical laws, that these laws can be defined, and that by relying on the logic of these laws man can influence the course of history. This discovery has wrought a tremendous change in the psychology of mankind. People have come to feel themselves powerful and mighty. They have acquired a sense of historical optimism.

This sense of historical optimism is inherent in the best characters of the art and literature of socialist realism. They are imbued with a desire to make history, and are in fact making it. They look upon the world with the eyes of masters and builders, who have set themselves the aim of transforming the world for the happiness of man and of making the Earth "the beautiful habitat of mankind, united in one family" (Maxim Gorky).

---

[1] Speech at the Plenum of the Central Committee of the Communist Party of the Soviet Union, June 19-21, 1963. Stenographic report, 1964, p. 243. See the full text of the speech in this collection.

In our times these innovatory qualities of socialist realism are of special value.

In the course of his development man has discovered not only the constructive but also the destructive forces. The progress of the technological and social revolution has posed before the modern world the problem of its very existence, and this has already given rise to pessimistic conceptions of the future, of mankind doomed to self-destruction.

In view of all this one is impelled to ask whether a genuinely humane art can reconcile itself to such conceptions, confine itself within the narrow limits of aestheticism and, moreover, preach indifference to reality and the social struggle. In our era we have particular need of an art that fosters an active attitude towards the world, an art that reveals the truth and affirms that the fate of man and the life of contemporary generations depend on people themselves. Precisely in this is expressed the highest degree of humanism in present-day art.

Of course art must give man joy and pleasure. But this must not be epicurian pleasure that weakens the will; it must be enjoyment that teaches people to love beauty, fight for it and increase the beautiful on Earth. Such is the broad programme of contemporary art which alone can make art rich and ensure man's respect for it.

There can be no doubt that for the optimism of its conception of the individual, history and reality, socialist realist art is indebted to the Marxist-Leninist outlook which is the philosophical basis of its creative method.

This outlook is the greatest asset of socialist realist artists. The experience of the fifty years of Soviet literature shows that the progressive outlook has always enabled the artist to discover and bring out social truth. But it should not be forgotten that a progressive outlook does not replace talent; it simply makes it more perceptive.

In 1905 Lenin wrote an article "Party Organisation and Party Literature".[1] The views he expressed there on the significance of a progressive outlook and partisanship in art became fundamental for socialist realist aesthetics. Georgi Kunitsyn's article "Lenin on Partisanship and Freedom of Creativity" is a study of these views and is included in the

---

[1] See pp. 22-27 of the present volume.

collection. All we wish to do here is to highlight one or two features of Lenin's work. Defining the principle of partisanship, Lenin pointed out that literature was first of all a part of the general proletarian cause linked with its other parts: politics, philosophy, ethics, etc., but, at the same time literature had its own peculiarities.

Lenin repeatedly stressed that literature was a special form of social awareness. For instance, in a letter to Inessa Armand, Lenin spoke of the difference between the publicistic characterisation of "class types" and their portrayal in art "because there the whole *essence* is in the *individual* circumstances, the analysis of the *characters* and psychology of *particular* types".[1]

Lenin's teaching on partisanship in art was directed both against bourgeois objectivism, which was the philosophical bastion of the naturalist theories, and against bourgeois subjectivism, which was the philosophical basis of many of the modernist schools.

Theoreticians of naturalism in the second half of the nineteenth century and today have been trying to show that they completely exclude the subjective factor from art and that their function is to portray life precisely as it is in reality, without adding any personal touch or fancy. In other words, life dictates, and they simply make a faithful record of what is dictated. Therefore, according to the naturalists, science and art should neither condemn nor stimulate, but simply portray and explain. Lenin's works reveal that such ideas are illusory.

Whereas the naturalists prostrate themselves before reality, representatives of many a modernist school have transferred all their attention to the artist. They are interested not in reality but in the way it influences the artist. They talk a great deal about the specificity of art and the right of the artist to reshape reality. The modernists believe that the function of art is to reflect not the existing world but the vagaries of the artist's soul. Lenin's works demonstrate the poverty of that aesthetic conception.

The Leninist principle of partisanship in art is the path to truth. The artist relying on this principle portrays reality more faithfully than the bourgeois objectivist, for he aspires to comprehend the laws of social development and does not

---

[1] Lenin, *Collected Works*, Vol. 35, p. 184.

shrink from taking part in social struggle. Such an artist defends the most progressive ideas and represents the most progressive class.

But, we repeat, a progressive outlook is no substitute for talent, which is the first requirement for creating a significant work of art. A progressive outlook makes talent more perspicacious, arms it with a true understanding of reality and aids it to portray reality faithfully in works of art.

It is from the same point of view that the artist should consider the significance of the creative method. The method becomes his aesthetic platform and, in particular, the basis of his understanding of the point and purpose of his work. It, too, is no substitute for talent, and it is certainly not a collection of recipes for creative work. It is appropriate to recall what Konstantin Fedin said at the Second Congress of Writers: "They expect us to provide them with recipes!... Art is not made to recipes."[1] One can make a thorough *study* of *Don Quixote*, but this will not tell him *how to produce* anything as great, for a real work of art is always a discovery and an invention.

Talent, or the artist's mastery, consists of two components: the ability to study and comprehend reality, and the art of translating his impressions into works of art.

Talent is a rarity, said Lenin. Talent is to be trusted, for it is perspicacious and enables the talented to see further and deeper than the untalented. All this is true. Many have written about it. But one cannot rely simply on native talent. The direction of talent is also a kind of talent.

Gorky was always calling on writers to undertake a persistent and systematic study of life. At the same time he was a merciless enemy of writers who were the slaves of reality, oppressed by its complications and contradictions, and who regarded precise, almost documentary description of life as the sole aim of art. "As silly as fact," was Balzac's aphorism that Gorky loved to repeat.

In combating naturalistic and subjectivist tendencies Gorky laid constant and sometimes excessive stress on the role of the subjective factor in art, thus opposing the countless theoreticians who, in the twenties expressed a distrust of artistic fantasy. There is nothing beautiful in nature,

---

[1] Second All-Union Congress of Soviet Writers. Stenographic record, 1965, pp. 501-02 (Russ. ed.).

Gorky used to announce categorically at the time; the beautiful is created by man. There is more beauty in a volume of Pushkin's verse or in a novel by Flaubert than in the icy twinkling of the stars or the mechanical rhythm of the ocean waves. John Ruskin was profoundly right when he said that the English sunsets became more beautiful after Turner had painted them. In another work of that period Gorky wrote that Levitan did not discover the beauty of the Russian landscape, but introduced it as his own human gift to Nature. Gorky was apparently himself aware of the inadequacy of his formulations and admitted that he was wrong in some way, but that he erred on the side of the idea that was especially dear to him—the idea of the active role of the artist in the world. What is, then, the place of the artist? The writer, Gorky wrote in 1927, must not become dissolved in reality (as the naturalist does), nor stand apart from it (which many modernists advocated), but raise above it, be its master.

For Gorky, therefore, works of art were not the reflection of the existing world plus the inner world of the artist; they were something different, a new world produced by impressions of real life processed in the artist's creative laboratory.

Art has frequently been compared with a mirror. The inaccuracy of this comparison was noticed even by the nineteenth century classicists: a mirror presents a cold reflection of whatever stands before it, but art always selects, analyses and reshapes reality in order to penetrate more deeply into its essence.

Socialist realist art is not restricted to a clarification of truth; it asserts truth and strives to ensure its domination in life. In this it follows the best traditions of critical realist art. In the mid-nineteenth century Chernyshevsky wrote about the aims of art: "Portrayal of life is a general characteristic of art and comprises its very essence; but works of art often fulfil another mission—they explain life. In many cases they pronounce *judgement* on the phenomena of life."[1]

"Judgement" in this case is understood as the right to condemn or approve various phenomena of life. Thus the aesthetics of critical realism embraced both a critical and an assertive principles in art.

---

[1] N. G. Chernyshevsky, *Collected Works*, Vol. 3, Moscow, 1949, p. 92 (Russ. ed.).

What place is occupied by these principles in the aesthetics of socialist realism, and which is predominant?

In their first definitions of the new method Gorky and other writers laid great stress on the assertive principle, sometimes contrasting socialist realism to critical realism in which the critical element had pride of place. At the First Congress of Writers in 1934, however, Fadeyev warned against a too literal interpretation of Gorky's words, pointing out that socialist realism not only asserted the new forms of social relations but at the same time was the most critical type of realism.

Many historians, sociologists, writers and philosophers speak of the complexity of society's life in the twentieth century. What social perceptiveness, analytical daring one therefore needs if he is not to give way before this complexity and not to be lost in it! We often admire the boldness with which an author reveals the seamy sides of life or his insight when he feels the musty smell of inevitable decay where others only see life full of vigour. But even greater daring is required if one is to have a look into the future and discover what is to come. In both cases a deep analysis of social life is needed. Socialist realism welds together the assertive, critical and analytical principles, with the result that an excessive stress on any one of them cripples the method.

The unity of these elements in socialist realism does not remove the problem of their balanced interrelationship.

For the socialist realist writer there are, of course, no taboo subjects. But he must not forget his responsibility to the people. He must not and cannot pour salt on a wound simply to see a man tremble with pain. He must, if he is to be true and objective, possess a sense of history, be able to see the scale of the events he depicts and the place of the fact he describes in the general system of other facts.

Socialist reality—the struggle for the practical achievement of communist ideals—has created a new type of artist, an active social worker, citizen and fighter. He takes part in the struggle for the minds and hearts of millions; he works to uphold the main ideological principle of Soviet literature —devotion to Party and people. For such a writer artistic freedom is something quite different from what it is for the bourgeois writer.[1]

---

[1] For further details see Georgi Kunitsyn's article in this collection.

In the capitalist world the writer frequently feels himself to be an outsider. The typical image of the artist in the imperialist epoch was the "superfluous man", standing outside society, a heretic, often something of a bohemian, almost always a rebel and often a man who despised life and the people around him. Many artists in capitalist society sincerely believed that in order to protect their artistic immunity they must stand apart from the mainstream of life. The English writer, Arnold Kettle, has described such an attitude, and his words contain much bitter truth.

In the socialist world the relationship between the writer and society has radically changed. In socialist society the government is *his* government, and the writer often sits in parliament and takes part in the making of important government decisions. He plays a direct part in moulding the spiritual culture of his people. He himself changes the world. Indeed, the highest praise that can be given to the writer was expressed in the words of Gorky when, having read Leonov's novel *Sot,* he said that the author knew reality as well as if he had himself created it. The builders of an invisible fortress, the fortress of the soul of the people, was what Alexei Tolstoi called Soviet writers in the bitter years of the Great Patriotic War.

The image of the new man, our contemporary, is the greatest achievement of Soviet literature and the most graphic expression of its innovatory quality. It embodies the spiritual and moral beauty of Soviet man, the builder of socialism and communism. At the same time it expresses national self-awareness, the moral and aesthetic ideal of the Soviet peoples.

The positive hero of Soviet literature is not always the "ideal" hero, but he tends towards the ideal by developing the better sides of his character and spiritual outlook. This is the logic of such development, which is not unhindered, but full of contradictions and accompanied by flights and falls.

The beauty of the positive hero is revealed not only in his definite ideal qualities but also in the process of their shaping accompanied by inner struggle and the triumph of sound, progressive forces and tendencies over everything that hinders or might hinder their victory. Such are the best heroes of Dmitry Furmanov, Alexander Fadeyev, Nikolai Ostrovsky, and many other Soviet writers.

The fine traits of the positive hero, evinced not only in his thoughts, but also in his deeds, and the very process of his development give the reader the most convincing evidence of the possibility of a similar course for himself. In this lies the "secret" of the educative power of the positive hero, the educative aspect of his impact upon the reader. In this way Soviet literature takes part in the formation of the man of a communist society.

* * *

We have only dwelt on one or two aspects of the formation of socialist realism and on its major principles, which bring out most clearly the essence and innovatory quality of this creative method in literature and art, and also in literary and art criticism.

We should add only that the aesthetics of socialist realism acknowledges the existence of objective laws in art and the possibility of their cognition, and that, while stressing the specificity of these laws, it does not oppose them to other laws of social life, but makes an effort to study their interaction and influence on each other. This is what makes socialist realist aesthetics so viable.

In its postulates and conclusions it relies on the following principles: (1) art reflects actual reality and lends an attentive ear to the "language of the subject" it portrays, to use Marx's expression; (2) an artist possessing talent and having a definite world outlook is not a passive medium who can only listen to and transfer what life gives him ("the dictation of reality", as György Lukács put it), he creatively reproduces and reshapes what he sees, comparing the existing reality with his ideal of it; (3) reproduction in art is not mere copying or imitation but a special "aesthetic actuality" (Herzen, Winkelmann), a means of studying, understanding and transforming life; (4) a work of art is genuine only when it reveals to men something new, enriches their emotions, mind and will, and evokes the artist in them.

The basic principles of socialist realism are sufficiently general to give art unlimited scope for revealing all its peculiarities as a definite form of man's spiritual activity. This is very convincingly proved by the experience of Soviet art. The existence of one creative method common to all national literatures and all Soviet writers and artists, does not exclude the development of specific national styles, the appearance of numerous stylistic schools and the diversity of individual manner in all genres of literature and art. Socialist realism, run the Rules of the Union of Soviet Writers, "affords the writers every opportunity of exercising creative freedom and initiative with regard to content and form and of displaying individual talents, it also presupposes richness and variety of artistic means and styles and promotes innovation in all branches of art."

The contributions to this volume by Nikolai Okhlopkov, Pavel Korin, Semyon Freilikh and several other writers provide ample evidence that the article of the Rules cited above has been confirmed in practice during the fifty years of development of the multinational Soviet art and of all national literatures comprising one single Soviet literature.

* * *

Lenin spoke of the necessity to create an art that would be accessible and intelligible to the masses, and which they would love. One of the most significant aspects of the revolution is that it opened up the possibility of creating such an art, taught people to understand literature, and provided them with every opportunity to display their artistic talents and participate in the creation of such a literature and such an art.

Fifty years of history have given convincing proof of the significance of Soviet literature and art in the spiritual life of the people and also of the fruitfulness of the creative method of socialist realism. The treasure store of Soviet art and literature is growing enriched by works that have played an outstanding role in the ideological and aesthetic education of many generations of Soviet people; they have given and continue to give the reader the joy of communion with the world of beauty and truth, moulding their aesthetic ideals in the spirit of communism. We may cite Mikhail Sholokhov's novels *And Quiet Flows the Don* and *Virgin Soil Upturned,* Nikolai Ostrovsky's *How the Steel Was Tempered,* Alexander Fadeyev's *The Rout* and *The Young Guard,* Leonid Leonov's *The Russian Forest,* Anton Makarenko's *The Road to Life,* Boris Polevoi's *Story About a Real Man,* Alexander Tvardovsky's *Vasily Tyorkin* and *Distance Beyond Distance,* Chenghis Aitmatov's stories, and plays by Konstantin Trenyov and Nikolai Pogodin; these are all works that played such an important part in the spiritual development of the Soviet peoples that we may consider their appearance not only as landmarks in the history of literature, but as important events in the whole spiritual history of Soviet society.

Interest in the best works of Soviet literature abroad, the formation of socialist art and literature in other socialist countries, the influence of Soviet literature and art on the most progressive tendencies in literature and art of many countries of the world, the triumphant success of Soviet musicians, song and dance companies, ballet and theatre in tours abroad—all this is evidence of the significance of the October Revolution for the history of world artistic culture. At the same time all this brings one to the logical conclusion that the creative method of socialist realism was bound to appear and become a new and fruitful stage in the artistic development of mankind.[1]

The influence of the socialist school on the development of world art is growing irresistibly. And this means, as Soviet scholars have correctly pointed out, that revolutionary ideology is making incredibly wide inroads in literature; indeed, a great artistic revolution is in progress, with beneficial results that can scarcely be overstated.

Mikhail Parkhomenko and Alexander Myasnikov

---

[1] For further details see the article "Socialist Realism and the Artistic Development of Mankind" in this collection, pp. 232-50.

V. I. Lenin

PARTY ORGANISATION AND PARTY LITERATURE

The new conditions for Social-Democratic work in Russia which have arisen since the October revolution[1] have brought the question of party literature to the fore. The distinction between the illegal and the legal press, that melancholy heritage of the epoch of feudal, autocratic Russia, is beginning to disappear. It is not yet dead, by a long way. The hypocritical government of our Prime Minister is still running amuck, so much so that *Izvestia Soveta Rabochikh Deputatov*[2] is printed "illegally"; but apart from bringing disgrace on the government, apart from striking further moral blows at it, nothing comes of the stupid attempts to "prohibit" that which the government is powerless to thwart.

So long as there was a distinction between the illegal and the legal press, the question of party and non-party press was decided extremely simply and in an extremely false and abnormal way. The entire illegal press was party press, being published by organisations and run by groups which in one way or another were linked with groups of practical party workers. The entire legal press was non-party—since parties were banned—but it "gravitated" towards one party or another. Unnatural alliances, strange "bed-fellows" and false cover-devices were inevitable. The forced reserve of

---

[1] The October revolution of 1905.—*Ed.*

[2] *Bulletin of the Soviet of Workers' Deputies*, an official newspaper of the St. Petersburg Soviet of Workers' Deputies. It appeared from October 17 to December 14, 1905. It had no permanent staff and was printed by the workers themselves in the printing works of various bourgeois papers. Its last, eleventh, issue was seized by the police while being printed.—*Ed.*

those who wished to express party views merged with the immature thinking or mental cowardice of those who had not risen to these views and who were not, in effect, party people.

An accursed period of Aesopian language, literary bondage, slavish speech, and ideological serfdom! The proletariat has put an end to this foul atmosphere which was stifling everything living and fresh in Russia. But so far the proletariat has won only half freedom for Russia.

The revolution is not yet completed. While tsarism is *no longer* strong enough to defeat the revolution, the revolution is *not yet* strong enough to defeat tsarism. And we are living in times when everywhere and in everything there operates this unnatural combination of open, forthright, direct and consistent party spirit with an underground, covert, "diplomatic" and shifty "legality". This unnatural combination makes itself felt even in our newspaper: for all Mr. Guchkov's witticisms about Social-Democratic tyranny forbidding the publication of moderate liberal-bourgeois newspapers, the fact remains that *Proletary*, the Central Organ of the Russian Social-Democratic Labour Party, still remains outside the locked doors of *autocratic*, police-ridden Russia.

Be that as it may, the half-way revolution compels all of us to set to work at once organising the whole thing on new lines. Today literature, even that published "legally", can be nine-tenths party literature. It must become party literature. Contrary to bourgeois customs, to the profit-making, commercialised bourgeois press, to bourgeois literary careerism and individualism, "aristocratic anarchism" and the drive for profit, the socialist proletariat must put forward the principle of *party literature*, must develop this principle and put it into practice as fully and completely as possible.

What is this principle of party literature? It is not simply that, for the socialist proletariat, literature cannot be a means of enriching individuals or groups; it cannot, in fact, be an individual undertaking, independent of the common cause of the proletariat. Down with non-partisan writers! Down with literary supermen! Literature must become *part* of the common cause of the proletariat, "a cog and a screw" of one single great Social-Democratic mechanism set in motion by the entire politically-conscious vanguard of the entire working class. Literature must become a component of organised, planned and integrated Social-Democratic Party work.

"All comparisons are lame," says a German proverb. So is my comparison of literature with a cog, of a living movement with a mechanism. And I daresay there will always be hysterical intellectuals to raise a howl about such a comparison, which degrades, deadens, "bureaucratises" the free battle of ideals, freedom of criticism, freedom of literary creation, etc., etc. Such outcries, in point of fact, would be nothing more than an expression of bourgeois-intellectual individualism. There is no question that literature is least of all subject to mechanical adjustment or levelling, to the rule of the majority over the minority. There is no question, either, that in this field greater scope must undoubtedly be allowed for personal initiative, individual inclination, thought and fantasy, form and content. All this is undeniable; but all this simply shows that the literary side of the proletarian party cause cannot be mechanically identified with its other sides. This, however, does not in the least refute the proposition, alien and strange to the bourgeoisie and bourgeois democracy, that literature must by all means and necessarily become an element of Social-Democratic Party work, inseparably bound up with the other elements. Newspapers must become the organs of the various party organisations, and their writers must by all means become members of these organisations. Publishing and distributing centres, bookshops and reading-rooms, libraries and similar establishments must all be under party control. The organised socialist proletariat must keep an eye on all this work, supervise it in its entirety, and, from beginning to end, without any exception, infuse into it the life-stream of the living proletarian cause, thereby cutting the ground from under the old, semi-Oblomov,[1] semi-trader's Russian principle: the writer does the writing, the reader does the reading.

We are not suggesting, of course, that this transformation of literary work, which has been defiled by the Asiatic censorship and the European bourgeoisie, can be accomplished all at once. Far be it from us to advocate any kind

---

[1] *Oblomov*—a landowner, the main character in a novel of the same title by the Russian writer Ivan Goncharov. Oblomov personifies routine, stagnation and incapacity for action.—*Ed.*

24

of standardised system, or a solution by means of a few decrees. Cut-and-dried schemes are least of all applicable here. What is needed is that the whole of our Party, and the entire politically-conscious Social-Democratic proletariat throughout Russia, should become aware of this new problem, define it clearly and everywhere set about solving it. Emerging from the captivity of the feudal censorship, we have no desire to become, and shall not become, prisoners of bourgeois-trader literary relations. We want to establish, and we shall establish, a free press, free not simply from the police, but also from capital, from careerism, and what is more, free from bourgeois-anarchist individualism.

These last words may sound paradoxical, or an affront to the reader. What! some intellectual, an ardent champion of liberty, may shout. What, you want to impose collective control on such a delicate, individual matter as literary work! You want workmen to decide questions of science, philosophy, or aesthetics by a majority of votes! You deny the absolute freedom of absolutely individual ideological work!

Calm yourselves, gentlemen! First of all, we are discussing party literature and its subordination to party control. Everyone is free to write and say whatever he likes, without any restrictions. But every voluntary association (including the party) is also free to expel members who use the name of the party to advocate anti-party views. Freedom of speech and the press must be absolute, but so must the freedom of association. I am bound to accord you, in the name of free speech, the full right to shout, lie and write to your heart's content. But you are bound to grant me, in the name of freedom of association, the right to enter into, or withdraw from, association with people advocating this or that view. The party is a voluntary association, which would inevitably break up, first ideologically and then physically, if it did not cleanse itself of people advocating anti-party views. And to define the border-line between party and anti-party there is the party programme, the party's resolutions on tactics and its rules and, lastly, the entire experience of international Social-Democracy, the voluntary international associations of the proletariat, which has constantly brought into its parties individual elements and trends not fully consistent, not completely Marxist and not altogether correct and which, on the other hand, has constantly conducted periodical "cleansings" of its ranks. So it will be with us too, supporters of bourgeois "freedom of criticism", *within* the Party. We are now becoming a mass party all at once, changing abruptly to an open organisation, and it is inevitable that we shall be joined by many who are inconsistent (from the Marxist standpoint), perhaps we shall be joined even by some Christian elements, and even by some mystics. We have sound stomachs and we are rock-like Marxists. We shall digest those inconsistent elements. Freedom of thought and freedom of criticism within the Party will never make us forget about the freedom of organising people into those voluntary associations known as parties.

Secondly, we must say to you, bourgeois individualists, that your talk about absolute freedom is sheer hypocrisy. There can be no real and effective "freedom" in a society based on the power of money, in a society in which the masses of working people live in poverty and a handful of rich men live like parasites. Are you free in relation to your bourgeois publisher, Mr. Writer, in relation to your bourgeois public, which demands that you provide it with pornography in frames[1] and paintings, and prostitution as a "supplement" to "sacred" scenic art? This absolute freedom is a bourgeois or an anarchist phrase (since, as a world outlook, anarchism is bourgeois philosophy turned inside out). One cannot live in society and be free from society. The freedom of the bourgeois writer, artist or actress is simply masked (or hypocritically masked) dependence on the money-bag, on corruption, on prostitution.

And we socialists expose this hypocrisy and rip off the false labels, not in order to arrive at a non-class literature and art (that will be possible only in a socialist non-class society), but to contrast this hypocritically free literature, which is in reality linked with the bourgeoisie, with a really free one that will be *openly* linked with the proletariat.

It will be a free literature, because the idea of socialism and sympathy with the working people, and not greed or careerism, will bring ever new forces to its ranks. It will be a free literature, because it will serve, not some satiated heroine, not the bored "upper ten thousand" suffering from fatty degeneration, but the millions and tens of millions of

---

[1] There must be a misprint in the source, which says *ramkakh* (frames), while the context suggests *romanakh* (novels).—*Ed.*

working people—the flower of the country, its strength and its future. It will be a free literature, enriching the last word in the revolutionary thought of mankind with the experience and living work of the socialist proletariat, bringing about permanent interaction between the experience of the past (scientific socialism, the completion of the development of socialism from its primitive, utopian forms) and the experience of the present (the present struggle of the worker comrades).

To work, then, comrades! We are faced with a new and difficult task. But it is a noble and grateful one—to organise a broad, multiform and varied literature inseparably linked with the Social-Democratic working-class movement. All Social-Democratic literature must become Party literature. Every newspaper, journal, publishing house, etc., must immediately set about reorganising its work, leading up to a situation in which it will, in one form or another, be integrated into one Party organisation or another. Only then will "Social-Democratic" literature really become worthy of that name, only then will it be able to fulfil its duty and, even within the framework of bourgeois society, break out of bourgeois slavery and merge with the movement of the really advanced and thoroughly revolutionary class.

Printed on November 13, 1905   Lenin, *On Literature and Art,* Moscow, 1967, pp. 22-27

LENIN ABOUT THE ART OF A NEW WORLD

Excerpts from the book *On Literature and Art*

"...Spectacles are not really great art. I would sooner call them more or less attractive entertainment. Nor should we be oblivious of the fact that our workers and peasants bear no resemblance to the Roman lumpen proletariat. They are not maintained at state expense but on the contrary they themselves maintain the state by their labour. They 'made' the revolution and upheld its cause, shedding torrents of their blood and bearing untold sacrifice. Indeed, our workers and peasants deserve something better than spectacles. They are entitled to real great art. This is why we put foremost public education and training on the biggest scale. It creates a basis for culture, provided of course that the grain problem has been solved. On this basis a really new, great, communist art should arise which will create a form in correspondence with its content" (pp. 253-54).

———

"But our opinion on art is not the important thing. Nor is it of much consequence what art means to a few hundred or even thousand out of a population counted by the millions. Art belongs to the people. Its roots should be deeply implanted in the very thick of the labouring masses. It should be understood and loved by these masses. It must unite and elevate their feelings, thoughts and will. It must stir to activity and develop the art instincts within them. Should we serve exquisite sweet cake to a small minority while the worker and peasant masses are in need of black bread? It goes without saying that the following is to be understood

28

not only literally but also figuratively: we must always have before our eyes the workers and the peasants" (pp. 250-51).

———

"For art to get closer to the people and the people to art we must start by raising general educational and cultural standards" (p. 251).

———

"Revolution unleashes all forces fettered hitherto and drives them from their deep recesses of life to the surface. Take for example the influence exerted by fashion and the caprices of the tsarist court as well as by the tastes and whims of the aristocracy and the bourgeoisie on the development of our painting, sculpture and architecture. In society based on private property the artist produces for the market, needs customers. Our revolution freed artists from the yoke of these extremely prosaic conditions. It turned the state into their defender and client providing them with orders. Every artist, and everyone who considers himself such, has the right to create freely, to follow his ideal regardless of everything.

"But then we are Communists, and ought not to stand idly by and give chaos free rein to develop. We should steer this process according to a worked-out plan and must shape its results" (pp. 249-50).

———

"We are not utopians, however, and we know the real value of bourgeois 'arguments'; we also know that for some time after the revolution traces of the old ethics will inevitably predominate over the young shoots of the new. When the new has just been born the old always remains stronger than it for some time; this is always the case in nature and in social life. Jeering at the feebleness of the young shoots of the new order, cheap highbrow scepticism—these are, essentially, methods of bourgeois class struggle against the proletariat, a defence of capitalism against socialism. We must carefully study the feeble new shoots, we must devote the greatest attention to them, do everything to promote their growth and 'nurse' them." (Lenin, *Collected Works*, Vol. 29, p. 425).

———

"We give little attention to that aspect of *everyday* life inside the factories, in the villages and in the regiments where, more than anywhere else, the new is being built, where attention, publicity, public criticism, condemnation of what is bad and appeals to learn from the good are needed most.

"Less political ballyhoo. Fewer highbrow discussions. Closer to life. More attention to the way in which the workers and peasants are *actually* building the *new* in their everyday work, and more *verification* so as to ascertain the extent to which the new is *communistic*" (p. 117).

"The first was the plethora of bourgeois intellectuals, who very often regarded the new type of workers' and peasants' educational institution as the most convenient field for testing their individual theories in philosophy and culture, and in which, very often, the most absurd ideas were hailed as something new, and the supernatural and the incongruous were offered as purely proletarian art and proletarian culture" (p. 129).

"We are too great 'iconoclasts in painting'. The beautiful must be preserved, taken as an example, as the point of departure even if it is 'old'. Why turn our backs on what is truly beautiful, abandon it as the point of departure for further development solely because it is 'old'? Why worship the new as a god compelling submission merely because it is 'new'? Nonsense! Bosh and nonsense! Here much is pure hypocrisy and of course unconscious deference to the art fashions ruling the West. We are good revolutionaries but somehow we feel obliged to prove that we are also 'up to the mark in modern culture'. I however make bold to declare myself a 'barbarian'. It is beyond me to consider the products of expressionism, futurism, cubism and other 'isms' the highest manifestation of artistic genius. I do not understand them. I experience no joy from them" (p. 250).

(Gorky recalls his meeting with Lenin at the Fifth Party Congress).

"And this bald, thickset, vigorous man, speaking with a

burr immediately began talking about the imperfections of *Mother*, rubbing his Socratic brow with one hand, tugging at my hand with the other, and looking at me with a friendly twinkle in his amazingly lively eyes. He had read the book in the manuscript borrowed from I. P. Ladyzhnikov. I told him that I wrote the book in a hurry, but before I could explain why I had hurried, Lenin nodded and explained it himself: it was very good that I had hurried with it, the book was needed, many of the workers had joined the revolutionary movement impulsively, spontaneously, and they'd find it very useful reading *Mother*" (p. 244).

———

(Gorky recalls his conversations with Lenin in the first years of Soviet power).

"The problem of proletarian literature interested him.... He stressed, insistently and frequently, the importance of Demyan Bedny's work from the point of view of propaganda, but said: 'He's a bit crude. He follows the reader whereas he should be a little ahead of him'" (pp. 247, 248).

"Yesterday I happened to read in *Izvestia* a political poem by Mayakovsky. I am not an admirer of his poetical talent, although I admit that I am not a competent judge. But I have not for a long time read anything on politics and administration with so much pleasure as I read this. In his poem he derides this meeting habit, and taunts the Communists with incessantly sitting at meetings. I am not sure about the poetry; but as for the politics, I vouch for their absolute correctness" (p. 158).

———

(V. I. Kachalov recalls).

"... It was an important meeting in the Hall of Columns of the Trade Unions House. The atmosphere in the artists' room was animated; Vladimir Ilyich and Gorky were speaking. Alexei Maximovich turned to me and said: 'I'm having an argument with Vladimir Ilyich about the new theatre public. There can be no doubt that the new public is no worse than the old; in fact, it is more attentive. But what does it want? I say all it wants is heroic drama. But Vladimir Ilyich insists that it wants lyricism, too, and Chekhov, and the truth of everyday life.'"

31

ON SOCIALIST REALISM

The art of writing consists first of all in the study of language, which is the basic material of any book and especially of *belles-lettres*. The French expression *belles-lettres* means "beautiful words". By beauty is meant that combination of different materials—sounds, colours, words —that gives to what the master creates a form which has the power to influence the emotions and mind arousing wonder, pride and joy at man's creative ability.

The true beauty of language is created by the precision, clarity and sonority of the words that go to form the pictures, characters and ideas of a book. The writer, who is a genuine artist, must have a wide knowledge of the lexical resources of our rich vocabulary and the ability to select the most precise, clear and powerful words. It is only combinations of such words and their proper distribution within sentences, from a semantic point of view, that can give an exemplary form to the author's ideas, create vivid pictures and carve out living figures so convincingly that the reader finds himself visualising what the author is portraying. The writer must realise that he does not simply apply his pen to paper but uses words to paint people, not as an artist does, in immobility, but in constant motion, in action, continually getting in conflict with one another and taking part in the struggles between classes, groups and individuals. But there can be no action that does not evoke reaction. Hence it is clear that in addition to the necessity of studying the language and developing the ability to select the simplest, most graphic and colourful words from a literary language, which, while perfected to a high degree, is nevertheless littered with empty and ugly words, the writer must also have a good knowledge of the past history and of the social phenomena of contemporary society, in which he is called upon to fulfil his dual role of midwife and grave-digger. This last word may sound gloomy, but it is quite in its place. It depends on the will and ability of the younger writers to give it a cheerful meaning, for we need simply recall that our young literature has been summoned by history to destroy and bury all that is inimicable to men, inimicable even when they might still love it.

Of course, it is naive and comic to speak of "love" in a bourgeois society in which one of the basic moral tenets is "Love thy neighbour as thyself", hence asserting that Man's love for himself is the perfect model.[1] A class society could obviously not come into being or persist if it followed the commandments "Thou shalt not steal" or "Thou shalt not kill".

In the Union of Socialist Soviets even Young Pioneers learn to understand and do fully understand one evident and awful truth: the civilisation and culture of a bourgeois society are founded on incessant savage struggle between a minority of sated "neighbours" and a majority of starving "neighbours". It is quite impossible to "love thy neighbour" when at the same time one has to rob him and, if he resists, to kill him. As the bourgeois "system" developed, the poor and hungry have, throughout the ages, cast up from their own number various robbers, on land and sea, and also various humanists—men who, being themselves insufficiently sated, have pointed out to both well-fed and hungry the need to restrict this self-loving.

Because the activities of the robbers cast too obvious a light on the basis of the government of the rich, the latter found it necessary in part to kill them off and in part to draw them into the activity of governing. In ancient times, for instance in the Middle Ages, the tradesmen and merchants, fighting the guildsmen and peasants, chose the robbers as their "leaders"—hence their Dukes, dictators, "Princes

---

[1] "Love of oneself is a basic tenet of Divine Law, since from it develops our love for our neighbours," *Tserkovny Vestnik* (Church Bulletin) No. 45, 1909, in the article "On the Burning of Corpses", unsigned but probably by Professor Yevseyev.

of the Church", etc.—and this technique of mercenary self-defence against the workers has persisted to the present day, when bourgeois states are headed by bankers, arms manufacturers, bold adventurists and other "socially dangerous" elements.

The humanists, too, disrupted the tradesmen's tranquillity, so that those who were most stubborn in advocating the need to restrict the self-love either were destroyed by the bourgeoisie by various techniques, even down to burning alive at the stake, or, like nowadays, they were lured by various temptations, such as appointment to lofty positions, so that having climbed there, the humanists began to protect the bourgeois system and its calm. We can see something similar in the activities of various European ministers manufactured by the tradesmen out of former socialist workers.

But all this does not lead the bourgeoisie to "peaceful co-operation between classes" nor the desired "harmonious class relationships"—"harmonious" meaning a situation in which the minority, having "full political power", may do all that it finds profitable, while the majority—the hungry "neighbours"—humbly carries out the wishes of the sated bourgeois of all nations, sated with and dulled by the "joys" of their criminal existence. History has constantly and incontrovertibly demonstrated the laughably ephemeral quality of the prosperity of even such "gold-plated" adventurist businessmen as was the famous "match king" Ivar Kreiger and the like.

Eloquent witness of the fleeting nature of the businessmen's well-being is the increasing number of suicides among them. But those who put an end to themselves do not in any way influence those who remain alive and mechanically, with idiotic consistency, carry on with their base and senseless affair of organising a new and bloody slaughter, the slaughter that will, in all probability, wipe out that caste of men whose self-love has caused all the misery and grief of the working man.

The young Soviet writer will be greatly aided in mastering the truth of reality—his material—if he imagines himself as swaying between two forces, one that acts on his mind and the other on his emotions. For history has placed him in precisely such a position in the era of the collapse of capitalism and of more and more frequent and bloody clashes between the proletariat and the bourgeoisie, on the eve of world-wide class struggle and the inevitable victory of socialism. But although the din of newly joined battle is great, it is still drowned by the dull croaking of the petty bourgeois who, cowering in the rear of their bigger fellows, have always been accustomed to do a little haggling and thieving and are, by their very nature, unfit to do battle. When the big owners begin to fight, the petty ones become marauders, slaying and robbing the wounded, stealing from the corpses and by such a process becoming, not infrequently, themselves big. Everyone knows that bourgeois "wars beget heroes", but even more often they produce swindlers. Moreover, the heroes usually remain torn to pieces on the field of battle, while the more agile swindlers re-emerge as owners and legislators and, having learned how profitable mass slaughter can be, they start to organise a new similar business, for an industry working for war is especially profitable. There is a god, whose name is Profit, whom alone the bourgeois worship and to whom they offer the bloody sacrifices of millions of workers and peasants.

The petty bourgeois and, in addition, many workers, poisoned by physical proximity to petty bourgeois, are living buried to their necks in a swamp and complaining of the damp. These senseless complaints mingle with the heroic calls of the revolutionary proletariat and drown them. While complaining of the discomfort of living in their foul and crowded swamp, they make very few attempts to haul themselves out on to a high and dry place, and many are even convinced that the swamp is indeed "heaven upon earth".

But although picturesqueness is essential to the writer, let us be a little less picturesque.

Our Soviet writer must firmly realise that the majority of his contemporaries—the material for his work—are people brought up by ages of merciless struggle with one another for a crust of bread, and that all his "neighbours", indeed every one of them is consumed by a desire for material prosperity. This is a quite natural desire, based on a biological need for food and a comfortable shelter, etc., and this need is common to all animals and insects. The fox and the kite, the mole and the spider all build nests or lairs, but some predators and parasites kill more than they can devour. The whole of mankind's culture is built on a desire for material welfare, but its parasite—the bourgeoisie—who has complete power and limitless possibilities of exploiting the workers and peasants, has abused the instinct for satisfying basic needs by creating that tempting surplus which is known as "luxury". The corruptive influence of this surplus is recognised by the bourgeoisie itself: in ancient republican Rome, for instance, there were laws against luxury, and in the Middle Ages the bourgeoisie of Switzerland, France and Germany fought against the growth of luxury. The bourgeoisie has always consumed more of other men's labour than was necessary even for the satisfaction of its most whimsical needs; it has caught a passion for the easy gain, for hoarding money and possessions; it has infected itself and the whole world. And this infection has resulted in the present idiotic scene: in the capitals of Europe there are whole streets of shops trading in articles of gold and precious stones, "luxury trinkets", to create which the precious energy of the working class has been wastefully squandered, while the working class itself has not enough to eat, is completely deprived of the opportunity to develop its own needs, abilities and talents. The petty-bourgeois passion for senseless accumulation of possessions, the sick passion for personal property, has become ingrained in the working class, too.

Do not think that I am opposed to luxury in general. No, I am for luxury for all, but against the idolising of material things. Manufacture things as well as possible, so that they may last and save you additional labour, but do not make a "graven image" out of a boot, a chair or a book that you have made—that is a good "commandment"! And it would be an excellent thing if our young workers learned this commandment.

Those who idolise material possessions, calm and comfort "whatever may happen" even in these days of the general decadence of bourgeois culture continue to believe in the possibility of a personal stable, easy and "sweet" life. It is hardly necessary to repeat that the basis of such faith is self-love, ingrained in men from time past and supported by the church, whose "saints" are typical examples of lovers of self and haters of mankind. In secular philosophy the principle of self-love or, in other words, individualism, has found ardent support from that sapient German bourgeois, Immanuel Kant, whose thought processes are a model of mechanical thinking and who is as alien to life as a corpse.

This is an out-of-date faith and, like all faiths, it is blind. Nevertheless it stirs people up, inspiring them with the absurd and false belief that each one of us is the "beginning and end" of the world, "unique", the best and the most precious. And this estimation of one's own importance especially clearly reflects the influence of personal property. Uniting people only physically and mechanically for purposes of attack, for the exploitation of the unarmed or poorly armed, it keeps each one of them in a state of constant readiness to defend himself against his "neighbour", another private owner with a similar point of view. Though it unites the bourgeois externally for aggressive purposes, property divides them internally for purposes of self-defence, for it is a case of "every man for himself", and this creates the life of a beast. The saying *homo homini lupus est* was brought to life precisely by the morals of property owners.

Zoological individualism is a disease with which the bourgeoisie has infected the whole world and from which, as we see, it is itself dying. It goes without saying, that the sooner it dies the better for the working people of the world. They have the power and will to hasten this death.

For the young Soviet writer the subject of the petty-bourgeois world is difficult and dangerous because of its power to corrupt and infect. The novice, the "beginner" has not had the opportunity of observing the petty bourgeois in all his "power and glory"; he knows its recent history only from books, and hence badly. The disturbing, disintegrating and sick life of the European bourgeoisie is hardly known to him, and again only from books and newspapers. There are still numerous survivors of the shattered petty bourgeoisie living in his own country; they pretend, more or less cunningly, to have become "social animals", have even wormed their way into communist circles, and protect their "self" with all the power of guile, hypocrisy and falsehood that they have inherited from centuries past. Consciously and unconsciously they sabotage, idle and swindle, and produce wreckers, despoilers, spies and traitors from their midst.

Quite a lot of books have been and are being written about these remnants of the human trash thrown out of the Soviet land, but nearly all of them are insufficiently forceful and give a very superficial and dull portrait of the enemy. They have an anecdotal character, being based on isolated incidents, and do not convey the atmosphere of historicism which is essential in a work of art, so that the socialist didactic significance of these books is very minor. Obviously in as short a span as fifteen years you will not create Molières and Balzacs nor rear authors of *The Inspector-General* or *Messieurs Golovloff*, but in a land in which the energy of the working class has built new towns, gigantic factories, is changing the physical geography of their country, linking seas by canals and irrigating and populating deserts, and giving it fabulous riches by revealing countless treasures in the depths of the earth; in a land where the working class has brought forth from its midst hundreds of inventors and dozens of major scientists, and where every year half a million boys and girls receive a higher education—in such a land one can make the highest of demands on literature.

In this young literature there has already been quite a number of valuable achievements; its scope in presenting reality is constantly growing wider, and it is only natural to wish that the presentation itself were deeper. And it will indeed grow deeper if the young writers will realise the need to learn, to enlarge their knowledge, develop their ability to comprehend and study the technique of the highly important and responsible form of revolutionary activity that they have chosen to undertake.

When subjected to the tension of the two forces of history —the bourgeois past and the socialist future—men visibly vacillate. Their emotional nature tends towards the past, and the intellectual, towards the future. They shout a great deal and in loud voices, but one does not sense a calm confidence that they have made a firm and decisive choice to follow a well-defined path, even though history has made it perfectly plain.

Bankrupt and decrepit individualism is still alive and active, manifesting itself in bourgeois ambition, the desire to move forward to a position of eminence, and in work that is "ostentatious", insincere, slovenly and compromising to the proletariat, and especially in work that follows "the line of least resistance". In literature this line is one of criticism of the past. As mentioned above, the revolting face of the past is known to our young writers only superficially and theoretically. The ease with which the past can be critically portrayed tends to deflect authors from the necessity of drawing the grandiose phenomena and processes of the present.

The young authors still lack the power to inspire the

reader with hatred of the past, so, in my opinion, they not so much make him recoil from it, as constantly remind him of it, underlining, fixing and preserving it in his memory.

If the poisonous, grinding baseness of the past is to be revealed and comprehended fully, it is essential to develop the ability to look upon it from the height of the achievements of the present and the noble goals of the future. Such a view from above must and will evoke a proud and happy enthusiasm that will impart a new tone to our literature, aid it to create new forms, and evolve the new school it needs—socialist realism—which can obviously be based only on socialist experience.

We live in a happy land where there is someone to love and respect. Love for our fellow man must and will arise from a feeling of astonishment at his creative energy, from people's mutual respect for their unbounded collective power, which is creating socialist ways of living, and from devotion to the Party, which is the leader of the working people throughout the country and the teacher of the proletariat of all countries.

1933

TO AFFIRM LIFE AS ACTION AND CREATIVITY

Now a few words about realism as the basic, broadest and most fruitful literary trend in the nineteenth century and extending into the twentieth. Its most characteristic feature is sharp rationalism and criticism. The creators of this realism were largely men who had outgrown their background intellectually and who could clearly see the social and creative impotence of their class disguised under its crude physical strength. They might be termed the "prodigal sons" of the bourgeoisie since, like the hero of the biblical parable, they escaped the sway of their fathers and the yoke of dogmas and traditions. To their credit it can be added that very few of them ever returned to the paternal foyer to partake of the fatted calf. A significant role in moulding our attitude to European literary realists of the nineteenth century has been played by bourgeois criticism, which examines the merits and defects of language, style and theme but has never been interested in revealing and bringing to light the social ideas underlining the factual material of the works. The social significance of the works of Balzac was appreciated only by Marx and Engels. Critics kept silent about Stendhal. In our country foreign literature is very little read in the original, and even less is known of the biographies of the Western authors and of their development and technique.

The literature of the bourgeois "prodigal sons" was extremely valuable by virtue of its critical attitude to reality, though the authors of the stories and novels did not, of course, point a way out of the filthy anarchy created by the bloated and overfed bourgeoisie. Only very few and mostly second-rate authors followed the dictates of popular philosophy and influential criticism and attempted to assert some incontrovertible dogmatic points which, by reconciling the irreconcilable contradictions, would serve to disguise the obvious and base fallacies of the bourgeois social system. In the nineteenth century, science and technology particularly rapidly extended and strengthened the material basis of the capitalist states, but the literature of France, which was dominant in Europe, was not in the least enraptured by the mechanical activity of the European bourgeoisie and made no attempt to seek a justification for its "mechanical" growth.

The basic and major theme of nineteenth century literature was a pessimistic realisation of the instability of the social existence of the individual. Schopenhauer, Hartmann, Leopardi, Stirner and many others lent support to this realisation by their doctrine of the cosmic absurdity of life—a doctrine that took its root, naturally, from that same awareness of social defencelessness and social isolation of the individuals. In the new actuality created by the ruling proletariat in the Union of Soviets, even the individual lost in the icy wastes of the Arctic and living under constant threat of death still does not feel himself to be alone and helpless.

The nineteenth century was predominantly the age of pessimism. In the twentieth century this doctrine degenerated, quite naturally, into the propagation of social cynicism, into complete and decisive denial of the "humanism" upon which the philistines of all countries prided themselves and which they paraded with such guile. Schopenhauer's clerical, hypocritical ethic of sympathy and compassion, which found many adherents, was histerically and furiously rejected by Nietzsche and, still more resolutely and practically, by fascism. The fascism of the Hitlers was a manifestation of pessimism in the bourgeoisie's class struggle for the power that was slipping out of its weakened but still tenacious clutches.

One should add that the feeling and even realisation of the extreme instability and lack of equilibrium of the social existence of the individual was not unknown even to the most talented of the servants of capital. Almost all the "great" and "famous" representatives of the nineteenth century bourgeoisie, whose memoirs, diaries and letters were published posthumously, spoke of the incorrigible vileness of the way in which bourgeois society is organised.

Among the services rendered by the ruling proletariat of the Union of Soviets, we must most certainly include its unbelievably heroic part in ridding the world of the must and rust of pessimism.

The realism of the bourgeois "prodigal sons" was critical realism. In revealing the vices of society and describing the "life and adventures" of the individual caught in the confines of family traditions, religious dogmas and legal norms, critical realism could not show man a way out of his bondage. The contemporary world was easy to criticise but there was nothing positive to assert except the obvious absurdity of social life and, indeed, of "existence" in general. There were many who vociferously asserted this, beginning approximately with Byron and on to Thomas Hardy, who died in 1932; from Chateaubriand's *Mémoires d'outre-tombe* and others to Baudelaire and Anatole France, whose scepticism is very close to pessimism. Various writers substituted Catholicism for pessimism, but, as we say, "horse-radish is no sweeter than radish"; almost all churches have been equally persistent in instilling into man a feeling of his impotence in the struggle for life. The harmful influence of religion is especially clearly demonstrated by its endeavours to restrict all efforts that are not in accord with the material and selfish interests of the princes of the church. One of the Popes, "the Vicars of Christ on Earth", was quite right when he said: "Christianity is extremely advantageous to the priesthood." In this country a great deal is eagerly written about socialist realism, and not long ago one of our authors made an interesting discovery in an article he published on Gogol. Gogol was a socialist realist. This is an interesting statement, because it shows what poppycock such home-made literary criticism can lead to and illustrates how little the author feels responsible to his readers for his own words.

Literary realism concerns the real facts of man's activity in life. In the era of *The Inspector-General* and *Dead Souls* no one, as far as is known, could observe facts of a socialist character anywhere at all. And for this simple reason Nikolai Gogol could not reflect such facts in the social activities of Khlestakov, Chichikov, Sobakevich, Nozdryov, Plyushkin and his other characters....

In literature, socialist realism can appear only as a reflection of the facts of socialist creativity provided by practical experience. Can such a realism appear in Soviet literature? It not only can, it must, for we already have the facts of revolutionary socialist creativity, and their number is growing rapidly. We live and work in a land where feats of "glory, honour and heroism" have become such common facts that many of them are not even mentioned in the press. They are not noticed by writers because the writers' attention is still directed along the old channel of critical realism, which rightly and naturally "specialised" in the "negative features of life". Here it would be appropriate to mention that certain distorting features—weakness of vision, falsity and hypocrisy—are also explicable by natural causes, and that these causes may be removed.

One of the most serious causes of the conservative persistence of critical realism is our writers' low professional and technical skills or, to put it more simply, their lack of knowledge—ignorance, inability to see, to comprehend, to know. And this is often combined with a yearning towards the past, towards the old man whose life has but one "prospect"—the crematorium. To this one must add the line of least resistance: wood is easier to work than stone, stone than iron, iron than steel, and life in a little wooden house is easier to describe than life in a stone or concrete multistoried block....

From the article "Talks with the Young"

1934

As a process of the evolution of matter, which is the basis of all forces, life is magnificently simple; as the process of development of social relations, it is complicated by all manner of falsehood and baseness. Truth demands simplicity, falsehood—complication. This is clearly testified by the history of literature.

In ancient times, when labour techniques were primitive and people had as yet not become firmly separated into master and slave, the oral art of the working people created remarkably vivid images in legends and folk tales. The general theme of oral literature was man's struggle with nature or with the magicians who discovered its secrets and his dream that one day the working people would become masters of the forces of nature. This was a universal theme.

The "universal" in the poetry and prose of the classics rises high above the general bourgeois level. Those literary works of past ages can be called "universal" which reflect in the most pessimistic way how the individual senses the tragic complexity of social existence and feels aware of his own insignificance in the process of history. This feeling was experienced and variously expressed by the masters, but it was also common to the slaves, prompting both into the fantasies of idealistic philosophy and the mists of religion. In the first century B.C. the sculptor Glycon portrayed Hercules accomplishing his last feat. In his hand the heroic labourer holds the apple of immortality, but his pose and his face do not express the joy of victory, but weariness and despondency. It is interesting to notice that the bourgeois, who defeated the feudal lord, has made no artistic record of the "victor's triumph".

The struggle is unceasing and the victories stable, but there is no celebration, or it is short-lived and garish as was the recent base and bloody triumph of the *thrice-accursed* Hitler, who personifies the power of the major German bourgeoisie. In nineteenth and twentieth century Europe the genuinely artistic image of the *individual* was either the critic of bourgeois society or the whiner who complains at the difficulties of life, the man who wants to live independently of the first aspect of nature, the material, and the second, the social; the man who wants to live "alone unto himself", as suggested to him by the mechanical thought processes of the old man of Königsberg, founder of the new philosophy of individualism.

But there is one country in which the bourgeoisie has been defeated. This is a fact of "universal" significance not only for the proletariat of all countries, but for the fundamental forces of the bourgeoisie, for the masters of its science and culture, whose number exceeds the demands of the bourgeoisie, and who have the only way to artistic freedom—the way of the revolutionary proletariat—suggested to them by their dramatic position in society and by the logic of history.

History has laid the task and obligation on the writers of the USSR to produce a fundamentally universal literature. This must be a literature that can stir the proletariat of all countries and stimulate its revolutionary awareness of its rights. We already have the material for highly artistic poetry and prose; it is quite new material, which has been provided and is constantly being provided by the revolutionary creative courage of the workers and peasants and by their many-sided talent. It is the material given by an unhead-of victory—the victory of the proletariat and the establishment of its dictatorship. The essential and historical significance of this victory completely excludes from our literature the themes of the hopelessness and absurdity of individual existence, and of suffering blessed by the pernicious falsity of Christianity. Man's suffering has almost always been portrayed in such a manner that it evokes a fruitless, useless "compassion", and very rarely in a way that engenders in the ordinary builder of culture a desire to avenge his violated human dignity or hatred for his suffering and for its source, the creators of the vile horrors of life.

One hundred and seventy million people have rejected the shameful obligation to suffer for the comforts and pleasures of the ruling class. They have not yet managed to get rid of all the external causes of the discomforts of life, because they have not yet had time and, also, because of their passivity and the philistine aspirations that many still share to taste the cheap "pleasures of life". The urgency of such aspirations is explained by the fact that although we have defeated the petty bourgeois physically, his spirit continues nevertheless to "exist" among us, exuding its stupefying odour of decay.

The material of literature is man, with all his many aspirations and activities, and in the process of growth or decline. We have the material, but we study it badly and lack the ability to present it in the forms of high art. Ability proceeds from knowledge; therefore we must arm ourselves with knowledge and learn to work skilfully and honestly. We must learn a great deal, and in our circumstances this is not

44

difficult, for the ruling proletariat has destroyed all the obstacles preventing youth from following the road to science and art.

The writers of the Soviet Union have been put in the centre of things, at the heart of a process of world-wide significance. This is the process of the creation of a culture based on the elimination of private ownership of land and the instruments of labour, and on the destruction of all forms of social parasitism. But while, in fact, included in this process, the Soviet writers, in their attempts to depict it, still regard man—the living force of the process—superficially and negligently, even with indifference. They speak of him in words of hollow, cold admiration, but it seems beyond them to describe him as he really is. They do not understand that *genuine art possesses the right to exaggerate*; that the Herculeses, Prometheuses, Don Quixotes and Fausts are not "the fruits of fantasy" but perfectly legitimate and essential poetic exaggerations of actual facts. Our actual, living hero—the creator of socialist culture—is very much greater and loftier than the heroes of our stories and novels.

In literature he should be portrayed as even greater and more lofty. This is dictated not only by life itself but by socialist realism, which must think hypothetically, and hypothesis, conjecture, is the sister of hyperbole, exaggeration.

Not long ago a most interesing and penetrating book—D. Mirsky's *The Intelligentsia of Great Britain*—was published. It describes the English intelligentsia and, among other things, it says: "Being powerless to direct the history of society, the bourgeoisie is also powerless to know it, in so much as it does not know that link which, if pulled upon, draws up the whole chain. But as the bourgeoisie cannot find the link, and does not even know that it exists, it is powerless to prove either the effectiveness, or the actuality of its opinion, and so is condemned to occupy itself in weak fingering with its paralytic fingers a number of arbitrarily selected abstractions and arbitrarily chosen categories."[1] This is an extremely true idea, especially when applied to social phenomena. The perceptive faculties of the bourgeoisie have been blunted by ages of grinding the stern and revolting "truths" of life into the dust and lies of religion and

---

[1] Dmitri Mirsky, *The Intelligentsia of Great Britan*, London, 1935, p. 178.

philosophy, into the lies of petty liberal "humanism" and, nowadays, into the crude lies of fascism. Unfortunately, there are grounds for alleging that most of our literature also declines to perceive the laws of development showing preference for shallow, superficial judgements.

In thousands of voices Soviet man, builder of the new culture, is saying to the writers: I was a shepherd, an anti-social lawbreaker, the hired hand of a *kulak*, but I have become an engineer, a doctor, a scholar, a naturalist; I was a peasant woman labourer, a servant girl, a domestic beast for my husband, but I have become a professor of philosophy, an agronomist, a Party organiser, etc. In saying this they talk only of the fact of their physical movement from one section of society to another, unable and sometimes not even wishing to discuss the chemistry of that fact. It is the business of the revolutionary artist, the "engineer of the soul", to reveal the psycho-chemistry of this transformation from hired manual labourer to master of culture, to reveal the logic underlying this phenomenon, to show the role played by the proletariat's class ideology faced with the opposition of the petty bourgeoisie with its zoological emotions.

The essence of the fact is not simply that the shepherd is building machines or the farmhand is directing a factory. After all, the big bourgeoisie has increased its numbers and continues to do so not only by natural birth rate but by selecting and sucking into its greasy and sticky mass the most talented and energetic of the workers, peasants and petty bourgeois. The inexhaustibly large world of the working people has always abounded in talents, and thousands of them, having become worshippers of the culture of the men of property, brought fresh blood to the enemy class and strengthened its power over the world. Only very few, maybe dozens have used their talents to help the pro-letariat become class-conscious and aware of its revolution-ary rights and demonstrated to it the historical necessity of struggling against the plunderers of the world, the manu-facturers of poverty and degeneration for the workers. Some writers in contemporary Europe and America are beginning to describe the capitalists' manner of devouring the talented people of the enemy class. They describe it because they can already sense the drama of their position in a society of two-legged beasts in gloves and top-hats, in the company

46

of rulers that are once again organising massive, world-wide slaughter of millions of workers and peasants.

The task of our Soviet literature is to show how the men and women farmhands, into whom church and family had for centuries instilled scorn and enmity towards their fellows of other tribes, religions and languages, have discovered among all the peoples of tsarist Russia a common proletarian sense of inborn, class kinship; how a consciousness of unity of purpose has appeared in the multinational Soviet Union; how this consciousness awakens and directs talent; how it arouses a thirst for knowledge, heroism in labour and readiness to fight for the mighty cause of the proletariat in every corner of the earth. The main theme of all-Union literature is to show how abhorrence of poverty turns into abhorrence of property. This theme conceals the infinite variety of the other themes of genuinely revolutionary literature. It contains material for the creation of the "positive" man—the hero, it contains the "historical truth" of the epoch, which is the revolutionary expedience of the proletariat's energy, directed towards the transformation of the world in the interests of the free development of the creative forces of the working people. . . .

From the article "Literary Diversions"

1934

There was a time in antiquity when the toilers' oral lore was the sole organiser of their experience, the translator of ideas into images, and stimulator of the collective's labour energy. This is something we must realise. In our country the target has been set of providing equal educational opportunities to all; all members of our society are to be equally acquainted with the successes and achievements of labour, for the purpose of transforming human labour into the art of controlling the forces of nature. We have a more or less sound knowledge of the process of the economic— and hence political—stratification of people, and of the usurpation of the working people's right to freely develop their minds. When priests made understanding of the world their own business, they were able to monopolise it only by means of a metaphysical explanation of phenomena and the resistance offered by nature's elemental forces to the aims and the energies of the working people. Begun in antiquity and continuing down to the present time, this criminal exclusion and expulsion of millions of people from the business of understanding the world has led hundreds of millions of people, divided by concepts of race, nation and religion, to remain in a state of abysmal ignorance and horrifying intellectual blindness, in the darkness of superstition and prejudice of every kind. Having destroyed capitalism throughout tsarist Russia and placed political power in the hands of the workers and peasants, the Party of Communists-Leninists, and the Workers' and Peasants' Government of the Union of Socialist Soviets, who are organising a free and classless society, have made it their aim to emancipate the working masses—through bold, wise and indefatigable efforts—from the age-old bondage of the obsolete history of the capitalist development of culture, which is now manifestly revealing all its vices and creative impotence. It is from the heights of this great aim that we, honest writers of the Union of Soviets must consider, appraise and organise our activities.

We must realise that it is the labour of the masses that is the chief organiser of culture and the creator of all ideas—those that have for ages detracted from the decisive significance of labour, the source of all our knowledge, as well as the ideas of Marx and Lenin, which are instilling a revolutionary consciousness in the proletarians of all lands, and in the Soviet country are elevating labour to a force that is the basis of creativeness in science and art. If our work is to succeed, we must realise that in our country the labour of semi-literate workers and a primitive peasantry, now organised on socialist principles, has created tremendous values in the space of only sixteen years and has armed the country excellently for defence against enemy attack. A proper appraisal of this fact will show us the cultural and revolutionary power of a teaching that unites the entire world proletariat.

All of us—writers, factory workers, or collective farmers —are as yet working poorly, and cannot fully comprehend all that has been created by and for us. Our working masses do not as yet properly understand that they are working for themselves. The consciousness is latent on all sides, but has not yet burst into a bright and cheerful flame. But nothing can take fire till it has reached a certain temperature, and no one has ever before been able so successfully to raise the temperature of labour's energy as the Party organised by the genius of Vladimir Lenin.

The principal hero of our books must be labour—i.e., man as organised by labour processes—man who in this country is equipped with the might of modern techniques and is, in his turn, making labour easier and more productive and raising it to the level of an art. We must learn to understand labour as a creative act. Creativity is a concept which we writers use too often and with hardly the right to do so. Creativity is that degree of intensity in the work of the memory at which the rapidity of its operation produces from its store of knowledge and impressions the most outstanding and characteristic facts, pictures and details, and puts them into the most precise and vivid words that all can understand. Our young literature cannot yet boast of that quality. Our writers' store of impressions and knowledge is not extensive, and one does not yet discern a striving to build up and deepen that store.

The main theme in the nineteenth century European and Russian literature was the individual, as opposed to society, the state and Nature. The chief cause of the individual's opposition to bourgeois society was a peculiar abundance of negative impressions contradictory to his class ideas and traditions of life. The individual felt keenly that these impressions were retarding the process of his growth and crushing him, but he had but a poor understanding of his own responsibility for the vulgarity, baseness and criminality of the foundations of bourgeois society. Jonathan Swift lashed at the whole of Europe, but the bourgeoisie of Europe believed that his satire was directed against Britain alone. By and large the rebellious individual, who criticised the life of his society, rarely and poorly realised his responsibility for the shameful practices of society. A deep and proper understanding of social and economic causes was even more rarely the basic motive of his criticism of the existing order. His criticism sprang most frequently either from a sense of the hopelessness of his existence within the iron cage of capitalism or from a striving to avenge his failures in life, and the humiliation it had inflicted on him. It may be said that when an individual turned to the working masses, he did not do so in the interests of the latter, but in the hope that after destroying bourgeois society the working class would ensure his freedom of thought and wilfulness of action. I repeat: the basic and chief theme in pre-revolutionary literature was the drama of the individual, to whom life seemed cramped, who felt himself superfluous in society and sought to find some convenient place for himself, and, since he could not find one, suffered and perished, either after reconciling himself to a society that was hostile to him or by turning to drink or suicide.

In our country, the Union of Socialist Soviets there must not, and cannot be superfluous people. Every citizen has complete freedom to develop his abilities, gifts and talents. The only demand presented to the individual is that he should be honest in his attitude to the heroic work of creating a classless society.

In the Union of Socialist Soviets the entire mass of the population has been called upon by the workers' and peasants' government to participate in the building of a new culture. Hence each and every one of us is responsible for all errors, shortcomings, spoilage in production, and all manifestations of philistine vulgarity, meanness, duplicity and unscrupulousness. This means that our criticism must be genuine self-criticism, that we must evolve a system of socialist ethics to regulate our work and mutual relations.

In describing facts that reveal the workers' intellectual development and show how the age-old petty proprietor is turning into a collective farmer, we writers confine ourselves to mere reporting, for it is in very inadequate terms that we depict the emotional processes underlying these changes.

We still have a poor perception of reality. Even the external appearance of the country has changed strikingly and the impoverished patchwork of the land has gone. No longer do we see a light-blue strip of land sown to oats alongside a golden band of rye, a greenish strip of wheat, patches overgrown with weeds, and on the whole a sorry-looking expanse of parcelled land. Today vast expanses of land present a single pattern and colour. Villages and towns are dominated not by churches but by big, public buildings. Giant factories reflect the sun in their huge expanses of glass, while ancient churches, toylike in appearance and pagan in their motley variety, testify to our people's talents, which used to find expression in church architecture. However, the new face of our land and the striking changes in it are not reflected in our literature.

We live at a time when the old way of life is being radically refashioned and a sense of dignity is awakening in man who is realising that he is a force actually changing the world. . . .

Life around us provides ever more "raw material" for artistic generalisations. Neither the drama nor the novel have so far produced a sufficiently vivid depiction of Soviet woman, who is playing such an important part in all spheres of socialist construction. It is even noticeable that dramatists have tried to create as few female roles as possible. Why it is so is difficult to explain. Although woman's social status in our country is equal to man's, and women have given full proof of the variety of their gifts and their capacity for work, this equality is very often and in many respects formal and external. Men have not yet forgotten, or have prematurely forgotten, that for dozens of centuries women were trained for sensual diversion and as domestic animals capable of "keeping house". This old-standing and shameful debt of history to one-half of the world's population should be paid off by the men of the Soviet country first of all, so as to set an example to all the other men in the world. Here, too, literature should try to depict women's work and mentality in such a way as to raise the attitude towards women above the accepted philistine attitude which has been borrowed from the lower animals.

Further, I think it is necessary to point out that Soviet literature is not only Russian literature, but all-Union literature. Since the writers of the fraternal republics, who differ from us only in language, live and work under the impact and beneficent influence of the idea that unites the whole world of working people that capitalism has divided, it is clear that we have no right to ignore the writings of the national minorities simply because we Russians are more numerous. The value of art is gauged not by quantity but by quality. If the giant Pushkin belonged to our past, it does not follow that Armenians, Georgians, Tatars, Ukrainians and other nationalities are incapable of producing great masters of literature, music, painting and architecture. It should not be forgotten that throughout the broad expanse of the Union of Socialist Republics a rapid renascence of the whole mass of working people is in progress towards an honest and human life, the free creation of new history, and the creation of socialist culture. We can already see that the greater its advance, the more powerfully does this process reveal the gifts and talents latent in 170 million men and women. . . .

With all its diversity of talent and the growth in the number of new and gifted writers, Soviet literature must be organised as a united and collective whole, a mighty weapon of socialist culture.

The Union of Writers is being formed not merely for the purpose of physically uniting writers, but to enable them, through a professional association, to feel their collective force, define the diversity in that force's creative powers and its purposes with the utmost clarity, and blend all those purposes harmoniously into one unit, directing the country's creative energy.

We are speaking, of course, not of limiting individual creativity but of providing it with the greatest possible opportunities for untrammelled development.

We should realise that critical realism stemmed from the individual creativity of "superfluous people" who, incapable of fighting for life, finding no place for themselves in that life and more or less clearly aware of the pointlessness of living merely for the sake of one's own existence, understood that pointlessness only as the absurdity of all social phenomena and the entire historical process.

While in no way denying the tremendous work done by critical realism, and fully appraising its formal achievements in the art of verbal imagery, we must realise that we need such realism only in order to throw light upon survivals of the past, and to wage the struggle for their eradication.

This form of realism, however, has not served, and cannot serve, to educate socialist individuality, since while criticising all things, it affirmed nothing or, at worst, returned to an affirmation of all it had itself denied.

As can be seen from the example of our heroes of labour the flower of the working mass, socialist individuality can develop only in conditions of collective labour, whose lofty and wise aim is to emancipate working people all over the world from the power of capitalism that distorts men.

Socialist realism proclaims that life is action, creativity,

52

whose aim is the unfettered development of man's most valuable individual abilities for his victory over the forces of Nature, for his health and longevity, for the great happiness of living on earth, which he, in conformity with the constant growth of his requirements, wishes to cultivate as a magnificent habitat of mankind, united in one family.

From the report to the First
All-Union Congress of Soviet
Writers

1934

It seems to me that the state of criticism and its aims have been defined in forms that are too "general" and too familiar to writers and critics to arouse any lively or active interest or provoke fruitful discussion about socialist realism as a method and technique of literary creativity or about the aesthetics and ethics of Soviet art.

Much has been and is being written about socialist realism, but there is no single and clear opinion, and this explains the sad fact that at the Congress of Writers the critics did not even make their existence known. We need a firmly established "working verity" broad enough to embrace and elucidate the purpose of all the processes at work in our country and all the acts of resistance to the creativity of the ruling proletariat. It is obvious that such a "working verity" should inevitably admit of variety of opinion; hence the need to make an exact and firm definition of what is inevitable and admissible. I think that socialist realism should take as its point of departure Engels's proposition: life is continuous and uninterrupted motion and change. In Nature there is the mechanical energy of physics and chemistry; in human society the friction, the clash of class forces and the labour activity directed towards the creation and enlargement of the material culture, bourgeois and class self-interested. The facts of history have established that in a bourgeois society the intellect has acted as a "catalyst" which, with varying degrees of success, has aspired to link and unite, i.e., to reconcile, and in the social sphere reconciliation is subordination of one force to another. Individualists should be shown that in capitalist conditions the intellect is least of all concerned about its rapid growth and seeks only stable equilibrium.

The realism of bourgeois literature is critical realism, but only to the extent that criticism is necessary for class "strategy": for revealing the mistakes of the bourgeoisie in the struggle for the establishment of firm power. Socialist realism wages a struggle against "survivals of the past", against its corrupting influence, and for uprooting these influences. But its major task is to evoke a socialist, revolutionary understanding and comprehension of the world.

I believe that ideas of this sort could provoke protests, annoyance and useful discussion among writers and critics. Our writers think and talk least of all about the aims and tasks of literature; hence an attempt should be made to stir up a more lively and profound interest in the matter in which they are engaged.

In general we ought as often and as persistently as possible to draw writers' attention to the following: the predictions of scientific socialism are being more and more widely and deeply brought about by the activity of the Party; the organising force of these predictions lies in their scientific foundation. The socialist world is being built and the bourgeois world is crumbling just as Marxist reasoning foresaw.

Hence a completely legitimate conclusion may be drawn: an artist whose imagination is properly directed and relies on a broad knowledge of reality and an intuitive wish to give his material the most perfect possible form and supplement data with what is possible and desirable, is also able to "foresee"; in other words, socialist realist art has the right to exaggerate, to "fill out". "Intuitive" should not be understood as meaning something ahead of knowledge, something "prophetic". It provides the missing links and details to experimental searches when they have been started as hypothesis or image. Our writers should be made acquainted with the revolutionary hypotheses of science ... which can be confirmed experimentally and serve as "working verities". . . .

From a letter to A. S. Shcherbakov, February 19, 1935, Moscow ider of will her to lead society to what aims, to say before...

Anatoly Lunacharsky

ON SOCIALIST REALISM

The task of literature has always been to organise the class for which it speaks. Even when literature has called itself "art for art's sake" and carefully disengaged itself from any political, religious or mundane cultural aims it has in fact served them, for so-called pure literature is also a certain reflection of a certain condition of the class that proclaims it.

The mighty, youthful classes, whose task is that of reshaping the whole of society and introducing new methods of making Nature serve man, are inclined towards realism. This is perfectly understandable; they need to orientate themselves on their environment and to have a precise knowledge of themselves, of Nature, of the social forces that are inimicable to them and of what they are fighting for.

In its time, the young bourgeoisie also evinced a love of realism in all forms of art. But the bourgeoisie has outlived its time, and we can analyse what this realism was at various stages of its development.

At first it was progressive realism. The bourgeois satirists made fun of the upper classes, defended the bourgeois "virtues" and presented the bourgeois ideology in ringing and vivid forms, attempting to make it the ideology of the oppressed mass following in its wake. But this youthful period passed. Realists of another sort appeared. These simply orientated themselves on their environment, merely drawing bold pictures of reality. But their pictures were meaningful, even though the greatest representatives of this second stage of realism (for instance, Balzac or Dickens) had no precise idea of whither to lead society or what aims to set before it. They could not distinguish clearly where their real enemy lay and even were not quite certain in whose name they were in fact writing. Nevertheless they considered themselves to be serving a certain artistic verity and made wonderful sketches of their environment from which it was sometimes possible to draw an extremely far-reaching conclusion.

Strangely enough, but stated objectively, their greatest service was to the proletariat; not the as yet unsufficiently developed proletariat of their own times, but that of a later period, to whom such realists gave weapons for its arsenal.

Then we can distinguish a third stage when the petty bourgeoisie begins to bemoan reality, which it finds disgusting. The foul and impoverished state of society casts shadow even on Nature and on the Universe itself, and pessimistic realism appears (the best example of this is Flaubert).

Not far removed from this is naturalism, which sets itself the task of drawing a scientifically true picture of the society surrounding it, offering no guidelines and observing the maximum detachment. Zola tried to write in this way, but, as we know, he failed to sustain the role. Outbursts of indignation or woe were permissible, but good taste required detached photographic writing. . . .

In the USSR today bourgeois realism is considered reactionary. The bourgeois realist, who writes statically, describing things as they are rather than in their process of development, who has no inkling of the mighty process that moves reality forward and does not aim to become an active force in this process, is, of course, a whiner and a reactionary in our eyes.

Obviously in our work of construction there is much that is unfinished, and at every step one can come across imperfections and even ugliness as well as all manner of painful details. The artist must certainly not hush them up, but if he takes them as stages of a progression, as features that must be and are in fact being overcome, he reaches one conclusion, and when he takes them in isolation he arrives at a criticism of our entire struggle and a condemnation of what we are trying to build. This is self-evident.

From all that has been said it is clear that socialist realism differs sharply from bourgeois realism. The whole point is that socialist realism is itself active. It not only gets to know the world but strives to reshape it. It is for the sake of this reshaping that it gets to know the world, that is why all its pictures bear a peculiar stamp, and this is immediately felt. Socialist realism knows that Nature and society are dialectical and are constantly developing through contradictions, and it feels first and foremost this pulse, this passage of time.

Moreover it is purposeful. It knows what is good and what is evil and notes which forces hinder movement and which facilitate its tense straining towards the great goal. This illuminates each artistic image in a new way, both from within and from without. Hence socialist realism has its own themes, for it considers important precisely what has a more or less direct bearing on the main process of our life, the struggle for a complete transformation of life on socialist lines. . . .

We already have significant works of this sort—works of purposeful, active dialectical realism, socialist realism. Such, for example, is Maxim Gorky's chronicle *Klim Samgin*, the third volume of which has already been published. True, the novel deals with the recent past rather than the present, but it shows the coming ruin of a whole series of social forces and the growth of the iron seed of Bolshevism.

On a similar high level is Sholokhov's last novel *Virgin Soil Upturned*, which astonishes one by the accuracy of its images and also by the degree to which it is impregnated with the will, the sympathy, the understanding and the tense involvement of the author in the unfolding events. . . .

But here I might be asked, whether that is not a form of romanticism; if your realists do not simply describe their environment as it actually is but introduce a subjective element, isn't that a tendency towards romanticism? Yes, it is. Gorky was right when he repeated several times that literature must be above reality, and that the very knowledge of reality was necessary in order to overcome it; he was right when he called such militant and laborious overcoming of reality in its literary reflection—romanticism.

However, our romanticism is a part of socialist realism. To a certain extent socialist realism is unthinkable without an element of romanticism. In this lies its difference from detached recording. It is realism plus enthusiasm, realism plus a militant mood. When this enthusiasm and militant mood predominate, when, for example, we introduce hyperbole or caricature for satirical purposes, or when we describe the future that we cannot yet know, or when we round off a type that has not yet crystallised in reality and paint him in the stature towards which we aspire, we are, of course, giving emphasis to the romantic element.

But our romanticism never for a moment approximates to bourgeois romanticism. The latter arose from dissatisfaction with life accompanied by no programme for reshaping it and no hope of combating it. Bourgeois romanticism yearns for an unattainable dream. Therefore it takes on the character of pure art (consoling itself in the realm of beauty) or of mystic religious abstractions, or of hideously woeful nightmares.

It is true that the young bourgeoisie had more noble forms of romanticism. They consisted in embellishing with illusion its programme and its role in history. The best members of the bourgeoisie were by no means lying; they were true to their own lights and believed in the grandeur of their mission. Very often they looked for colour to the past, to moments in human life that they took to represent culminating points—classical times, the Middle Ages or, even more remote, Biblical times.

As Marx and Engels showed, the socialist movement has not the slightest need to adorn itself with such ancient plumes; but they nevertheless pointed out that if socialist movement wished to stand forth in all its glory it would borrow adornment not from the past but from the future. Such borrowing of plumes from the future is in no way falling into illusion.

The point is that our Soviet art is also dissatisfied with the present, hence its kinship with romanticism. But besides being dissatisfied with reality, it wishes to change it and knows that it can do so. The land to which one can sometimes fly in order to relax and gather strength—that land is the future: not the "foretaste of the harmony of coming bliss" that Shchedrin mocked at, but the dream of accomplishing our grand plans, whose foundation we are now working on, and about which Lenin said that it was hardly possible to think of a really good Communist lacking this ability to dream.

Such are the general features of socialist realism, the tendency that has already acquired quite well-defined forms. Of course, it will be some time before it will settle down

internally and the proletarian style, with its own peculiar
genre and exhaustive thematics, will be adequately established and complete. But such is the task of our Soviet
literature (and all other art forms), whose gradual implementation we shall watch with bated breath in the near future.

1933

Alexander Fadeyev

SOCIALIST REALISM

Let us begin by reviving a few simple truths that many people have begun to forget.

Is it true that a mastery of the socialist outlook of the proletariat, which is, historically, the most progressive and revolutionary outlook, is *essential* for every artist who wants to give *progressive* expression to the ideas, hopes, interests, feelings and passions of the new society? Yes, it is true.

But is it true that this is the sole and sufficient prerequisite for a progressive revolutionary *artist*? No, it is not true. Quite a few other conditions are required.

1. *It is necessary to have an artistic gift or talent*, i.e., that "peculiarity" which allows the gifted man, and not only allows but *compels* him to express his thoughts and feelings more or less fully, convincingly and aesthetically perfectly in artistic images. We know that the old, exploiting system, founded on the incredible oppression of millions, on the contradiction between physical and intellectual labour, on social inequality between men and women and on hundreds of other such contradictions, destroyed, strangled and enslaved millions of talents among the people. We know and can see in practice that the successes of socialism, overcoming these contradictions, already guarantee and will guarantee even more the tempestuous growth of millions of variously and vastly talented and gifted people. Nobody, moreover, is frightened by or finds aristocratic overtones in such expressions as talented scholar, talented administrator, talented locksmith, co-operator, inventor, commander, etc. It is only in art and literature that some

people are embarrassed, for no reason at all, by such descriptions. If one looks through recent critical literature one often comes across extremely good, clever and correct (as well as bad, silly and incorrect) comments on the mighty role of world outlook, on artistic method, and on the stylistic school to which this or that work might belong. But I often feel impelled to ask: "Listen, comrade, is this a really gifted work from the point of view of its artistic merits? Is it worth discussing questions of art in relation to this work? Perhaps apropos of this work one ought to raise other important questions, but of a quite different order?" That is the first point.

2. *It is necessary to acquire literary experience, abilities and skill.* Some of our critics have been utterly confused by the formalists. We are aware that artistic techniques, the art of writing, the construction of a work, the art of detail, and other important matters have been turned by vulgar formalists (and non-vulgar formalists are the same vulgar formalists, only garbed in thin sociological raiment and shielded by a couple of biographical points and three quotations from Marx) into something standing in its own right, divorced from the artist's world outlook and his ideology. But nowhere and at no time has Marxism-Leninism regarded artistic creativity as something *predestined* (requiring only the right ideological basis), or denied the importance of experience, skill, a mastery of writing technique, a knowledge of language, the ability to give the work a definite structure, etc. That is the second point.

3. *It is necessary to work hard, persistently and painstakingly.* For some unknown reason certain writers and critics do not consider the work of writing to be a variety of human labour. They obviously think that the Marxist world outlook or talent are sufficient to produce good works. This is a grave error that might prove fatal to them. That is the third point.

4. *It is necessary to have all-round knowledge, especially knowledge of facts and of what one is writing about.* Some of our critics have been absolutely confused by the adherents of LEF.[1] We know that these latter have made facts an

---

[1] LEF—the Left Front in Art—a literary group that was formed in Moscow in 1923. The basic tenets of the group were connected with futurism and other bourgeois formalist movements.

object of worship. But one would not give a brass farthing for a scholastic impotent "outlook" which fails to study facts from all points of view and define their place in the historical process which puts them in direct and indirect connection to each other. That is the fourth point.

If a work does not satisfy these four conditions, it is difficult to use it as a point of departure for a broad discussion of artistic method and style in general. A critic may tear it to pieces because of its deficiencies of world outlook, while the author's outlook may be no worse than that of the critic, but he may lack talent. The critic may rant about the dreadful contradictions in artistic method, and the author may be entirely in favour of the critic's method but may feel his lack of knowledge, experience or ability. The critic may utter shrieks about insidious "empiricism" and various other "isms", but the author has simply been too lazy to polish his work and has published it in a rough form, or has not studied his subject sufficiently well.

Hence it is obvious how naive were the articles discussing the artistic method and style of, for instance, the works of Isbakh, or of Chumandrin, or of Stavsky's *Village* or Luzgin's *Gramophone* or Altauzen's *Green Enthusiast* and many other similar works. For various reasons these and similar works did not reach the level of artistry that would make it possible and necessary to put questions of style and method.

Nothing that I have written here is designed to offend anyone or censure anyone's work. But I think it important to repeat certain simple artistic truths.

Insufficient attention to these simple truths has until now been a grave source of harm to many of our Soviet critics and writers.

A very large number of theoretical and critical works has been devoted to questions of artistic method, that is, to the question of how the artist's outlook, his attitude to life, is expressed in his artistic practice, and to what degree the outlooks of artists representing various classes and ages have determined their artistic practice. A lot of work has been done to survey the products of artists of former classes and ages in the light of historical struggle between basic philosophies of life. Proceeding from the premise that the philosophy of the proletariat is dialectical materialism, many of us have believed that a new, revolutionary artistic method ought to be the method of dialectical materialism in art. It is now obvious to all of us that such an attitude was pedantic and dogmatic and did Soviet literature a great deal of harm.

For very many of us the so-called method of dialectical materialism in art has become a stale and dull concept, a yardstick, a "talisman" to clasp in one's hand. Many young writers and even some of their seniors really begin to think that there exists a universal Marxist pamphlet or series of pamphlets that would "dispense" this dialectical materialism leaving it for them only to *apply* it to their creative work. On the other hand, for very many critics the "method" has become something that exists in its own right, an aim in itself. Hence, the basic aim of artistic activity is the achievement of an ideal and pure dialectical "method". There are, as yet, no writers, this group of critics alleges, who have achieved this method; but there is a very small number of those who "have approached" it, a definite number approaching it and a fair quantity of these who either have not even caught a glimpse of this "method", or are distorting it and struggling against it. Every sensible man, however, realises that the aim of revolutionary artistic creativity cannot be the achievement of some "distilled" method, but the artist's participation in the struggle of millions for a new, socialist society with the mighty weapon of artistic word;

that for this purpose the artistic word must be first of all revolutionary, convincing, wise and true;

that the concept of artistic method has arisen from the quest for ways that would *aid* the artistic word to be as convincing, as wise and as true as possible;

that the organic transition of the writers originating from the old intelligentsia to the positions of the working class, their assimilation of its philosophy (which is possible not via a pedantic, scholastic study of the founders of Marxism but through the practice of life itself, illuminated by the revolutionary theory of Marx and Lenin—a theory that condenses man's rich practical experience throughout history) is useful and necessary because precisely *this assimilation* assists every genuine artist in perceiving with maximum fullness, depth and accuracy all the richness of reality, the true essence of things, the fundamental tendencies of the development of human society and the rise of the new,

63

socialist society in the course of struggle with the old system of exploitation.

The process of assimilation of this philosophy has already been taking place for a long time before our eyes and on an unprecedented scale. For the majority of genuinely revolutionary authentic artists in our country this philosophy has already become the determining factor in their work, that is, it is becoming their artistic method.

It is precisely this circumstance that has given rise to and will continue to bring forth the truly (though sometimes underestimated) living riches and variety of revolutionary content and artistic form of our young Soviet literature.

Our epoch is so grandiose, our socialist country is making such gigantic historic strides, and the demands of socialism are so great that our literature cannot yet satisfy us. Compared to *such* successes and *such* demands it is still in its infancy. But if we cease to measure our *genuinely* Soviet and *genuinely* artistic literature by the wretched, abstract, scholastic and factional yardstick; if we cease discarding as useless anything that does not compare with the works of the two or three authors who have for some reason been proclaimed as "having approached" the sought-after "method"; if we realise that the true revolutionary method in art *is first of all an accurate artistic portrayal of reality in the process of development, of its basic tendencies, its living richness and the variety of problems that disturb the new mankind*; if we consider that in real life, in the hard struggle of communism against capitalism, it is not always that *such* portrayal appears in an ideally pure form, but it often bears the stamp of other influences or takes the shape of a struggle against other tendencies; if, in other words, we are able to detect the *major* tendency of art and not blame deficiencies of talent or ability on those of outlook or method —if we realise and take into account all this, we can easily see that our Soviet literature is developing more and more confidently and triumphantly under the aegis of *the new revolutionary artistic method: socialist realism*. And it could not be otherwise, for it is in this way that the *progressive, leading style of the epoch* is reflected in revolutionary literature. This is precisely why our literature is revolutionary. This is why it is diverse in form and rich in content.

Much has been written—and sometimes well—about the impossibility of *detaching* artistic method from the outlook of the artist. But many have forgotten that these two concepts must not be *blended* or *identified* one with the other, for they are two separate things. This can be verified particularly easily with reference to artists of past ages, for even the greatest of them never realised the true historical content of what they were writing about or the way in which they were writing. "A fusion of the great ideological depth of comprehended historical content with Shakespearean liveliness and saturation with action will be achieved only in the future", Engels wrote in a letter to Lassalle. What is more, a writer's artistic method has sometimes stood in contradiction to his philosophy. This was clearly enough demonstrated by Engels with regard to Balzac. Though a convinced legitimist and supporter of absolutism, Balzac nevertheless drew "typical characters in typical circumstances" with such strength and clarity that reading Balzac does more for one's understanding of the history of French society than dozens of political or economic works of that time. Many of Balzac's works still have enormous revolutionary-educative significance even today.

We know that there was a great contradiction between Tolstoi's idealist philosophy and the basically realist tendency of his literary works which made them "a step forward in the artistic development of humanity as a whole".[1]

Such contradictions between philosophy and artistic method to be observed in a number of authors must not be taken to mean that the author's world outlook is not important. We should not forget that the flaws of outlook have left, of course, their trace on the artistic method of those authors. If Balzac had had a full and historically correct *realisation* of the true content of what he was writing, this would have rid his brilliant works of many artistic discords and increased still more his significance for us. Tolstoi's reactionary utopianism and his moronic doctrine of non-resistance were also reflected in his masterly works and from this point of view reduced their value to us. The outstanding significance of Lenin's articles on Tolstoi lies in the fact that Lenin analysed his creative work historically in its contradictions.

The difference between socialist realism and the old realism consists, among other things, in that the contradiction

---

[1] Lenin, *Collected Works*, Vol. 16, p. 323.

between philosophy and artistic method in socialist realism will be less characteristic, since the subjective hopes and interests of the proletariat do not contradict the objective laws of historical development. The artist in socialist society has the actual opportunity for "a fusion of the great ideological depth of comprehended historical content with Shakespearean liveliness and saturation with action".

Some people deny the significance of a progressive revolutionary world outlook for the contemporary author. They reason like this: Homer, Shakespeare, Goethe, Cervantes and other great writers were not "*socialist* realists", but their works have lived for centuries, while many of our writers, although they are perhaps socialist realists, look rather puny when compared with the literary giants.

In the first place, it is beyond doubt that, all other things being equal, a progressive, comprehensively developed outlook has always *increased* the artistic force of the literary works of the past. And in the second place, I have already said that the level and degree of talent, the artist's genius also count. In other words, the superior quality of socialist realism is not always matched by equally great *talent*.

We should not forget that Soviet literature is still very young, and a genius is not born every day. But more geniuses will be born as millions of people are freed from the shackles of the past. Our literature is already incomparably superior to contemporary bourgeois literature. Socialism has the right to be proud that it has already produced quite a few very gifted revolutionary artists (e.g. Mayakovsky) and that it has Gorky, whose works have achieved the synthesis that Engels spoke of and will live for centuries. Gorky's works are a new step—of gigantic revolutionary and artistic significance—in the development of the whole of mankind because socialist outlook in them is combined with true genius.

We ought to discard as soon as possible the old "professorial" concepts of realism, romanticism, naturalism—concepts based on formal, external features and standing in direct contradiction to the Marxist-Leninist ideas on that score based on the objective historical analysis of art.

Marx, Engels and Lenin understood artistic realism as approximation to objective, historical truth, revelation of the essential aspects of reality, fearless exposure of contradictions, "a tearing away of all and sundry masks"[1] behind which the exploiting classes sought to conceal the exploiting nature of their rule, and, at the same time, as a bold *flight* of thought, as a passionate revolutionary dream springing from reality and waiting for its implementation tomorrow. From this point of view the so-called romantic breakthrough into the future is an aspect of genuine realism.

Realism that crawls upon the surface of things and phenomena, seeing only their isolated aspects outside their links with the process of history, and unable to foresee their development in the future, was branded by the founders of Marxism as vulgar, creeping "realism". We know that their pronouncements on romanticism were always directed against false "romanticism", against philistine exaggeration, poetisation and mystification of superficial, banal or else simply fallacious concepts of reality, against the flight from real contradictions to the shelter of elaborate phrases and against "casting a veil over the essence of things" (Marx). But the founders of Marxism-Leninism always commented enthusiastically on artists' bold prevision of the future and their revolutionary dream.

For Marxism-Leninism the greatest *realists* of past ages were the writers of wide scope and variety, extremely dissimilar outwardly: Homer, despite the mythological shell of his eternal creations; Dante, although he led his hero through the Inferno and the Purgatory; Swift, even though the real historical enemies and friends of his class were presented in the fantastic guise of Lilliputians, Houyhnhnms and Laputans; Shakespeare, although—awful to tell!—he believed in ghosts; Cervantes; Goethe, although this great genius sometimes yielded to German philistinism and appeared as a vulgar "romantic" or writhed in the grip of the "multiheaded hydra of empiricism"; Pushkin, Lermontov, Griboyedov, Saltykov-Shchedrin, Gogol—although, the latter combined objective, revolutionary unmasking of evil with reactionary romanticism, the two traits locked in furious combat with each other; Dickens, as long as he did not himself become a cricket on the philistine hearth; Heine, who was great when he ridiculed philistinism and did not stoop beneath its cheap, idyllic banners; Tolstoi, who combined "a tearing away of all and sundry masks" with "the self-

---

[1] Lenin, *Collected Works*, Vol. 15, p. 205.

improvement diet of rice cutlets"; Jack London, when he was not preaching escape from social contradictions by means of a petty-bourgeois flight to the "bosom of Nature" or entrapped by Nietzschean "philosophy"; Stendhal, Balzac, Flaubert—when the "objectivism" of the latter did not turn into the stale scepticism of a refined *rentier*; and many, many others.

These were the great realists of the past, for despite their social and individual difference, they all, to a greater or lesser degree, drew close to objective, historical truth, and in their major works, which have survived the centuries, they raised questions that still disturb mankind. On the other hand, they were all brilliant personalities, and besides the socio-historical differences their every work was distinguished by the author's bright *individuality*. Some people think that the method of socialist realism is necessary to make writers as like as two peas. But such standardisation and uniformity makes a mockery of both socialism and realism. *Socialist realism is, above all, richness of artistic individuality.*

For Marxism-Leninism the important thing is not labels or pigeon-holes but the objective, historical function of a given writer, and the degree and manner in which his works may be employed as an active force or as a cultural and aesthetic heritage. The basic formula of Marxism-Leninism, therefore, is an obligatory, historical and comprehensive analysis of each artist in the light of the conflicts of his time. In Marxist reasoning Schiller, for instance, was a typical "romantic" since, as Engels put it, he found "a refuge from trivial squalor in lofty squalor". But Schiller, the author of *The Bell, The Robbers* and *Wilhelm Tell,* was for his time a *revolutionary* romantic of the bourgeoisie and, as such, played an historically progressive role (by the end of his life, incidentally, Schiller became a typical reactionary romantic). As a *revolutionary* romantic he still has an educative significance for us, especially for the young. But in view of the defects already outlined his educative significance for our times cannot be *as great* as, for instance, that of Shakespeare or Balzac.

From the Marxist-Leninist point of view Zola, for example, is often seen as *vulgar, creeping* realist, but by no means always. To the extent to which he succeeded in giving broad generalisations, and to which his works served to reveal social inequality and the rapacity, licentiousness and moral decay of the bourgeoisie at the time of the Second Empire in France, he played an historically progressive role and still has educative significance. Nevertheless it is obvious that his realism is inferior to that of, say, Balzac. Engels said that Balzac was worth more than all the Zolas put together.

In a Marxist-Leninist analysis Blok was a typical representative of bourgeois-aristocratic decadence. But we know from his diaries and from his works how passionately this extraordinarily talented artist tried to break out from the narrow confines of the literary trend to which he belonged, and what realistic power he achieved in those of his works where he managed to overcome the restrictions of his literary trend. His poem *The Twelve* was, in its own way, a revolutionary outburst and played a *revolutionary role*.

Marxism-Leninism has several times demonstrated what a reactionary "romantic" obscurantist Dostoyevsky was when he tormented himself before his "little god" and derided revolution. But Dostoyevsky was a realist of genius in his depiction of the torments and sufferings of people who were humiliated and maimed by the social system of exploitation.

All this leads to one conclusion:

In real life artistic phenomena do not always appear in a perfect, "pure" form. The concept of "method" that sorts writers into pigeon-holes without revealing their objective historical function should be fearlessly consigned to the devil.

And this is equally true of contemporary Soviet artists.

The predominant trend in Soviet literature is socialist *realism*. Why? Because in Marxist-Leninist reasoning gunuinely artistic realism is fidelity to historical *truth* and perception of the basic *tendency* of the development of reality in its struggle with the forces of the old order. Why is it that today this genuine realism is in fact socialist realism? Because our country is the country of triumphant socialism, and because the contemporary artist adopts the socialist point of view when he truthfully depicts reality in the light of the basic tendency of our epoch.

Canonisation of individual genres, forms, temperaments, manners and techniques is alien to socialist realism. Socialist realism is characterised by rich variety. It includes epic, lyric, drama, tragedy and comedy, satire, the multivolume novel and the essay, the poem and the epigram, the psychological novel and the adventure story, the passionate revolutionary dream and the merciless "tearing away of all and sundry masks" from the face of the enemy, lofty revolutionary ardour and sober analysis, the struggle of passions and merry laughter, strict fidelity to real life and the fearless flight of fancy.

Canonisation of theme is also alien to socialist realism. By calling upon the writer to show what is *new* and socialist in life—for it is in the practice of millions that the genuine truth of socialism is revealed—socialist realism expects him to reflect the unending variety of human life, the entire historical experience of mankind, all the problems and questions that agitate the new man. The world-wide internationalist struggle of the working class and its great Party for a communist system; the decay, fanatic resistance and ruin of capitalism; the socialist transformation of millions of peasants and other intermediate social strata; the liberation of peoples from the cursed national oppression; the new, socialist labour as opposed to the drudgery under the yoke of capitalism; the exposure of all ideas that disguise exploitation or "embellish" it—such as the ideas of individualism, religion, racial and national "superiority"; passionate propaganda of the great liberating ideas of socialism; the Civil War and the imperialist war; succession of revolutionary generations; the emergence of the new, socialist individual and collectivism; the mighty, popular movements of bygone ages; scientific discoveries and research; love, birth and death—all the variety of the life and struggle of millions of people in the singular-historical battle of socialism with capitalism must and will provide the "theme" for socialist realism.

The large majority of genuinely revolutionary authentic artists of our country with the great Gorky at their head are creatively working along these very lines, rejecting "pure" or abstract styles, overcoming their own contradictions and errors, resisting harmful tendencies, bearing more or less noticeable traces of the past and showing greater or lesser talent.

1932

Alexander Tvardovsky

THE MAIN THEME

Speech at the Third Congress of Writers of the USSR

Comrades! The main theme of our Congress is the seven-year plan and the tasks of literature. Although this theme has been mentioned often enough, it has not yet, in my opinion, been declared with full force, has not concentrated within itself all the many-sided, large and complicated questions of our development in a new stage.

I do not mean to say that we have not heard good, sensible and vivid speeches from this platform, especially by representatives of national literatures and, indeed, by some Muscovites and Leningraders.

The point is that we seem still to be paying a sort of tribute to the inertia of our yesterday's existence.

This is first of all borne out by the main report with all its imperfections that I cannot, incidentally, in all conscience lay at the door of Alexei Surkov alone, since the preparation of this document was carried out in a way that would have caused disapproval of even Gleb Uspensky's peasant who insisted that it would be no letter if the whole village was writing it.

This tribute to inertia is visible in some delegates' contributions as lifeless "local reports", boring "statistics", etc.

From this inertia comes the lack of cohesion, the fractional nature, the accidental and unnecessary appearance of certain points—in a word, just what happens in many of our novels and stories, where the theme is defined and everything seems to be in its proper place, but the reader gets no deep satisfaction.

Obviously, I am not taking upon myself the task of "putting things right", as they say; I simply want to state how I understand the matter and what seems to me to be the essential thing about it.

The essential thing for us is to realise seriously what is our task in the seven-year plan, which, incidentally, while we sit and discuss things here, is already going full blast, to realise seriously that our task is to fight for a high "general level" of quality in all the many branches of literature, incomparably higher than what we had in the past.

The period of comprehensive communist construction does not mean simply the new conditions in which literature exists; it means a new measure of demand made on us by the people of our country, which divides us decisively from the period that has just passed.

We cannot go on living in the old way, is what we must say to our literary past and even to our today—and we will not!

That is what seems to me to be the most important thing in the work of this Congress and, of course, I am certainly not being original in thinking in this way. But the point is that the essence of this task must be felt deeply, and not just put into words, it must become a personal task for each one of us, and not merely "the task of the whole collective".

So we are talking about the quality of literature, the significance and impressive power of the ideas and images that it must bring to the people of our time. Here we must clarify and define one or two things in the simplest of terms.

In all fields of human activity, quantity and quality exist in a certain balance, in equilibrium, as it were. More and better—that is what is said with regard to all the material values that are created by human labour. But it sometimes happens that "more" is of greater importance than "better", and quantity—even if temporarily—is preferred to quality.

But in spiritual activity, especially literature and art, preference is always given only to quality. And what is more, quantity in this field has definite limits to its growth, which must not apply to quality.

What does a theatre-goer care about "700 plays written in the period under discussion"? He would have been satisfied with just seven good plays that he would want to see time and time again.

However much one may love poetry, does he need hundreds of volumes of poems written in that same period? Does a reader need 365 novels per year? Whatever the variety of taste and choice, that is an unnaturally excessive number—the only sort of literature that can be consumed in such quantities is the American detective stories that Kornei Chukovsky was telling us about.

So, when it comes to literature, the first and most important thing is quality—hardly a new idea, but what can you do if it is not yet fully clear to all of us even in the face of the growing level of demand that our readers are putting and will continue to put on us? How many times we have heard the expression "more and better" at this Congress, with "more" receiving greater emphasis, since it is much easier to achieve than "better". This is something that our present 5,000 Union members can guarantee, especially as the possibilities of printing and publishing in this country are colossal.

The task of literary education and artistic growth of Soviet writers arises directly from the general major task of raising the quality of our Soviet literature.

I shall not dwell on how imperfect and sometimes harmful I personally consider the various "official measures" in this connection.

Obviously, in our literary business it is not "official measures" that are decisive, but the *model*, a concrete example of great mastery. The importance of a model is vital and immutable.

We need only to look at Sholokhov. Sholokhov has not only given us *And Quiet Flows the Don* and other works; without particularly thinking about it he has, incidentally, created a whole school of notable Soviet prose-writers. Perhaps they have not as great talent and follow in his wake, but they have immeasurably widened the field encompassed by Soviet writers. They exist, they have their readers; they represent diverse aspects of a vast literary process.

Let us take another example, Marshak. The high standard of Soviet verse translation from foreign languages and from the languages of the fraternal republics represented by our brilliant masters in this skill, is undoubtedly in many ways indebted once again to the "model"—the unusually brilliant pen of Marshak, poet-translator following, in his turn, the Russian classical tradition of artistic translation. The same might be said of the pleiad of talented children's writers and poets that was engendered by Marshak's "model".

The number of "model" writers of their sort is not, of course, confined to these two—I merely name them as examples of totally different styles of our rich and diverse literature.

Is the task of creating "model" works the privilege of just a narrow and small group of the "chosen"? Of course, not! Today it is Sholokhov; tomorrow, someone else we do not yet know. But this is not some sort of impersonal duty that with our customary "verbosity" we can place on the shoulders of the "entire collective" as though this were a kind of god on whom we can rely to carry it out, so that we can relax. No, "God won't help if you have no head on your shoulders", as the saying goes.

I wanted to stress this need for a deep *personal* understanding of the problem facing literature on the threshold of communism in order to prepare the way for an even more important assertion.

We often speak of our collective responsibility for the fate of literature and of the responsibility of each of us for "literature as a whole", etc.

Here I want to say—I have already partly said this—that however paradoxical it may seem at first glance, the highest form of collective responsibility in our work is a real awareness of one's responsibility for oneself, not for "literature as a whole". And take note that we haven't really very many writers that cope with this sort of responsibility. But, I might say, we have more who eagerly take upon themselves responsibility for "literature as a whole"—for supervising it, instructing it and directing it.

In short, being responsible "for oneself" is difficult like hell and demands the utmost expenditure of mental and even physical energy, long years of apprenticeship, the biggest and better part of one's life and complete disinterestedness, even in one's thoughts.

At one point Goethe says that if the artist completing a work thinks of the rapture with which people will greet it, and then himself feels this rapture in anticipation, he might as well give it all up, because nothing of any value will come of it. And only if he is prompted to return to it not by any external motive but by his personal involvement (perhaps it won't meet with any success, but this is how *I* want it, this is how it *must* be written)—only then is it possible that something might come of it.

"I want to serve my country with my pen," authors often write in their first raw verses or prose. This sounds extremely noble. But in fact it is immodest and conceited. Even the skill to wield an axe, to say nothing of the pen, is not something that comes easily to a man. The art of writing takes years and years of conscious, unsparing labour to master even for a man with talent, and not only labour but personal risk too, because even with all conditions observed it is a dangerous business. Sometimes it costs a man too much to make this choice.

These and many other similar thoughts come to one's mind when we talk about bringing up the next generation of writers. For one reason or another many young writers join our ranks not as a result of profound experience of life or manly soul-searching: is this a vocation or just an idea I have in my mind?—but as a result of a simple-hearted attraction to the "beautiful and easy" life of a writer. We must not promise them an easy life in literature—there is no such thing! And there cannot be such a thing for any writer of talent. The writer might feel delight, even ecstasy, in the very process of work, but his life is never easy, nor can it be, even under communism.

It wouldn't be a bad thing to keep in mind Tolstoi's advice: if you can live without writing, don't write. It is obvious, that the necessity for the appearance of any book or manuscript also matters.

In our world it is usual to harrass and hustle people who have not written anything for a long time or who have written little. But in some cases this is quite unnecessary; let them not write, so much the better, for can there be any value in something that is penned not because of an irresistible spiritual urge, a passionate desire to write, but—not to put too fine a point of it—because of considerations of professional obligation? And as for people who without our prompting want nothing in the world so much as to write, who have something to write but simply cannot get it written—then such harrassing and hustling is simply cruel.

This is the sort of thing one has to talk about, bearing in mind all the time the same problem of raising the standard of our Soviet literature and its prestige in our own country and throughout the world.

We are talking about the personal moral obligations and norms of the writer's work that must bring it close to the concept of communist labour.

Naturally, we must take these moral, ethical norms over from the experience of the great masters of the past—our own countrymen and those of all other nations. They lived in different times, set themselves different tasks and had different philosophies of life consonant with their time, but their unselfishness, noble self-abnegation in their beloved work and inspired service to great art still preserve their significance as the highest example and standard.

Generally speaking, we ought to conduct all our discussions as though we were in their presence; we must not forget what a mighty inheritance we have. Allow me to remind you that in the coming year, 1960, we shall be celebrating, among others, two dates of truly world significance; the fiftieth anniversary of Lev Tolstoi's death and the centenary of the birth of Anton Chekhov. This lays many obligations upon us. It will be the second year of our great seven-year plan, and in it there will be these two red-letter days of our national Russian culture and of the whole of Soviet culture. What are we writers going to think of ourselves at that time in relation to our aims and prospects of achieving them?

However, whether we are good or bad, neither Tolstoi nor Chekhov will do for us what we ourselves must do. They did their bit and did it splendidly, and we—such as we are and such as we must be in the face of the tasks posed to us by our great times—we must do ours.

And if this is so—let us get down to work. Work that is not easy, even tormenting at times, but joyous, inspired by the realisation that we are taking part in the great cause of building a communist society on earth and making the spiritual world of the people of that society more rich, fascinating and beautiful.

Is this not the most important thing, the essential thing for each of us individually, for each of us *personally*! And the degree to which this thing, most important and basic for all of us gathered together in this hall, is to become a personal acknowledged aspiration will determine to a considerable extent how close every one of us approaches his own cherished model, be it in poetry, in prose or in drama.

It might, of course, be quite appropriate and even useful

to debate the advantages of romanticism over realism, or the other way about, but it is a fact that when I, as a reader, have to do with a book that captures my heart and gives me the lively joy of getting to know life in its vivid images, I worry least of all about whether this is pure romanticism or realism with a touch of romanticism, or something else. I am simply grateful to the author for what he has given me.

Who in fact is going to object against romanticism if it gives birth to splendid works of art and sings the glory of our times; or against realism if it presents trustworthy and highly impressive pictures of real life? No one, of course. But when I am treated to some stilted writing, in which life is presented in such conventional passages of so-called "elevated" style that I want to shut my eyes with awkwardness, and I am told that I ought to read this, that it is romanticism, then I say, "No." And if I have before me some copying of life, pitiable and unimaginative, dull as a house-register on a screen, scantily illuminated with paltry thought, and am told that it is realism, I reject it. As a reader I refer to both in the words of Sobakevich: "I wouldn't eat a frog, even if it were coated with sugar, and I won't take oysters, either. I know what an oyster reminds me of...."

This age favours us writers.

It offers us whatever material we wish to choose from, whatever suits our taste or fancy. And nobody is standing over us and saying: "You must write like this, not like that."

Write as your conscience dictates; write what your knowledge of the aspect of life you have chosen allows, and do not be frightened in advance of editors and critics. There is one rule that I always observe in my work as editor and author: a good book, even if it is, as we say, a cutting one, has always greater chance than a bad one, and better able to overcome all obstacles in its path to the reader. I personally do not believe that there are manuscripts of genius that cannot find their way to the reader. I don't believe it!

We are richer than we think; we have even more riches than we boast of. I for one am convinced that no imperfections of our organisational forms and methods of rearing writers and guiding literature will prevent what ought to appear out of the wealth of genius of our peoples who are now in the best period of their history, approaching communism. And it does not matter that we are going to spend less time praising ourselves—let us even exercise the greatest severity in evaluating our modest achievements of today—no harm will come, for there is someone who will give us all and each one of us individually his due—this is our demanding but very fair and sympathetic reader, our great people, our Communist Party.

1959

Konstantin Fedin

SPEECH AT THE PLENARY MEETING
OF THE CENTRAL COMMITTEE OF THE CPSU

June 18-21, 1963

I confess that I was at a loss before I could decide on precisely what theme to concentrate in my speech to the Central Committee of the Party, because so many problems, questions and tasks had already been touched upon in recent discussions of Soviet art. But in the end my experience of art itself prompted me that the least good work flows from the pen at times when the author is anxious—God forbid!— not to leave anything out. Not even a bad writer in a very long book has yet managed to "tell all". On the other hand, every good critic knows that it is absolutely wrong to judge a book by what it gives insufficient attention to or does not deal with at all. So I have to limit myself to one question: which do I consider to be the most important among all the problems that are now so deeply stirring the entire artistic world?

I gave myself a very general answer: the most important thing is our constant, urgent concern for the successful development of Soviet art. I really could not restrict it further. But as I proceeded to break down my theme into sections, I stopped at what seems to me to be one of the most vital aspects nowadays—our conflict with Western modernism in connection with the method of socialist realism. So I decided to speak to you on this subject. I would like to make one qualification: when I speak of art, I have in mind literature, painting, sculpture, music and the stage, though I rely most of all on the experience of literature.

It is not the first time for Western modernists to enter battle with Soviet literature. The days when they simply denied the existence of any sort of literature in our country are now long since gone. And the more aggressively they now campaign against our writers, the more obvious do they make the growing significance of Soviet art, both here at home and in the international field.

The positions from which Western modernist critics attack Soviet art (it makes no difference which aspect—our views on the role of literature, our subject matter, literary form, sometimes even our use of language) are mostly founded on a formalist basis. And whichever aspect of Soviet art the critics touch on, their greatest annoyance and dissatisfaction is always evoked by the very close link between the Soviet writer and the Communist Party. The very possibility of the Party directly influencing literature is considered inadmissible. The Western critics, who proclaim rising above politics as an artistic ideal, obviously think that they achieve this ideal when they attack Soviet art for its devotion to the Party.

This gives great opportunities for guile, but there may also be some misunderstanding.

For example, one cannot but attribute to guile the recent noisy proclamation in the West of "Soviet avant-gardism". This myth was very clearly exposed as enticement to popularity-seeking, which unfortunately deceived two or three of our gifted young poets. But myths arise and are dispelled. Avant-gardism remains an historical product of the West. Soviet literature remains true to type.

It seems to me that in the West a significant proportion of the conflict with our conception of art arises precisely from inadequate evaluation of the historical development of artistic phenomena. Inadequate knowledge of them may, of course, be the result of deliberate distortions of history by the propagandists. But it is difficult to attribute to anything other than misunderstanding the persistent desire of certain Western art experts to apply to nearly all countries of the world their pet theory of successive development of artistic forms. According to such a point of view, every national art that does not copy the latest Western fashion in art should be considered underdeveloped. But should one really expect that in countries now struggling for liberation from colonialism art will inevitably develop by the same stages as it has developed under capitalism? Is it credible that art in socialist countries should follow each vagary of

Western artists who cast about in that old world of theirs? Surely it is the history of a people that determines the specific path of its artists.

Soviet art was born not in the bookworm's study, nor in the hermit's cell. In the stern days of the Civil War, older Russian writers—who were much younger in those days— found themselves faced with a choice: on which side of the barricade will they take up their stand? And they made their choice. If they happened to choose wrongly, they found enough strength to correct their error. The outstanding Soviet writer, Alexei Tolstoi, has given us in his stories stern and stirring evidence of such agonising searchings. It was he who in the early twenties sang a hymn to the new reader: "The new reader is he who has come to feel himself master of the Earth and the City. He who in the last ten years has lived ten lives. He who has the will and the courage to live. . . ." Tolstoi asserted that within his heart of hearts the writer heard the reader's call saying: "You want to hand on to me the magic wand of art. . . . Then write honestly, clearly, simply, majestically. Art is my delight."

Alexei Tolstoi was not alone in hearing this call. Kuprin also fell into tragic error, but he overcame it and returned from the West to his native land. In his old age Bunin felt the tragedy of his situation, and from distant emigration he sent moving letters to young Soviet writers, and books with kind dedications inscribed in them.

All experience is made up of positive and negative features. The fate of the older writers, their tragedies, were lessons for the Soviet writers, as was that greatest of all historical lessons, learned in the seething ferment of a revolutionary people. They were building a new world together with the people; they were defending the land of October and together with the people they travelled the road, soaked with the blood of the best of our countrymen, to victory in the Great Patriotic War. For almost half a century our literature has been inseperable from the history of the Soviets, and it has been the will of the Soviet peoples that this history should be personified at its every step by the Communist Party, standing at the helm.

What hopes can anti-communism have of "sowing discord" between Soviet art and the Party? History cannot be reversed. True, the Western propagandist is not so naive as to call upon our artists to break with the motherland of socialism—this method has entered the annals of the intervention. The favoured butt of Western criticism is socialist realism and one of its components, the attitude to the past, the problem of traditions.

Clearly the dominant artistic tradition of Soviet literature is realism of the classics of the last century and the turn of the century (the works of Gorky). The enthusiasm with which Gorky gathered together and united the forces of young Soviet art and, at the same time, worked out the principles of socialist aesthetics, is unforgettable. It remains still in the hearts of Soviet writers.

The principles of the artist's approach to the presentation of reality in works of art have taken years to mature. Literary experience and the achievements of talented writers have provided the material for the building of the Soviet artistic world. Marxism and the revolutionary genius of Lenin have inspired the theoreticians and critics, expecting them to generalise philosophically the new phenomena of Soviet art and determine what they have in common with the artistic heritage and what makes them quite specific. In this way the foundation of an ideological and artistic outlook—the method of socialist realism—was laid down in Soviet literature. More than one decade has gone by since socialist realism itself became established as a creative tradition in literature and art.

What strikes one in the angry retorts of the opponents of Soviet art is the three-word phrase "socialist realist tradition". These words provoke furious reactions from our Western critics, to whom they are a constant source of annoyance. The reason for their fury is, of course, the word "socialist", but to speak out against socialism is to take up openly a political stand. In addressing the artist it is much more "a-political" to attack "realism" and "tradition". So the critics cry out in unison that realism is out of date, and that to follow any traditions is to be conservative. They neglect to mention the abundance of realist artists in the West (possibly because there are quite a few progressives among them with more than a little sympathy for socialism) and seem not at all embarrassed by the incongruity that results.

They are in for embarrasment, however, when they decide to sing the praises of, say, poetic form that is free from rhyme, stanza and generally accepted rhythm, and forget to mention or are quite ignorant of the fact that this, too, is tradition. It was used a hundred years ago, to go back no further, by the American poet Walt Whitman, then by the Belgian Émile Verhaern and host of other Western poets; and then at the end of the last century the German poet Arno Holz, in a completely "non-innovatory" way, founded his "new form of lyrics" on rhyme "subjectively perceived by the individual". Yet this is how the Western objectors to realist traditions hope to allure "underdeveloped" Soviet literature.

Our young poets are aware that free verse was employed quite often by proletarian writers in the early days of Soviet literature. This sort of verse, combined with other techniques, was also used by Mayakovsky—with the basic difference that he, while remaining a highly individual poet, was alien to subjectivism. His voice, like a megaphone, amplified the tumultuous and resolute voice of the revolutionary mass. His verses were new in content and social meaning, and therefore Mayakovsky's innovation assumed a perfect form and did not remain merely a vehicle for experiment. Mayakovsky has also become part of the Soviet socialist tradition.

They try to frighten us by saying that socialist realism measures individualities by one yardstick and thereby belittles the personality of the artist. Here we cannot help recalling, even without paraphrase, the well-known comment of Lev Tolstoi with reference to the decadent writings of Leonid Andreyev: "He scares us, but we are not afraid." We are not afraid because socialist realism embraces an endless variety of artistic talents, which differ from each other not only in national flavour but, even within each equal Soviet nation, by their timbre, the perspective of their view of the world, their artistic manner, and the techniques of their mastery. The Party has never ceased to stress the variety of forms and trends within the single mainstream of socialist realism, and it continually urges the artists to perfect their techniques. Let us call to mind just one example, the strongly romantic stream that flows unabated in our prose, as it has done ever since it first sprang up, and alongside it, the deep lyricism of recent works of prose-writers who, for strength of feeling, are equal to their fellow artists, the poets.

When our literature was taking its very first steps, Gorky used to say that in the Land of Soviets the significance of the individual personality in the process of history was constantly growing, and that this was *thunderously*, to use his expression, confirmed by the actual history of those difficult times. Present-day communist construction gives immeasurably more vivid evidence of the significance of the individual personality in every sphere of human activity. The individual is not divorced from society, and society is built on the model of its best members. The name of Man is raised high in the Programme of the Communist Party. Individual development of every man and perfection of his moral qualities are the deep concern of the entire socialist system of government and society.

The Western world cannot possibly consist of propagandists of anti-communism alone, just as by no means all of those active in the field of art support unreservedly the modernist tendencies. Many of the critical comments made in the West about Soviet artistic life arise from a constantly increasing interest in it. There is a growing number of international occasions in which more and more people active in the arts in both socialist and Western countries take part.

Soviet writers consider it essential to intensify this sort of intercourse. They are guided by the necessity to aid all peoples in their struggle against a new destructive war that threatens mankind. While there continue to be class societies beyond the frontiers of socialist countries, there can be no talk of any "ideological fusion" of the artistic intelligentsia of directly opposite camps. As life goes on the righteousness of some of its social phenomena is confirmed by history, and the falseness of others is revealed to more and more people. We cannot call a halt to our disagreement with our opponents, nor can we break off our discussions in the sphere of art. Socialist realism continues to assert itself—of this we are convinced—and we cannot cease to speak up in its defence with the passion without which a genuine artist cannot exist.

We are building a new world. We are building a new man within that world. And the duty of the Soviet artist is to contribute to this glorious effort!

Mikhail Sholokhov

INTRODUCTORY SPEECH
AT THE SECOND CONGRESS OF WRITERS OF THE RSFSR

(An extract)

When we are abroad we are often asked—sometimes with malice, sometimes with a genuine desire to understand—for an analysis or, as it were, a layman's explanation of what socialist realism is. I shall not risk stealing the bread from the mouths of our theoreticians, and in any case, like all practical men, I am not very good at scientific formulations. But I usually answer such a question in the following way: socialist realism is the art of the truth of life, comprehended and interpreted by the artist from the point of view of devotion to the Leninist Party principles. To put it even more simply, it seems to me that any art that actively assists men to build a new world is socialist realist art.

Whoever wishes to understand what socialist realism is should pay careful attention to the enormous experience Soviet literature has accumulated over almost half a century of its existence. The history of this literature *is* socialist realism embodied in the vivid images of its heroes and in the visual representations of the popular struggle.

Let the path followed for half a century by Soviet literature and, in particular, by one of its leading echelons—Russian literature, stand before our eyes today as we discuss the future of art. We have enormous wealth behind us. We have something to be proud of, something to counterpose to strident and sterile abstractionism. And although we can see how much remains to be done if we are to be worthy of popular trust, and although we are far from being satisfied with our work, we should never forget how much our literature has already contributed to mankind's spiritual wealth, nor how great and unquestionable is its authority throughout the world.

SPEECH ON ACCEPTANCE OF THE NOBEL PRIZE

On this solemn occasion I consider it my pleasant duty to express once more my gratitude to the Swedish Royal Academy for awarding me the Nobel Prize.

I have already had the opportunity to state publicly that it means for me more than international recognition of my professional services as a writer. I am proud that this award has been made to a Russian writer, a Soviet writer, for I stand here as a representative of the large body of writers in my native land.

I have also expressed my satisfaction that the award is, in an oblique fashion, yet another affirmation of the genre of the novel. I have recently had to listen to or read a number of speeches which, to be quite frank, astonished me. The speakers claimed that the novel form was old-fashioned and no longer in tune with the demands of contemporary society. But it is the novel that enables the writer to give the fullest possible portrayal of the world of reality and to project on this portrait his own attitude to reality, to its burning issues, and also the attitudes of his fellow thinkers.

The novel, as it were, best predisposes the writer to a deep perception of the vast life around us, rather than to attempts to put forward his tiny "self" as the centre of the Universe. This is the genre that by its very nature offers the greatest scope to the realist artist. Many young art movements reject realism on the grounds that it has outlived its time. Unafraid of accusations of conservatism, I hereby proclaim that I hold the opposite point of view and am a convinced supporter of realism in art.

People nowadays often talk about the so-called literary avant-garde, by which they mean the latest modish experiments, especially in the realm of form. But in my opinion the genuine avant-garde is represented by those writers whose works reveal new content, the characteristic aspects of our day. Realism in general, and the realist novel in particular, are based on the artistic experience of the great masters of the past, but in the course of development they

86

have acquired essentially new, specifically contemporary characteristics.

I am speaking of the realism that expresses the idea of life's rejuvenation, its refashioning for the good of mankind. I am speaking, of course, of the realism we now call socialist. Its specific feature is a view of the world that rejects mere contemplation of or retreat from reality, and calls to battle for the progress of mankind, makes it possible to achieve aims dear to the heart of millions and illuminates the paths of the struggle.

Mankind does not consist of a host of isolated individuals, floating, as it were, in a state of weightlessness, like cosmonauts outside the reach of gravity. We live on the earth and are subject to its natural laws and, as the gospels say, sufficient unto the day is the evil thereof, the cares and the needs, the hope for a better future. Immense strata of the population of the earth are moved by the same desires, live by the same interests, which unite them far more than they divide.

These are the working people, the people who, with their hands and their brains, create everything. I belong to those writers who find the greatest honour and the greatest freedom in the totally unlimited possibility of using their pens to serve the working people.

It is from this that everything stems. Thereon is based my opinion, the opinion of a Soviet writer, on the place of the artist in the present-day world.

We live in restless times. And there is not a nation on earth which would want war. Yet there are forces that hurl whole nations into the war flames. Is it possible that the ashes should not sear the heart of the writer—the ashes of the boundless holocaust of the Second World War? Is it possible for the honest writer not to speak up against those who would like to doom mankind to self-annihilation?

What, then, is the vocation, and what are the tasks of the artist who sees himself as a son of his people, a tiny unit of mankind, and not as some deity indifferent to the sufferings of men, elevated to Olympus, above the clash of opposing forces.

To speak to the reader honestly; to tell people the truth—sometimes harsh, but always courageous; to strengthen human hearts in a belief in the future, in their own strength, in their ability to shape that future. To be a fighter for

87

peace throughout the whole world and, by his words, to raise up such fighters wherever those words might reach; to unite men in their noble and natural desire for progress. Art has a mighty power to influence the minds and hearts of men. I believe a man is worthy of the title of artist if he directs this power towards the creation of the beautiful in the souls of men, towards the good of mankind.

In the course of its history my people has not progressed along the beaten track. Its paths have been those of explorers, pioneers of life. I have always seen my task as that of a writer who, by all that he has written and all that he will write in the future, pays tribute to the labouring people, the constructive people, the hero people that has never attacked anyone but has always been able to conduct a worthy defence of what it has created, to defend its freedom and its honour, its right to build the future of its own choice.

I should like my books to help people to become better men, to grow purer of heart. I should like them to evoke love of one's fellow men and the will to struggle actively for the ideals of humanity and progress. And if I have succeeded to any extent, I am content.

My thanks to all those present in this hall, to all who have sent me greetings and congratulations in connection with the Nobel Prize.

1965

Pavel Korin

THOUGHTS ON ART

The fate of art is bound up with the fate of mankind. Chronicles, records and works of research do not always give us as deep an understanding of the history of mankind as do ancient slabs of stone; traces of the Assyrian or Egyptian designs; fragments of ancient columns, preserving still the warmth of the sun and the touch of the hands which polished them; the magical fantasy and primitive boldness of the Aztecs' images of the gods of life and death; the irresistible flamelike upward thrust of Gothic architecture; the Renaissance frescos singing triumphant hymns to the glory of man; the line and colour of ancient icons or the indignant paintings of progressive Russian artists which are evidence of their civic courage and spiritual anguish.

It is as though we were looking into the eyes of the artists some familiar and some unknown, who open up to us the heart of their peoples, the soul of their epoch. The immortal power of art, enshrined in stone, colour and sound makes us relive again and again the joys and sorrows of mankind.

It is difficult for an artist to speak about art. I do not think this is a paradox. It is difficult to speak about something one cherishes and loves. There are words which, it seems to me, ought to be pronounced very softly, under one's breath, so great are they—words like artist, art, motherland. One should simply hold them within oneself, like a gift of life too great to be repaid.

So if I take up the pen, it is from a desire to share with you some thoughts about present-day art. My article will not be a learned treatise, nor a programme; rather it will be thoughts at a halt, when a long road is behind but the summit still lies ahead, and from the height gained by our art, the height of the ideals and aims of our times, we feel the need to look around us, to look back and throw a glance into the future. After all, the present is always a bridge between what is past and what is yet to come.

I shall not claim, of course, to deal with all the important problems of art in our day or, even more, to solve them. But there is one thing I do not want any doubts to remain about, and from the first page I shall speak with the words of Montaigne in my mind: *"C'est ici un livre de bonne foi, lecteur."*

The Art of the Present

Every epoch creates its own art. Great epochs, in which men live a particularly tense and concentrated life and in which vast social movements take place, stirring to activity millionfold masses, call into being great and elevated art. Remember Phidias and Michelangelo, Shakespeare and Beethoven.

When I think about our own times and our own art, I always try first of all to define what Goethe called "the demand of the day, the demand of the epoch" which is the highest, immutable law of art.

I see the demand of the epoch in that unrivalled urge for freedom and happiness which has seized the peoples of all the continents on earth. The ideals of independence and justice, the noble ideals of humanity and progress enable men to walk erect where, to the shame of the civilised world, they have known the overseer's whip and the axe of the executioner. Our age is devoted to the sacred struggle of mankind for freedom and dignity. The bastions of oppression are crumbling. Before our very eyes the banner of national independence has become the rallying banner in a mighty struggle for the victory of truth and justice for hundreds of millions.

The entry into battle of whole peoples—such is the beatiful and invincible sign of our times. This heroic struggle imbues the works of classical art with a new light and endows them with new life. For what heart, thirsting for freedom and ready to lay down life for it, can fail to respond to the thunderous chords of Beethoven's *Egmont* as a challenge to heroic feats? And who can fail to see Michelangelo's slaves, tensed and exhausted, as symbolic representations of the titanic efforts and sacrifices on the road to liberty? And the words of Prometheus, as he flung down a challenge to the gods, are comprehended today as a proud resistance to all tyranny, as an oath of faithfulness to the chosen cause:

I have no wish to change my adverse fortune
Be well assured, for thy subservience.[1]

The Prometheuses of ancient and modern Greece; the Prometheuses of all countries in which man is oppressed, in which he is engaged in the struggle and must conquer— this is no myth, no legend. It is life itself, worthy of becoming legendary.

The people of our country are following the struggle now going on in the world with close attention. Our native land, in which different nations are united in equality and brotherhood, is a shining prototype of man's life in the future. No one in our country is spurned because of the colour of his skin. We are all one people, united before the world. From ancient times we have been able to sense the wounds of the oppressed, and this ability to sense, deepened by a passionate desire to change the people's anguished fate, to transform life, is one of the noblest revolutionary traditions of Russian art and literature. Radishchev wrote: "I looked around me, and my soul was tormented by the suffering of mankind."

The creation of a new world and the birth of a new man is the essence of the historical process of our age and the basic content of the art of our times.

One single, inescapable alternative faces each artist in our times: stagnation or progress; slavery or freedom; hatred of mankind and the division of peoples or the spirit of unity, friendship and brotherhood; ideals of justice for all men and the triumph of peace or the threat of war; an art of militant humanism, truth and beauty—for without truth there can be no beauty—or an art divorced from life, remote from mankind, formal and abstract in its essence.

Before such an inexorable choice, the words of Maxim Gorky, addressed to creative men, ring out loud and clear: "Whose side are you on, 'masters of culture'?"

---

[1] Aeschylus, *The Prometheus Bound*, Cambridge, 1932, p. 121.

Making the choice today is not simply a question of artistic individuality. It is above all a question of conscience. And if genuine art has always cried out in favour of truth and peace, then today it must be an active fighter for truth and peace if it wishes to bear the name of art. It must be clear to all that both collectively and individually we bear the responsibility for the fate of peoples and for the fate of art, and each of us is bound by invisible threads to millions of lives and millions of hearts.

It is difficult to understand how is it possible not to see that the atomic bomb spells annihilation to the splendid creations of popular genius; how is it possible to be blind to the self-sacrificial, heroic efforts of men who have risen up in the name of independence; how is it possible to be deaf to the groans of enslaved peoples and to engage with indifference and cold blood in creating the empty forms of abstraction, which only by error could be called art, and which is nothing but a parody of art, betraying spiritual poverty and spiritual misery.

I am convinced that the flourishing of abstractionism, which is so passionately opposed by Renato Guttuzo in Italy and by Rockwell Kent and other celebrated artists in America, cannot be long-lived. Its course has no aims and no prospects; it leads to a dead-end, to nowhere.

I am confident of the victory of art that speaks to men in the voice of liberty and peace and whose sacred dedication is to the loftiest ideal of the epoch—a free man in a free world.

What, then, must it be—art in tune with the times?

Gorky wrote that heroic deeds demand heroic words. The great epoch of struggle demands a great art and dictates its scale. We should remember that contemporary art is a mighty unifying force, and must strive towards a lofty, heroic, passionate art that will resound like the *Marseillaise* and the *Internationale*.

Let me hark back to those far off and unforgettable years when my friends of the School of Art, Sculpture and Architecture and I were young and our country was going through stormy and troubled times.

For us artists the victory of the people in revolt signified triumph for the heroic in art. Life around us was beautiful and tragic. It called us to an art that would match life in the force of emotions and the power of philosophical content: a monumental art that was courageous and inspiring, pathetic and passionate.

I recall that we were often hungry, as by night, in cold studios, we painted posters after sketches by Mayakovsky and Cheremnykh, made pictures for the ROSTA[1] windows and dreamed of an art that would stir the heart and evoke heroic enthusiasm, the sort of art that gave birth to Bach's Passions, *The Citizens of Calais* by Auguste Rodin, the sculptures of Michelangelo, the titanic music of Beethoven, the painting of Alexander Ivanov and Vasily Surikov, like Rude's flaming *Marseillaise*.

Our imagination created cities of the future that would surpass Campanella's *City of the Sun* by the place allotted in them to art.

And with all our straining powers we sought to find and embody in art that most important quality that makes man significant—grandeur of spirit, a heart aflame.

In my view, future belongs to monumental art. The concept of "monumental" is a broad one which does not lend itself to a definition limited by strict formula. At times of the greatest upsurge of its spiritual life, mankind has created art works of such social moment that men of all times have accepted them with gratitude and ecstasy.

When I speak of the monumental, I see rising before me the Parthenon and Winged Victory of Samothrace, Dante and Michelangelo, Tintoretto and Goya, Velazquez and Shakespeare, together with the glory of Russia, Rublyov and Dionysios, Alexander Ivanov and Vrubel. The monumental is inseparable from lofty ideas, from passionate feelings, from expressive perfection of the language. Thought and image are the heart of art, the law of the monumental. The monumental is the character of creation. And only the mighty language of monumental form, I believe, can enable one to speak to the millionfold masses of the people "in the lofty harmony of song".

But when I look at our contemporary art I feel alarmed by one thing. It seems to me that for the past few years our art has been developing more like studio art. We need one, no doubt, though our aesthetic thinking should not end here. Streets of tiled-walled houses, motorways, city entrances, stations, squares, stadiums, swimming pools, aero-

---

[1] ROSTA—Russian Telegraph Agency.—*Tr.*

dromes, schools—everything that many people see daily should serve the artist as a stimulus towards creation and aesthetic transformation. Beautiful mosaics, gorgeous frescos could and should become an organic part of urban ensembles; they must accompany man's work, festivities and life. And that wonderful world of the beatiful, the world of mastery and love that we meet—alas!—most of all at exhibitions and museums of applied art, should be made accessible to our citizens not only in the art of major public forms, but also in modest articles of everyday personal use. One involuntarily calls to mind the wise words of Anatole France, who said: "There are not two forms of art, applied and fine." One cannot dissect that single organism into two halves without doing damage to each of them.

Our cities must become exhibitions of outstanding works of monumental art, like the towns of the Renaissance, where the statues at the crossroads, portals and cathedrals call to mind the names of their creators: Michelangelo, Donatello, Ghiberti.

The plan for propaganda of monumental art put forward by Vladimir Ilyich Lenin at the dawn of the new world must be carried out with revolutionary passion and scope worthy of the epoch.

On Realism

The basic text of our world is truth.

Our art must be the art of truth, realist art. But the character of realism is determined by the times, by the age that dictates its aesthetic demands.

Realism should be spelled the way Maxim Gorky spelled it: Great Realism.

Gorky spoke of the necessity for romanticism and of the essential presence in our works of "the third reality", the reality of the future. This means that romanticism, breadth of vision, a desire to go "onward and upward" are inseparable from a true reconstruction of life.

Truth, after all, may be conceived in different ways. But we must not confuse the great truth of art, the truth of the age or the truth of mankind with the petty half-truth of accidental and isolated facts or with worthless verisimilitude. The truth of an age may be expressed only by him who has a clear idea of the aspirations and aims of that age. The task of the artist, and his problem, is to show not the accidental and particular, but the essence, the purpose and the ruling tendencies of his time.

I call to mind one of our most outstanding artistic successes: Vera Mukhina's *Worker and Farmgirl* (1937). This sculpture is a symbol of the times and a glorious hymn to man. What passion and fervour this work conveys! This is the *Marseillaise* of our age, second not even to Rude's.

Somewhat earlier another outstanding work, Ivan Shadr's sculpture *The Cobblestone Is the Weapon of the Proletariat*, entered Soviet art. It pays tribute to the proletariat's sacred struggle in a way that only a truly revolutionary artist can do.

Our best works of art combine romantic imagination with sharp insight into the subject. I remember how deeply impressed I was by Boris Ioganson's *Interrogation of Communists* (1933). This painting holds great truth and power. Two men stand in the face of death surrounded by enemies. Yet there is no pessimism in it. There is conviction stronger than death, and there is the sort of lofty tragedy that we meet in Ilya Repin's canvases.

This is realism.

We have sometimes heard sceptical comments that Soviet painting is in no way different from that of the nineteenth century, that is, that plastic thinking has not progressed, and realist painting has been replaced by photography.

The absurdity of such a point of view is obvious to anyone who is familiar with the process of genuine creation, to everyone who knows the history of Soviet art and its best representatives.

G. Korzhev's cycle *The Communists* is an excellent example of the eternally revolutionary and innovatory force of realism. The corner-stone of every genuinely realist creation is a poetic idea, a poetic concept which, in turn, determines its plastic realisation.

As regards the "photographic" nature of certain canvases seen at exhibitions, everything depends on the artist. The subject alone can never save the artist if there is no deep truth of feeling and expression. For the artist, everything is important—line, silhouette, brush-stroke—everything that goes to make up the arsenal of artistic techniques and helps to achieve the truth and expressiveness of the image. We have, of course, unimaginative works, cold and dull, which are evidence of the authors' fossilised thinking and of their tendency to give a superficial and illustrative representation of life, rather than generalise its phenomena and interpret them through images. And we may also come across canvases with soulless dummies on them, which the author believes are the embodiment of some topical idea. This is a false trial, as false as the creation of vague obscure symbols and no less obscure allegories which are supposed to represent the "cosmos" or the "family", or "fury No. 1".

If images are to be true, the artist must learn a great deal, digest, assimilate and embody all this. To feel deeply is as difficult as to create. A man who is unmoved by his task or his theme can stir no one.

When I think about our times and about art worthy of the age, I recall the summit of realism, Italian art of the Renaissance.

Michelangelo. What a heart the man must have had! I once said to myself in the Sistine Chapel: "Remember the passion and the mighty tragedy of these images! Remember this!"

I saw that Michelangelo had created man as he ought to be. I realised that every great artist—be he painter, poet or musician—not only expresses the hopes of his age but also looks into the future. Hence the elated mood that grips our imagination.

In the Sistine Chapel I saw painting raised to its greatest summit of spirit and form. And when later I stood before the works of Titian, Tintoretto, Raphael and Veronese I felt the unifying force that bound them together: the spirit of great ideas, simplicity, proud courage, inspiration and breadth of vision. Everything in their works is integral and perfect. Tintoretto may be felt in contour and shading, in the posture of his characters and the composition of the painting. If you look at an arm, you feel that this is a hero's arm. This is great realism. And we must have a realism of this scale in Soviet art, so that we, too, may feel and express ourselves with similar force and passion.

I do not wish to be understood too narrowly. There is another side to realism, when the artist portrays man just as he is but, at the same time, reveals the full truth about him and pronounces his sentence on man and his age. Velazquez' portait of Pope Innocent X belongs to this category. It is striking. Rarely can we find such a superb psychological realist, or such truth about a man, conveyed in such a perfect artistic form, or such a typical image of intransient significance for all men. In 1935 I wrote to Nesterov: "To look at this portrait of Innocent X is like reading *Macbeth, Lear,* or *Hamlet.*"

We should try to discover the source of the unfading impact of this marvellous painting, to carry it with us in our memory as an example of the heights to which a realist painter may rise.

It is this sort of realism we must aspire to.

That is extremely bold and daring, you may say. But I find myself forced to agree with Johannes Becker, when he says: "We must dream more boldly than ever before; we must dare to entertain dreams of such great and limitless boldness as no other generation before us could ever have displayed."

From the National Towards the Universal

The drawing together of nations in the struggle for independence, the preservation of peace and the strengthening of friendship is the adornment of our epoch and has enormous significance for art.

And it seems to me that our multinational art must take and is already taking a universal character. This universal character must have a national and no other basis. From a national basis to a universal character—such is the line of development. One cannot take the specifically national as a final aim and limit oneself to it.

There is nothing new in my words. Just look at history for a moment. Rembrandt remains a Dutchman in art, and you would hardly say he belongs to any other nationality. Velazquez and Goya were Spaniards through-and-through— in world outlook and the language of their art. Dürer embodies the German Renaissance, just as Raphael and Leonardo da Vinci do the Italian.

These great artists expressed on a national basis universally human ideas, near and dear to the whole of mankind.

The genuinely national artist is one who is closely and essentially bound to his people, understands its historical destiny, its historical aims and path, is devoted to the higher interests of his nation and expresses his thoughts and feelings in the native language of his people.

The canvases of Martiros Saryan are filled with light and sunshine, happiness and joy at the blinding beauty of Armenia. They enchant us with their sincerity and deep feeling. Armenia stands out from his canvases enhanced with poetic force and transformed by the painter's love for her. This is thoroughly national, and at the same time is intelligible to all, for the feeling of love of one's country is common to all men.

The national aspect is an essential trait of every true artist. This is a general law of art. The feeling of belonging to one's nation is not something that can be introduced intentionally or achieved artificially. One simply has to love one's country, one's people, with an active love—without boasting, or closing one's eyes to imperfections; our pictures and the whole of our art should bear witness to this love.

Everyone cherishes the splendid creations of his people. I love the Kremlin, with its towers and cathedrals, St. Basil the Blessed and the majesty of the architecture of ancient Rus. But a man would be spiritually empoverished and blind if, while paying homage to the creations of his own people, he lost the ability to admire the harmony of the Parthenon, the flight of Gothic arches or the beauty of Georgian and Armenian old fortresses.

The Demand of the Age and Questions of Creation

The demands of the age make me consider such eternal problems as tradition and innovation in art, modernity and mastery. I deem it necessary to discuss these matters, though lack of space compels me to do this in a brief and concise form.

The revolutionary energy of our times and the assertion of a new world, justice and humanity have defined a new logic of art and changed our attitude to it, without denying, however, the achievements of bygone ages in both form and content.

Art grows out of tradition. The great art of days gone by was founded on tradition. The creations of Phidias and Raphael, the works of Andrei Rublyov, Alexander Ivanov and Vasily Surikov were nourished on the traditions of previous times. Our attitude to the immortal masters must also be worthy of them; it must be active and creative. Our love for great masters should not be simply mute adoration, it must inspire the artist's progress along the tortuous and sometimes tormenting path of artistic doubts, discoveries and achievements. The artist cannot be the prisoner or the slave of tradition. The genuine artist accepts tradition but remains free. He must find his own path in art, his own attitude to life and his own plastic language. He who blindly follows tradition cannot become a great artist.

We rate the art of ancient Rus very high, but who would dream nowadays of reviving the epic art of the fresco, following minutely the manner of Rublyov or Dionysios? We cannot turn the warm blood of precious experience into the cold, lifeless pattern for future imitation.

What should we really take from the past and make our own?

First of all, fidelity to the lofty ideals of the time, that we meet in the masters of the Italian Renaissance and in our own Russian artists.

We must adopt creative daring and sweep that astonish us in Tintoretto, in the mosaics of Montreale and Chefal, and in the work of Theophanos the Greek.

From the great masters of the past we can learn their astonishing purposefulness, their will to create, their skill. Let us think of Michelangelo's *Slaves*. The sculpture is breathtaking for its power of expression. It is genuine art, achieved by a master in a purposeful and thoughtful combat with his material. The will of the artist is present in everything, for it is not enough to think of a poetic idea, you have also to find an adequate form of expressing this idea. And this demands great effort.

We should respect the great masters of the past, but every Soviet artist must have his own vision of the world. The true artist always creates something of his own and takes an active part in the formation of a tradition that will be followed by succeeding generations.

The true artist is always a new, highly individual phenomenon in art. Surikov, for instance, introduced new forms of art; Nesterov, a new landscape, Serov, a new portrait. Saryan opens a window into a world perceived and created by him, the world of blooming valleys and snow-capped hills of Armenia. The graphic art of Lithuania and Estonia presents us with a poetic legend of its homeland and of the peoples of the Baltic Sea.

The genuine artist portrays a world he sees in his own way, endowing it with new content and beauty. Every real artist, therefore, is an innovator, for innovation is not something artificial, made to order. Innovation is related to the content, to the message of the work. The manner of thinking, the imagery must be novel. We artists of the twentieth century cannot slavishly imitate the artists of the nineteenth. The contemporary scene must be portrayed in a contemporary language. This does not mean transferring on to canvas certain formal attributes of the times nor, equally, deliberately searching for a fashionable style. The first approach would be merely illustrative and devoid of any creative fervour, and the second would amount to nothing but stylisation or mere imitation.

We have artists who have found new forms of capturing the epoch with power and inspiration. They are Mukhina and Shadr, Gerasimov and Ioganson, Deineka and the Kukryniksy, Plastov and Chuikov, Saryan, Favorsky, Vereisky, Shmarinov, Konenkov, Kibalnikov, Korzhev and many others. Artists blazing new trails do not recognise innovation as an aim in itself. Alexander Ivanov and Vasily Surikov were guided in their work by the ideas that formed their philosophy of life. The innovatory aspect of their work was the effect of their close ties with the epoch.

Closely related to the question of innovation is that of contemporaneity in art. These two streams have common roots and are subject to the same logical development.

Contemporaneity is the essence of art. But it cannot be achieved by formal reproduction even of topical features of the times. For the artist who really wants to go in step with his age, topicality should be a means and not the ultimate goal in art. Life moves constantly forward, and the artist who cannot sense and comprehend the basic tendencies but grasps at a few topical themes of today is doomed to oblivion tomorrow.

Beethoven did not consciously strive to be modern. He was simply unable to be otherwise. He thought deeply, and felt the pulse of his age, sincerely and passionately expressing what he felt; and no blows of fortune—lack of recognition, need, loneliness—could break his belief in the rightness of the path he had chosen.

Delacroix, when he painted *Liberty lending the people*, understood his age and created a picture that became a memorial not only to the revolution of the 1830s, but to revolutionary France herself.

One must always search for one's own and only theme, sparing neither time nor effort. One must seek it not on the outskirts of history, but at its heart, in its depths, at the mainstream. Where that active and impelling interest in life and contact with it are missing, the artist is bound to fall prey to banality, formalism or abstraction.

Indeed, which is more up-to-date—the art of the Italian Renaissance, Pushkin, Kramskoi's portraits, Nekrasov's poetry, Shevchenko, Isaakyan, Rodin, Rude or the surrealist creations of, say, Salvador Dali?

To answer this question one must clarify for oneself the essence of abstractionism, tachism, surrealism and the various other "isms" of the day that are now flooding Europe and America. It seems to me that all these trends are the sick reactions of people living in a world of contradictions and hatred, a world without a future. The advocates of abstract art are aware of the instability of this divided, rapacious and selfish world and are unable either to counteract its influence or stand up against it in their works. They have no ideals, and love neither man nor life. Their trickery (for what else can you call those dabs of paint put on canvas by mops or bicycle tyres?) is the despairing cry of fruitless souls in a doomed world.

So if we say that the works of Bach and Beethoven, Michelangelo and Raphael, Alexander Ivanov, Surikov and Serov, Gogol and Tolstoi are nearer and dearer to us and more modern than the "ultramodern" canvases of the formalists, this is because people of today and future ages will always feel their truth and immortal beauty.

Art acquires its power to influence only when the artist expresses his thoughts in a perfect artistic form. Even the most lofty idea cannot move or convince anyone if it is badly expressed. A mastery of technique is an essential prerequisite of movement towards the summit of art.

But mastery must be inspired by a lofty aim. I remember how I first sensed the gulf between inspired mastery and conscientious workmanship. In the Vatican in Rome, one is moved by Raphael's majestic style, harmony, clarity of spirit, artistic tact and simplicity. And alongside are the works of his pupils. Their frescos have many good points, but they lack the proportion, simplicity and majesty that rivet us to Raphael's works.

Mastery is a complicated concept. I think one should distinguish between great artists and great masters. It is the content that grips one. Take Bryullov, for example, a master of genius, whom I rate very highly. But when I think of his study of hands in the Tretyakov Gallery, it seems to me that the treatment is rather academic. There is another study of hands alongside, by Alexander Ivanov, and this is life itself.

Mastery of technique plays a necessary but subordinate, subsidiary role. Its emphasis and brilliance must be subdued so as not to overshadow the content.

Mastery is acquired through a study of life and through hard and strenuous work which should not be visible on the canvas.

I should like to dwell for a moment on another question of principle.

I am convinced that one cannot separate the artist a creator from the artist a man.

The role of art is enormous. It elevates and improves people; it provokes thought; it is a powerful source of ideological and aesthetic influence. So the artist himself must be pure of heart and great of spirit.

Some people wrongly believe that one may commit unworthy actions without their being found out or becoming generally known. It may happen that the facts will not be discovered, but the inner being of a man will inevitably be reflected in anything he creates. So he who does not respect his convictions or who hopes to profit by his talent, or who acts against his conscience for the sake of private gain cannot become an artist.

Today when Soviet art is called upon to bring the peoples of the world the word of peace and freedom, each one of us artists must strive to be up to this task, and to be Man in Gorky's definition of that word.

1961

ON CONVENTION

There are certain "connoisseurs of art" who think there is only one creative path in the theatre. They are prepared to formulate it as a constant, working artistic statute, binding for everyone. They judge the work of all theatres according to one formula. This makes me want to exclaim, with Zola, that: "I am always annoyed when I hear critics pronouncing sternly: 'This is theatre, but that is not.' How do they know? One single formula cannot embrace the whole of art!"

By all means let those theatres exist and perfect their style, which, while striving to make content and ideas the dominant elements, are at the same time trying to introduce on the stage that truth in which the actors painstakingly reproduce life, remaining true to nature, and the producer—in his *mise en scène*, stage-setting, "supposed circumstances", use of "accessary arts", décor, etc.—also aspires to be equally true to life. But it seems to me that the spectator should not be deprived of an opportunity to make use of his own creative imagination. I do not believe that the theatre should predigest everything and spoonfeed the audience. In the theatre, a hint or a detail, "a merest suggestion" can bring a play closer to artistic truth than a desire to say everything for everyone. A spectator may not actually walk out of a play in which everything is presented to him ready-made. Indeed, he may actually take pleasure in it, even if he realises that the theatre is portraying everything for him, presenting it all in a lifelike way down to the minutest detail, leaving nothing out. But he does not realise that he is being deprived of one of the greatest pleasures—the opportunity to take an active and creative part in the play by using his own powers of imagination and fantasy.

Here, too, there is convention, but not the sort that remains from the pseudo-classical and aesthetical-conventional theatre. More often than not there is also none of that healthy convention, born of popular tradition, that in my opinion is the essential element of artistry in the realist theatre. I don't think that, in the controversy about convention, it would be reasonable to give all the support to one theatre and to close one's eyes and firmly deny all the artistic, intellectual and emotional force of another. "Nothing angers me more than that narrow circle in which they want to imprison art," wrote Zola.

Let a theatre live and flourish, which strives to recreate the whole of life exactly and in detail, but does not fall into naturalism or pedestrian realism. The best exponent of such a direction is the Moscow Art Theatre, a theatre known to the whole world for its high culture.

Let there also be other theatres and other plays which, like the former, desire to present the spectator with nothing but the truth and to convey to him great ideas, but use different artistic forms and means. There are various creative paths leading to the same lofty aim.

We have more than once spoken of pernicious theatrical convention—the false, cardboard convention born of pseudo-classicism and the harmful convention of aestheticism and various other "isms". We have discussed the falsity of formalism and the limitations of naturalism. Formalism is a monster that devours content. Naturalism is a monster that indifferently munches the just and the unjust with an air of impartiality and objectivity.

But there is a totally different convention which, for the time being, until a more precise term can be found, might be defined as realist popular convention, the progressive convention of theatre art. This convention is an essential part of realism in the theatre.

Such convention gives the widest possible scope to artistic expression, suggesting appropriate artistic forms and means for most varied plays and performances.

At the very dawn of human history, when theatre audiences first began to share the rich inventiveness of ancient legends and tales clothed in dramatic form by Aeschylus, Sophocles and Euripides, the art of the theatre engendered and has been since elaborating *convention*.

Convention which is an indivisible part of the entire Greek theatre of antiquity has left its powerful imprint everywhere.

We feel it when we touch upon the dramatic unities; the theatre of antiquity was free in its choice of the time and place of action;

or mention the *chorus*, which served to express the thoughts of the people or the author's own attitude to the events described; the chorus, which was thematically linked with the character whom the actor was portraying and which in a number of cases took most active part in the action;

or call to mind the presentations of the ancient Greek theatre, which were played in broad daylight under the open sky, either on wooden platforms in town squares or in amphitheatres built on sloping hills and providing seats to such vast numbers of spectators that this alone made the theatre popular and democratic (according to archaeologist's calculations, the theatre in Athens accommodated twenty-seven thousand spectators and the theatre in Megalopolis, in Arcadia, forty-four thousand);

or analyse the artistic techniques with which the ancient dramatists elevated the characters in their tragedies above everyday life, above elementary resemblance of life and petty verisimilitude, translating the message and significance of the characters into poetic, artistic symbols without impairing the realistic essence of the images;

or mention the high dramatic tension of these plays.

Can we possibly discard all this as obsolete and use it only for references to the history of culture, simply because there are certain aesthetes who will say—"this is not new", or should we not re-examine it, extracting each fine grain, each precious stone of eternal culture and testing their brilliance in the bright rays of the people's present dreams of the theatre of the future?

Perhaps the most important thing that we can learn to create from the genius of the past is genuinely heroic images and events. Apart from showing men as they are, we must learn to show them as they could and ought to be.

Only to a certain limited extent can we say that such

images are taken from life, for since they are generalised and typified, they become larger than life itself.

In portraying a man with individual peculiarities, with his own impressions of life, aspirations and feelings, the ancient Greek dramatists exaggerated and sharpened their heroes' thoughts, desires, emotions and passions.

Here it would be appropriate to recall Lev Tolstoi, who believed that an irremovable element of the artist's nature is the ability "to see things not as they are", to see them more fully, to notice something vitally new, hitherto unexplored by man. In this sense, while remaining true to life, art becomes far more eloquent than any fact taken directly from life, and loftier and more real than everyday reality.

What in life is considered humdrum and banal, appropriate in a kitchen-sink drama or in a newspaper crime report, might become transformed into high tragedy of universal significance. After all, it was just such a garrison tale of a general who was deceived by his adjutant and strangled his wife out of jealousy that Shakespeare turned into a great tragedy of man's credulity. "Each one of his dramas," Belinsky wrote of Shakespeare, "is a symbol, a separate part of the world, concentrated by fantasy within the narrow confines of a work of art and presented as though in miniature."

In *The Thunder-Storm*, Alexander Ostrovsky transformed a reported event in the life of a merchant family on the Volga into an unusually powerful tragedy of Katerina, a woman whom no forces could reduce to submission.

Our dramatists can learn a lot from all this. But their purpose should not be that of blindly imitating the principles of ancient Greek tragedy. Neither should they put on buskins and eject all ordinary people from their plays and replace them by tyrants and semi-gods, or substitute the unusual and exceptional for the ordinary. They should use the acquired knowledge to discover the secrets and basic principles of the theatre, and boldly revive in Soviet theatre the genre of pure tragedy, especially tragedy in verse, drawn from life, but at the same time rising above life, greater than the simple facts of life and the chance fate of man. There is no need for buskins; their time has long since gone. We do not need artificial theatrical grandeur and passion. We should not take only the "lofty" and "noble" from life. In order to portray the many aspects of reality we should create not only such gentle, humanly naive works as, for example, Gogol's *Old-Time Landowners*—so incredibly moving in its simplicity and sincerity; we should recreate, on a new basis of exalted, tragic passions and bitter conflicts, such great and rounded characters as Gogol's Taras Bulba. Tragic heroines on our stage may not be so supercharged as Medea (though this is a great pity), but in no way should they be so completely ordinary and everyday, and certainly they should not have water running in their veins instead of blood, nor organised minds and hearts incapable of passion.

This is when you will recall realist convention. For you will hardly succeed in staging, say, *Medea* of Euripides, Shakespeare's *Othello*, Pushkin's *Boris Godunov*, Griboyedov's *Woe from Wit*, Lermontov's *Masquerade* or Gogol's *Taras Bulba*, unless you have recourse to the extremely impressive forms and means of the conventional theatre that correspond to the more than elevated inner world of each human character.

We must boldly revive and invent new elements of convention.

We are right to consider the tragic images of Aeschylus, Sophocles and Euripides and the comic images of Aristophanes as realistic. If the grass of the steppe ripples from the snoring of Taras Bulba and his sons, that is also realism. Gogol's *Viy* and *The Nose* are likewise realist productions, just like the weird sisters in *Macbeth* and the ghost of Hamlet's father.

Goethe's *Faust* is deeply realistic, reflecting the ruin of feudalism, a period of upheaval and world-wide historical significance. But you will remember how "unrealistic", from the point of view of pedestrian realism, is the very beginning of Goethe's *Faust*—the "Prologue in Heaven". What do pedestrian realists care that the legend of Faust is a pure folk-legend, which originated as a form of protest against religion? What do they care that Goethe introduced deep humanistic content into the traditional rites he used in the "Prologue"?

There is nothing you will not find in *Faust*! There are senior angels, the Lord himself, Mephistopheles, the Spirit of the Earth, the Master, Doctor Faust, Wagner, this philistine in science, the poor, modest maiden Margaret, Helen of Troy, the wife of the King of Sparta Menelaus, a choir of cherubs, the Emperor, an astrologer, courtiers, the Chancellor, crowds of people, dwarfs—everything that can be conjured up by rich, human fantasy, but which certainly could not find living space in narrow-minded realism.

Nevertheless, this is all convention, born of the contrast of living people with the fantastic. This is perfect realism, the realism of life, history and the times, moving eternally forward. It is the realism of the great life struggle of those who cannot content themselves with the soothing but shallow and banal ideas and emotions with which people like Wagner console themselves. This realism found brilliant expression in the words:

> *"Nur der verdient sich Freiheit wie das Leben,*
> *Der täglich sie erobern muss!"*[1]

And how much popular convention there is in the realism of Dante's *Inferno,* in the *Lay of Igor's Host* or in the *Iliad*!

All this offers an incredible variety of artistic forms you can employ in the theatre to reveal the most important phenomena of contemporary life and the greatest world events of our day.

With all the warmth of my heart (so much have these works given me during my lifetime), I cannot but recall the boldness with which the poet and dramatist Vladimir Mayakovsky employed the laws of convention of the mystery plays of the Middle Ages to create his remarkable and innovatory play *Mystery-Bouffe*, which was a discovery of new "theatrical lands". Mayakovsky rediscovered the marvellous world of theatrical convention, taking as its basis the popular presentations of the past, and perhaps it was at that moment that a new, innovatory popular convention was born, fathered by Mayakovsky in the early days of the October Revolution and brilliantly developed by other outstanding Soviet dramatists, right up to our own times.

Among those who, while in no way neglecting the best theatrical traditions of the past, have boldly and skilfully introduced into their plays this innovatory, *popular convention*, enriched by the new life, were Vsevolod

---

[1] *"Freedom alone he earns as well as life,*
  Who day by day must conquer them anew!"
                                        (Goethe, Faust, New York, p. 391)

108

Vishnevsky, Vladimir Bill-Belotserkovsky, Nikolai Pogodin, Ilya Selvinsky, Alexander Bezymensky, Leonid Leonov, Alexander Korneichuk, Mikhail Svetlov, Lyubomir Dmiterko, Valentin Katayev and Nikolai Erdman.

I well remember Vsevolod Vishnevsky, a courageous man undaunted by any obstacles and always ready to fight for his art (and not only for art).

His Narrators in *The First Cavalry Army* and in *Optimistic Tragedy*, and his Messenger in *The Last and Decisive* and *At the Walls of Leningrad* are an enormous artistic invention, that has become an everyday thing for us.

He has not been afraid of an obvious convention when, in *Optimistic Tragedy*, he made two sailors of the Baltic Fleet, who had already died, address the public like the living address the living and express their innermost feelings in the following extraordinary dialogue:

> *First Sailor*: (looking at the audience): "Who are these?"
>
> *Second Sailor*: "The public. Our successors. Our future, about which we used to think, if you remember, on board ship."
>
> *First Sailor:* "It's interesting to see the future as it really is. There are one and a half thousand people here watching us.... You'd think they'd never seen a sailor!"
>
> *Second Sailor*: "They are silent. They've come to see heroic deeds and heroic people."
>
> *First Sailor*: "Then all they have to do is look at each other."
>
> *Second Sailor*: "What polite silence! But can't someone get up and say something? (*Addresses one of the spectators.*) You, comrade, what are you frowning at? This isn't the War Ministry, it's a theatre.... Perhaps you think that in this case the War Ministry and the theatre have different purposes? Aha, you don't think so.... Now then, let's start! (*As though beginning to recite a poem.*) Forget what you are going to do this evening. The sailors' regiment, having followed its path to the end, is turning to you, to its successors...."

Beyond Vsevolod Vishnevsky's Narrators and Messenger I can discern the ancient theatre, in which the chorus, the coryphaeus and the messengers were so significant. His is the splendid convention of the mass, popular performances, but with new, contemporary functions, aims and role. The messengers have become central figures. They are completely living persons, not at all allegorical figures. Even earlier, Vladimir Nemirovich-Danchenko had introduced a wonderful Narrator, played by Vasily Kachalov, in Lev Tolstoi's *Resurrection*. This Narrator gave a commentary of events, introduced the characters, sat by their side, moved among them, unnoticed by anyone of them. This was a very bold convention.

It is a pity, by the way, that the producers following the Moscow Art Theatre traditions pay insufficient attention to the experience, legacies and traditions handed down to them by such a master of realist convention as Nemirovich-Danchenko.

In a few years, some dramatists have turned the role of the Narrator into that of the personality of the author. Strictly speaking this is the same Narrator, but with a broader function: he recalls the past relating it to our day, consults the audience or the characters, or "thinks aloud".

These peculiar, quite original and very human characters, introduced into the plays, have greatly expanded the authors' opportunities of taking part in action and counteraction, of fully or partially revealing their intentions, overtaking events, consulting the audience, taking the critical attitude of a bystander towards the characters or taking up active attitudes to events.

When our dramatists and producers intend to show by means of art the tremendous scale of such undertakings as the cultivation of virgin lands, or the construction of new industrial giants, or space exploration, they may use any form, but the most organic will be a monumental, elevated stage presentation or film, the style so successfully introduced by Dovzhenko.

I should like to repeat what Chekhov once wrote:

"Nothing needs refreshing so much as our stage.... You will not refresh the stage with silliness for one very simple reason: our theatre has already got used to silliness. We must refresh it by using the other extreme. And that extreme is Shakespeare."

Dramatists, producers and actors, let us learn from Shakespeare and Pushkin, from the ancient Greeks. Let us borrow those elements in the theatre that will not allow us to belittle in the slightest degree the contemporary events, but, on the contrary, will enable us to achieve mighty artistic generalisations and produce realist artistic symbols.

This is not the only way to picture our great times, but it is one most commonly forgotten when realism is divorced from romanticism, or deprived of those elements of convention which have been considered inappropriate to realism precisely because they are conventional.

We must fully understand Pushkin's idea of theatrical convention. He reasoned as follows: "Verisimilitude is still reckoned to be the major condition and foundation of the theatre. But what if we are shown that the very essence of the dramatic art does exclude such verisimilitude?"

"What sort of verisimilitude should we ask of the dramatic writer?" Pushkin asked. And he replied: "Drama was born in the public square for the entertainment of the people. Like children, the people demand interest and action and drama provides them with unusual and real events."

Yes, drama was born in the public square. And with it the theatre as the "entertainment for the people" was born.

Let us recall the convention of the pageants, open-air spectacles and shows of the past, whose inventiveness was spurred on not by poverty of the purse, but by rich creative imagination and the generous fantasy of the people. Remember convention that abounded in the brilliant, truly popular works of the classical dramatists. This was realist convention; far from neglecting life (as was the case in pseudo-classicist, formalist or modernist convention), it, in fact, sprang from life and drew its strength from it, though in no way copying it or mechanically reproducing it.

We have forgotten, for example, the most magnificent convention that comes from folk traditions, from the work of genuinely popular dramatists and poets, from the very first Russian theatrical performances, when the stage was filled with such symbolic personages as, for example, Wisdom, Faith, Hope, Conscience, and so on.

Healthy popular convention appeared in ancient Rus long before it came to the theatre, when there were only "rites and games" such as, for instance, the "nettle-eve" celebrated before sowing began, and similar to the ancient Greek games before the sowing season. This was a dramatic rite in which many people took part. Folk ritual games accompanied such items of work as harvesting, binding the sheafs, gathering in the stocks and carrying the grain from the fields to the barns.

Dramatic convention originated from the rites of spring, theatricised weddings, special theatrical accompaniments of folk songs, shrovetide celebrations, and many other "games" (some of which were introduced by Alexander Ostrovsky in his comedy *Poverty Is No Vice*).

The contemporary theatre ought to take over some of the traditions of past centuries, but adapt them creatively. This was boldly done by the rich-hearted poet and dramatist Victor Gusev when he wrote his dramatic poem *The Sons of Three Rivers* for the Mayakovsky Theatre. Gusev gave his dramatic poem this name because he describes the life and aspirations of three young men, born in the same year on the banks of three rivers—the Volga, the Seine and the Elbe. He made use of the traditions of Alexander Ostrovsky's *Snow Maiden,* Cervantes' *La Numancia* and Russian fairy tales, ancient epos and songs. It also calls to mind Daumier's *Europe*, Michelangelo's allegorical lands, and Titian's allegorical *La Bataille de Lepante*.

It would be interesting, I think, and would immensely expand our vision, so that we would be able to see the "whole world" and the "whole of mankind", if, for example, in plays describing virgin lands being put to plough, or the building of power stations to harness the mighty rivers, or the search for "the black treasure"—oil, etc., our authors reworked the classical traditions in a creative way and introduced "on a par" with living people such personages as Earth, Thunder, Drought, Rainstorm, the Nation.

But the important thing is to solve such problems *creatively*.

Imagination and fantasy were glorified by Shakespeare himself, who knew their gigantic power in the theatre.

Chorus (*exits*):
". . .But pardon, gentles all,
The flat unraised spirits that hath dar'd
On this unworthy scaffold to bring forth
So great an object: can this cockpit hold
The vasty fields of France? or may we cram
Within this wooden O the very casques
That did affright the air at Agincourt?
O, pardon! since a crooked figure may

> *Attest in little place a million;*
> *And let us, ciphers to this great accompt,*
> *On your imaginary forces work.*
> *Suppose within the girdle of these walls*
> *Are now confin'd two mighty monarchies,*
> *Whose high upreared and abutting fronts*
> *The perilous narrow ocean parts asunder.*
> *Piece out our imperfections with your thoughts;*
> *Into a thousand parts divide one man,*
> *And make imaginary puissance;*
> *Think, when we talk of horses, that you see them*
> *Printing their proud hoofs i' the receiving earth;*
> *For 'tis your thoughts that now must deck our kings,*
> *Carry them here and there, jumping o'er times,*
> *Turning the accomplisment of many years*
> *Into an hour-glass: for the which supply*
> *Admit me Chorus to this history;*
> *Who prologue-like your humble patience pray,*
> *Gently to hear, kindly to judge, our play."*[1]

As you can see, the powerful, inspired theatre of Shake-speare, based on popular traditions, summons the mighty fantasy of the audience to its aid.

The theatre asks the audience to see the plains of France and two mighty kingdoms on the tiny stage and to imagine that they see before them the dangerous channel and thousands of troops dispersed about the stage, though in fact it holds only a small company of actors.

But that is the true theatre and its King is the Actor who rules over time, place, numbers, everything.

In a flash the theatre can change the place of the action with just a single phrase, as does the Chorus at the beginning of Act IV in the same play, *King Henry V:*

> *"...And so our scene must to the battle fly;*
> *Where, O for pity! we shall much disgrace*
> *With, four or five most vile and ragged foils,*
> *Right ill-dispos'd in brawl ridiculous,*
> *The name of Agincourt. Yet sit and see;*
> *Minding true things by what their mock'ries be...."*[2]

Do not believe in the undue modesty of the theatre. Of

---

[1] William Shakespeare, *King Henry V*, London, 1954, pp. 5-7.
[2] Ibid., p. 92.

course, it sometimes indulges in buffoonery, histrionics, and exaggeration, but basically it requires very little to bear the audience aloft, to the very heights from which the whole world is visible. You want proof of this? Come with me to the Chinese theatre.

Here you see two armies engaged in battle, but represented by just two warriors. In fact, the size of the armies is very simply shown by the number of pennants around the waist of each of the two warriors. For they are the symbols of the armies.

Confess that although there are only two men on the stage before you, nevertheless when you see from the pennants round their waists how big their armies are, and when these "armies" begin to do battle with just two wooden swords as weapons, your blood runs cold, you catch your breath and clutch your neighbour's hand.

Fantasy engenders realism as no naturalism or pedestrian realism can do.

As a rule, the spectator has an enormous facility for creative imagination.

When I was putting on a "mass performance" in the open town square in the twenties, there was nothing on the scene but a few articles used in the action. There was no décor whatsoever. Indeed, there was nothing to hang scenery on, for above us there was the open sky. There were no wings. Indeed, there was nothing on which they could lean or to which they could be attached, for there was no stage and nothing around but the open square, with thousands of spectators on all sides. I shall never forget how these thousands of spectators, as though under the influence of a magician's wand, began to believe in everything that was happening on the stage, and began to see the place of action, even though this was only hinted at by the few props. This marvel of the theatre was accomplished with the aid of imagination, the most ancient dramatic force tested throughout the ages.

A small but precise hint is only needed for the audience to be carried away into the world of the play, a world that has not been faithfully copied by the author from life but filled out by his imagination.

Konstantin Stanislavsky wrote about imagination in his book *The Actor Prepares*.

"The play, the role, is the author's invention, a series of

magic and other 'if's' and 'supposed circumstances'. *There are no events of actual reality on the stage; actual reality is not art. This latter, by its very nature, demands artistic invention, and this in the first instance is what the author's work is.* The task of the actor and his creative technique is to turn the inventiveness of the play into a stage event, and in this an enormous role is played by the imagination. It is, therefore, worthwhile dwelling a little longer on it and looking more closely at its function in creativity."

It is, indeed, worthwhile. And here producers, actors and artists should dwell on the enormous role of the imagination, not only for the actor, but for the spectator, too.

Even in the most ultra-naturalistic theatre there is still a certain place for the spectator's imagination, though here it works in reverse, so to say. Thus, for instance, if he sees "real" forests, houses and apartments on the stage, the spectator nevertheless forces himself not to notice the "life-like" naturalism of these forests, houses and apartments. The theatre's desire to represent its props as real life provokes a natural protest from the audience against such deceit and they have to strain their imagination to keep up their contact of trust with the characters and not to notice the props. This is a Sisyphean toil. Or they haul on to the opera stage an enormous ship, a stage property "from life", and try to make the spectator believe it's real. But he knows that if this ship, so artfully made to look real, were in fact real, the whole stage would crumble beneath it, together with the unfortunate actors. The spectator has to have considerable imagination to sit out the performance. Or else he simply ends by disbelieving every single thing about the opera.

In the theatre they think that the spectator stays sitting in his place because he believes in the reality of the ship; but the spectator remains in his place precisely because he doesn't believe a thing; for years he has been thinking that this is quite normal and should be so in the theatre.

I repeat that if there is still room for the spectator's creative imagination even in the ultra-naturalistic theatre, then, in cases where the theatre consciously and intentionally arouses the spectator's imagination by special means already tested many times over, it may thrive and blossom with unrestrained freedom.

To be fair, the naturalistic theatre by no means always erects "ships" and "real houses" on the stage. It often gets by without scenic edifices on the stage, because by copying life it has to copy small rooms—perhaps a small drawing-room, with its furniture, flowerpot-stands and knick-knacks. It is not so upsetting as the big ship. But a copy of life remains a copy, and leaves almost no opportunities for the imagination to be aroused and soar to the heights of an inspired, poetic perception of life.

The photographic presentation of a "slice of life" with the maximum amount of verisimilitude ("Décor is the same as description in a novel," said Antoine) robs the spectator of the last morsel of imagination.

I recall Stanislavsky's words: "What can warm and stir us more than inventive imagination!"

Do you want to be bewitched and deeply stirred by imagination? Then come with me into the world of Cervantes' tragedy *La Numancia*.

You are indifferent to everything, you are tired after a day's work. Oh, you will soon find wonderful relaxation. You will come face to face with real art. *La Numancia* is tragic but filled with the loftiest optimistic passion, it sings the joy of battle for the happiness of one's people, for its independence and honour.

First, let us get acquainted with the wonderful personalities of Cervantes' tragedy.

At the head of the list of dramatis personae are the Romans, then the Numancians and suddenly there are such characters as:

Spain
The river Duero and three tributaries
War
Disease
Famine
Glory
A demon
A shrouded corpse.

This is straight from popular traditions. These are allegorical figures, but they are alive, and each of them has its problems, desires and aspirations; each has its flaming thoughts and intelligent feelings; they suffer and grieve deeply, but they are sustained by bright hope.

These are conventional characters, but they can be understood by the simple peasant and woodcutter, miner or worker. They have immense power which breaks the confines of the play, so that events become great, actions significant, ideas enormous.

But one has to imagine that he sees before him not an actor or actress but the river Duero with its three tributaries, or Famine, or War, or nothing more or less than the whole of Spain. . . .

In *La Numancia* the monologues not only express each personality's task in the play but also sketch quite definitely the "supposed circumstances" in which the characters act. And they sketch not only the "supposed circumstances", but also the "time" and "place".

The actor recites his monologue not simply to be heard, he wants the spectators to have a vivid picture of all that, say, Spain says. She has been more than once tortured by the enemy. Towns are cut off from each other. Brother hates brother. The barbarous Roman hordes have invaded Spain. Only Numancia defends its independence and freedom. The Romans have employed battering rams against the walls of Numancia and dug a moat and trenches around the fortress. Only one route remains open, the river Duero. As long as the river is not crossed by the enemy and sealed off, the fortress can hold out. . . .

The great Talma insisted that the actor must visualise his monologues; in popular performance this "duty" is equally entrusted to the spectator. This is the creative co-operation of actor and spectator, his participation in the play.

All this is not just an excursion into the past for the sake of the past. Such thoughts help me to see the future of the theatre. I see plays whose connection with everyday life is not destroyed but unusually expanded by the introduction of the many rich traditions of the popular theatre.

Like many producers I have a certain amount of experience in the realisation of such principles. I tried to put into effect certain elements of what I have said above. The trouble is that my attempts in this direction were, at that time, entirely or almost entirely isolated. And there was no one with whom I could discuss either the positive or the controversial results.

As for the audience, they received our experimental performances very willingly and easily, although they have been exposed to the systematic influence of the theatre that categorically rejects any kind of convention. They seem to have a natural and indestructible desire not simply to see a

117

performance, but to participate in it on a par with the actors.

I have done quite a few experiments in the search for "realistic convention" and have offered them to the audience to judge. And every time my appeals to the spectator's fantasy have been successful, sometimes more, sometimes less, depending entirely on the degree of success of the particular production. Spectators at our theatrical experiments always had the opportunity of disagreeing with the new elements that they saw in our plays, and even of returning their tickets and leaving the theatre. I must say that nobody availed himself of this opportunity, natural enough when something unusual is offered. For some "theatre connoisseurs", however, the success of the "realist conventional" performances seemed an extremely ominous sign of ... formalism.

Any attempt to find one's own way, to interpret a play in one's own fashion or to present a play in one's own style is frequently put under the heading of formalism.

Certain theatre-goers have definite tastes and are accustomed to definite images. They are not receptive to any "novelty". Their established "theories", are of no use when they try to find out why some "formalist" performances enable the spectator to relax spiritually and enrich him with great and deep impressions, rejoicing at the theatricality.

The spectators have always been the best friends of our modest experiments and quests.

Spectators, you are wonderful, beautiful people! How grateful I am to you. You have paid no attention to my occasional mistakes, miscalculations and failures, and you have always received my presentations, even the most controversial, with a belief in the many-sided and multiform power of the theatre, in which there are perhaps as many shades of colour as there are in nature, and as many marvels as there are in life.

The opportunity to enjoy art is open to all who can see the variety of colours and trends in art, and who are aware of its weeds.

If you happen to visit one of the mountain settlements in the Caucasus, and go for a walk to bring back some beautiful flowers, the inhabitants would warn you: "Don't leave them in your room at night—you will be poisoned by their scent."

There is art of this sort. But one must not turn away from the wide and varied, bright and fragrant world of healthy flowers just because there are poisonous ones.

I got interested in some of these "weeds" in art and made a study of them in certain of my presentations, following my own path.

In search of myself I often intruded into those spheres of art which were against my tastes, quests and my dreams of art. In this I must blame only myself.

Before I went to the Realistic Theatre I was a cinema film director. I directed Nikolai Erdman's *Mitya, Appetite for Sale*—from a pamphlet by Paul Lafargue (scenario by Erdman and Mariengof), *The Way of the Enthusiasts*, etc.

Before that I was an actor in the Meyerhold Theatre. After the theatre and all things "theatrical" I was particularly attracted to the cinema for its being down-to-earth and natural.

In my youth I was very attracted by Walt Whitman, and now, in the cinema I could at last give a free rein to my love of nature: of the sea, the stars, clouds, real storms, real thunder, and not a rumbling produced with the aid of metal sheets hanging in the wings. The dramatic unities looked pure nonsense in the cinema, which enabled you to capture the whole living world on a film and which transported you in a hundredth of a second from Moscow to somewhere in the Arctic, from the Arctic to Africa, from the snows to the burning sands.

The cinema rules the world as it wills. So we ought to build cinemas in such a way that the viewer can see what has been photographed on screens in front of him, on all sides and above his head. I wanted to do this when I first began making films. With all the passion of youth I shared these ideas with Alexander Dovzhenko, who was then taking his first steps in the cinema. Years later Dovzhenko proved by his splendid films that no complicated montage could give as large a picture of the world as one sound thought. Very recently I saw a caricature of Dovzhenko's and my youthful dreams when I saw the American circorama at the World Fair in Brussels. Possibly some part of the future belongs to this way of projecting films. The spectator is in the middle and all around him the film is being shown. He is the focal point of all that takes place on the screen. But what I saw was imperfect technically and extremely primitive artistically. Everything was shown at random, chaotically, with no composition and no central uniting point.

A running river, the rustling of the leaves in the wind, the drumming of the rain on the cottage roof, thunder—hardly audible, somewhere in the distance, and then right overhead. Lightning, downpour of rain, storms, fires, blizzards—could all of this be imitated in the theatre, no matter how technically equipped it might be? Should the theatre, forgetting its own great specific qualities and its own nature, compete with the cinema in such a direct and straightforward use of nature and life, at which the cinema has been so successful because of its specific qualities and creative character?

After all, theatre producers and artists, unable to find purely theatrical means of portraying certain scenes, have quite often made use of cinema screens and projectors. This was often done by Ervin Piskator, Meyerhold and many of his disciples, including me.

Was not this "borrowing" from another art a sort of compromise? Is the art of the theatre really poorer in artistic techniques than the art of the cinema?

Yes, the cinema is very much more powerful than the theatre, if we forget or neglect the great power of the theatre (all the more so since it is not static, but can grow if we wish).

The answer will be "No", if only we remember all the powerful techniques of the theatre, gather them together, study them, test them, select the most effective, and if we multiply and enrich them with new artistic discoveries and inventions. In fact, the art of the theatre not only will not give way to the art of the cinema, but will be unrestricted master on "its own ground". That is why it is worthwhile recalling and counting on our fingers all that has been discovered in past centuries by the popular theatrical performances. That is why we must passionately search for and explore new lands on the map of the theatre. For the cinema, too, it is worthwhile thinking about this, since although the theatre often looks towards the cinema, the latter very often simply copies the theatre. Moreover, it copies it badly, as badly as the theatre attempts to imitate the cinema.

Disregard of the specific qualities of an art and their

development exerts a fatal influence on this art, be it theatre or cinema, painting, music or sculpture. For each art has its own vast variety of forms which demand, in their turn, the establishment of certain specifications for each of them. Thus the colour films must be quite different in nature from that of "black and white" films. And a wide-screen cinema must have its artistic and not just technical peculiarities. To proclaim the slogan of realism without a concomitant study of the specific (but far from "eternal") qualities of each aspect and type of art means limiting oneself to vague and abstract formulations.

Realism is not on abstract term and should be amplified and qualified with regard to each particular art.

The concept of realism cannot be made general, standard and universal for easel and scenery painting, for the theatre and the cinema, for literature, music, sculpture, etc. The specific nature of each art must claim its rights, and each art must make its voice heard.

It is essential to purge the concept of theatricality in the realist theatre of fetishes and dogmas. When the theatre's concept of realism is dull and narrow, there is no room for "theatricality" in such a theatre.

Adherence to the main principles of realism being the general law, each art having its own specific qualities, provides its own forms of realism peculiar to it. And here enormous significance attaches to the ability of an individual artist to make *the fullest use* of the specifics of his particular art.

Let us take, for example, Charlie Chaplin. There is no doubt that his art is the fruit of critical realism and his attitude to the world and reality is basically similar to that of realist artists working in other branches of art. But his mask, his use of convention, his behaviour, peculiar gait, his entire appearance, although realistic in terms of cinema, would become unrealistic if mechanically transferred to some other form of art. Take the Chaplin image in cinema. One tiny deviation and it would become theatrical. Only the genius of Chaplin is able to make his conventional images absolutely real in the cinema.

Moreover, in all his films Chaplin is surrounded by partners whose manner of acting seems more natural, verisimilar and realistic. They walk normally and their entire carriage is just like that of ordinary people. From the point of view of the simple, normal and natural, Charlie is pure convention. Yet in the films he is a hundred times more realistic than all those around him. Thus realism makes a mockery of the dogma created seemingly to assist it. Chaplin widened immensely the actor's possibilities in the cinema as Eisenstein, Pudovkin and Dovzhenko did the producer's.

It is true that one cannot "divorce form from content" and analyse them separately, neither can one entirely depend on content in defining the manner of its artistic treatment.

In literary images, for example, Chaplin's mask would be pretentious, affected and unnatural. The same would apply in painting. His little men would look funny and misshapen in sculpture. Chaplin's mask is at home only in the cinema, although it originated in the theatre.

Here let me recall a serious artistic error I once made when I was captivated by the possibilities of cinematic art and decided to be absolutely "real" (which is possible only in the cinema) in the art of the theatre.

I was simply intoxicated with that tangible realism with which Alexander Serafimovich described people, animals, the smell of earth, saddles and air in *The Iron Flood*.

Do you know the smell of a soldier's cape that has many times been exposed to wind and rain? Do you know the smell of saddles and leather straps, or the scent of hay? Do you know the taste of soldier's porridge, reheated over a campfire? Can you imagine in a flash that you are by the sea in the early morning, and feel the light morning breeze on your face? Many are the beautiful and wonderful things a man can feel, if he loves and knows nature and life. So I wanted to do all this, as far as possible, in the theatre, so that the audience should forget completely that it was watching a play and feel itself totally in the midst of the men of the Taman Regiment in *The Iron Flood*.

However, I tried to do within the walls of the theatre, neglecting the specific conventionality of the latter, what it is possible to do only in the cinema.

On the other hand, I did not want to resort to the "conventionality" which, in the words of Lenin (at the First All-Russia Congress on Adult Education, in May 1919), degenerated in the formalist theatre and culture in general into "the most absurd ideas", "individual theories" and "something supernatural and incongruous". The Party began an irreconcilable campaign against such "experimentation".

Formalism was something I detested, but looking for the truth of life in art, I went into another extreme.

I did not always combat formalist "experimentation" cleverly or wisely, nor did I always find what could be opposed to it. But I always hated it and was organically repelled by "Gogol on bicycles", the circus-like tightrope stunt in Ostrovsky's plays at the Proletkult Theatre, or the green wig in the production of *The Forest* at Meyerhold's theatre (fortunately, that wretched wig did not prevent me from seeing Meyerhold's original interpretation of Ostrovsky's play). I was not yet ready for the struggle and did not have the necessary powers to fight loudly and boldly, for instance, against the "metro-rhythm" of the theatre directed by Ferdinandov, in which even the text of Ostrovsky's *The Thunder-Storm* was broken into minute passages, the actor mechanically rapping out each syllable; or against Forreger's theatre, in the Arbat Street. My youthful inexperience could not suggest me anything better to do than go along to the theatre and simply stop the performance by saying for all to hear that this was not theatre but a disgrace. Then I would invite the audience to go into the foyer and discuss Forreger's "theatrical principles". When they banned me from the theatre, I used to change costumes to avoid recognition by the attendants, I dressed up even in women's clothes. I simply could not stand this smug theatre believing itself to be aesthetic.

By the time I began to stage *The Iron Flood* I had already sown my wild oats and could look around with more sober eyes. I, too, began to be sharply criticised for being distracted by form, and even for "formalism". The leaders of RAPP[1] were particularly diligent in this. The discussion of my production of *The Running-Start* lasted three days in a row! I didn't expect that these coiffeurs who wanted to trim every artist in the same style had got so angry with me.

At the Realistic Theatre (formerly the Fourth Studio of the Moscow Art Treatre) I had to decide on the creative principles for each performance much more carefully. This was much more difficult than raising a hullabaloo. I had to find my bearings. In the early stages of such complete independence it is, apparently, not so easy to find the right road at once. So on seeing the work of young producers, we

---

[1] Russian Association of Proletarian Writers.—*Tr.*

should not think that their creative principles are final and would never change.

Preoccupation with naturalness, born of work in the cinema, neglect of the specific qualities of the theatre and the role of convention in it, plus the three-day discussion of *The Running-Start* directed part of my work on *The Iron Flood* along a false trail. Following on the soundness in concept, plan and performance of *The Running-Start*, I made of *The Iron Flood* a mixture of naturalism, romanticism and convention, the first component being predominant at times.

The artist Stoffer and I cut the auditorium by three ramps, with hillocks all around. The spectators' chairs were placed between these three ramps. Above their heads was a special ceiling on which stars, clouds, or clear blue sky could be projected. The action either took place simultaneously on all three ramps and the hillocks around them or moved from one place to another. The impression was produced of a great deal of air and space in the little theatre.

Where but a small hint would have sufficed, Stoffer and I tried to produce "real" roads winding between "real" hills and even mountains. . . . But all the spectators had to do was stretch out a hand and they could touch the "road" and convince themselves that the "bumps" in the road were stage props. Indeed, they need not do even that, for this was clear enough at a glance. We should not have tried to "deceive" the spectator, for the spectator would gladly build his own fantasies if given the merest hint. And these would be a hundred times more real to the spectator than the stage properties made to look like real life.

For the audience did believe the actor Romanovsky, for instance, when playing a villager in *The Running-Start*, he appeared wearing only short pants, leapt from the stage to the floor of the stalls and—began bathing in an imaginary river: he dived holding his nose and putting fingers in his ears, he snorted after his dive and shivered in the chilly air. Romanovsky did this so skilfully, and so wholeheartedly believed in the truth of his action, that no one doubted for a minute that he really was bathing, and that there was cold water there in front of the audience.

The audience always enjoyed the actor's art and awarded him warm applause, grateful for the opportunity to participate in the performance.

The theatre draws its power not only from individual outstanding artists, the brilliant and immortal actors, but also from the ordinary, capable exponents of the stage art who can achieve, with the aid of the audience, simply miraculous results. If it were not for them there might only be four or five theatres, if not less, in the entire world.

The more natural and true to life an actor is, the more his performance will bring the audience's creative fantasy into action, provided he does not "overdo" his role or use the hackneyed conventions of the "old time stage".

The playing must be highly artistic, and not scrupulously lifelike; hence if the truth is artistic, it will always leave room for the spectator's fantasy. Here we need negation, not of all convention, but of only that sort of convention that leads to formal acting and away from "sincerity of passions" and "true feelings".

Take naturalistic actors and see how they eat, drink, fall in love, fly into rages, weep and laugh—it all smells of sweat, is unaesthetic, coarse and revolting. And the theatre loses its point, fantasy is firmly under lock and key, inventiveness is lost in some neglected corner, the spectator's creativeness is bottled up, even though he is confronted by an experienced, senior and well-known actor.

On the other hand, the most frightful things, which it would be impossible to watch in real life, can be so portrayed by a genuine artist that they become a real pleasure to look at.

When the Kabuki Theatre was on tour in Moscow, the fine Japanese actor Ichikawa Sadanji played some high official who was overwhelmed by misfortunes and decided to commit suicide. So here he is sitting on a rug in the middle of the stage, his legs crossed under him, reciting a monologue, with a sharp knife in his hand, the handle wrapped in a scarf and just enough of the blade left exposed for him to commit *hara-kiri*.

With a swift motion, Sadanji thrust the sharp blade into his stomach ("apparently" thrust it), and then, with a few words of monologue, suddenly ripped the blade sideways towards the centre of his belly. Pause. Then the same motion, moving the blade towards the other side. Pause. Then again. Pause. And once more. Pause....

The whole audience held its breath. We had seen something poetic, elevated, triumphant. That's right, triumphant.

There was nothing frightful, revolting or physiological about it. That's the actor's art!

This made me recall the words of another great artist, Stanislavsky: "I am an ultra-naturalist of lofty emotions."

And that is what we had with Sadanji—life itself, plus "lofty emotions". The result is the great wonder of art.

This is what the theatre is able to do if we penetrate the secrets of its realist convention and poetry.

For the theatre to be great "in mind and body" it must affirm realism alone. And not realism in general, but socialist realism. It should be able to foretell what is to come, to understand the life and its leading tendencies, and to have ideological purpose corresponding to the Party line. Truth and life must rule the stage, but not as a mirrorlike, dead reflection. The theatre must make the spectator forget that he is confronted by actors. More than that, the spectator should be invited to fill out what the theatre gives him with the help of his fantasy and imagination.

There is no special theatrical truth, having an independent existence. It is simply that life demands from art artistic images of itself. And convention assists in this. And we have still a lot to do in this direction.

1959

Georgi Kunitsyn

LENIN ON PARTISANSHIP AND FREEDOM OF CREATIVITY

Marxist-Leninist aesthetics did not appear out of the blue. Progressive aesthetic thought had to travel a long and fruitful path before this aesthetic system could appear. The problem of freedom of creativity, for instance, interested the predecessors of Marxism and even theoreticians of earlier epochs. Since very early times people have been thinking about the social function of literature and art, and have been trying to find objective laws governing the reflection of reality in art. Of great interest, in this connection, are Plato's theory of the ideal republic and the place of the artist in it, and Aristotle's *Poetics*.

These contained conjectures that artistic creative activity depends on the society, but so far there was no correct understanding of the objective laws of the development and class essence of art. Ancient philosophers made many true observations on the process of artistic cognition, but they did not yet form a single aesthetic system.

We find the first attempts to examine the class character of art in the works of Marx, Engels and Lenin, who established that in a class society all ideology, including art, has a class character. The ideology of a slave-owning society is no exception. But class affiliation is not necessarily identical with partisanship. Partisanship, as Lenin pointed out, is the highest form of class affiliation, class affiliation fully realised. Even when party consciousness had already arisen and existed as an objective phenomenon, many artists reflected the interests of particular classes quite unconsciously, without rising to the level of partisanship. They even shared the misconception that art was not a class phenomenon, believing that they stood "above class" and "outside" politics, or simply refusing to recognise the existence of the classs struggle.

Lenin wrote that no man, if he understood the relationship of the classes, could avoid joining one class or another, or could shield himself from some kind of partisanship, whether in politics, literature or art. Hence partisanship is the conscious struggle of the theoretician or the artist, using the means of science or art, for the ideals and interests of his class, and is therefore indivisible from the class struggle.

Lenin defined equally clearly the conditions in which advocacy of the interests of a particular class becomes a conscious process for the ideologist. He wrote that partisanship is the concomitant and result of highly developed class antagonisms, of highly developed class struggle. Lenin's teaching on revolutionary situations and the socialist revolution and his analysis of bourgeois revolutions indicate when conditions are present in human history for highly developed class struggle and for partisanship which is the political expression of that struggle. This, incidentally, completely refutes those Soviet literary scholars who think that only communist partisanship exists. The appearance of partisanship as a new social phenomenon is connected with ideological preparation for the first bourgeois revolutions. Proletarian partisanship arose later.

It would also be incorrect to suppose that in the period of bourgeois revolution and afterwards, all bourgeois writers and theoreticians became party conscious. There are to this day many people in the capitalist world who do not understand the class nature of their creative work. Artists began to see the class nature of their work only with the intensification of bourgeois revolutionary feeling. It was in that epoch and not earlier that the initial conscious demarcation between the antagonistic feudal and bourgeois classes took place.

The epoch of socialist revolution represents the highest stage of the development of the class struggle, and its result and concomitant are the scientifically based principles of building the Communist Party whose aim is the liberation from exploitation of all the workers, not only the proletariat.

The class struggle in antiquity and in the early Middle Ages had an essentially different colouring. Even then ideology was class based; but partisanship as the conscious expression of the interests of a class arises only when one class begins to be aware of itself precisely as a class irreconcilably opposed to another class, which is also politically organised. Until then, the political struggle takes the form of a struggle between estates within a class, or between groups within an estate, though this, of course, is objectively an expression of the class struggle. Neither slaves in revolt nor rebellious serfs ever reached the level of a politically organised and class-conscious independent movement, though it was their struggle that destroyed slavery and serfdom and cleared the ground for more progressive social relations.

Apart from the problem of partisanship in art and literature, the period of ideological preparation for bourgeois revolution also brought forth—though on a different basis—the question of freedom of creativity. The people of the time regarded both questions as different aspects of the same problem: the relationship of art to society.

Lenin showed that it is impossible to live in a society and be free from it, and that true and total social freedom, including freedom of creativity, means scientifically based advocacy of the interests of the working masses, of the cause of the revolutionary proletariat; humanity's liberation from class exploitation. This is the political aspect of freedom. Naturally true freedom of creativity is possible only for artists holding this position. But the problem of freedom also has an epistemological aspect; the better the artist's knowledge of the subject, the greater is his freedom. In relation to creativity, this means the practical use of the objective laws and the aesthetic aspect of art. Devotion to the people is not enough to give the artist absolute freedom. He must also possess talent, that is, the ability to perceive and reflect reality through artistic images and penetrate aesthetic "secrets".

As regards Lenin's treatment of the relationship between partisanship and freedom of creativity, we may conclude that partisanship either paralyses freedom or, on the contrary, becomes its guarantee and its basis. Allegiance to a reactionary party directed against the interests of the people, is incompatible with freedom of creativity. Communist partisanship, being the highest form of devotion to the people, in no way restrains the artist's talent, but on the contrary guarantees it genuine freedom.

* * *

The questions of partisanship and freedom of creativity were more than once raised in the past. But how were they formulated and solved? Let us take the most prominent thinkers of the time when bourgeois ideology was taking shape in Western Europe and revolutionary-democratic ideology in Russia, and analyse in particular their treatment of freedom in a wide philosophical sense, and not only in relation to art.

One of the first attempts to solve this problem in modern history was made by Spinoza. According to him all things and phenomena exist in a world of contingency, but the basis of their existence is objective necessity. By recognising this necessity, man acquires a definite power over these phenomena and over himself.[1] This was, of course, a brilliant conclusion for its time. But Spinoza did not solve the problem, he merely indicated certain ways of approaching it. He could not go further than that, however, because he was unable even to attempt a materialist explanation of social life; his views on nature were of a metaphysical character. This, in turn, explains why Spinoza never gave a thought to the question of social freedom, or to the more specific problem of the freedom of artistic creativity. In terms of the epistemology of art, Spinoza's propositions had, in their day, a certain positive significance.

The influence of social interests on the aesthetic views of the artist was observed by Kant, who lived in a period of more highly developed class struggle in Europe. But he saw that influence as negative. Kant tried to prove the incompatibility of any interest (primarily a social one) with genuine art. He interpreted freedom of creativity as the artist's independence of society and even of personal interests. Kant's theory of the "disinterestedness" of art is an attempt to divorce the epistemological aspect of creativity from its social aspect. This, in fact, accounts for Kant's popularity among contemporary cultural figures in the capitalist countries, who are trying to get away from the pressing problems of society.

Engels wrote that "Hegel was the first to state correctly the relation between freedom and necessity. To him freedom

---

[1] Spinoza, *Philosophy of Benedict de Spinoza*, New York, "Of the Power of the Understanding, or of Human Freedom", p. 257.

is the appreciation of necessity".[1] However, the philosopher whose ideal was the Prussian monarchy was not looking for ways to achieve freedom for the people. This inevitably made it impossible for him to pose the question of freedom of creativity correctly. Having made a wealth of valuable generalisations concerning the process of artistic cognition, Hegel, like Kant, concentrated only on the epistemological aspect of art, giving it a specifically Hegelian interpretation based on self-knowledge of the absolute spirit. Art as a weapon of class struggle, as a powerful means of educating the masses, continued to await its discoverers.

This was the fault of almost all pre-Marxist ideologists, who dealt only with the freedom of creating artistic images, regardless of the class position of the artist or the class content of his work. At best they took some account of the artist's relation to society, censorship, or public opinion, but here, too, the artist remained the central figure, and his freedom of creativity was explained as a quality of human nature.

Isolated conjectures about the artist's link with the epoch, or the popular movements, or the social struggle could not introduce any significant change into the general picture. All these conjectures, prompted by the development of the class struggle, could not produce a revolution in aesthetics as a whole or in the treatment of its particular problems mentioned above. Pre-Marxist aesthetics can be credited, however, with raising these problems in one way or another. Closest to the point were Russian revolutionary-democrats Belinsky, Dobrolyubov and Chernyshevsky, who made an attempt to link the artist's freedom of creativity with the interests and point of view of the working masses. In their works, however, they mostly use the terms "people" and "popular consciousness", and not "class", but their concept of "the people" means, in essence, the peasant class, which in their day formed the vast majority of the population of Russia. In his policy statement "On the Role of Popular Consciousness in the Development of Russian Literature", Dobrolyubov advances an idea that the writer's loftiest duty is to give a true portrayal of life in accord with the interests of the people, to fight for their liberation and make progressive culture accessible to them.

---

[1] Engels, *Anti-Dühring*, Moscow, 1969, p. 136.

Nevertheless there is certain one-sidedness in the views of the revolutionary-democrats when they discuss freedom of creativity. The anthropological principle, which they often applied in science, is visible also here. Their main stress is largely on freedom as the manifestation of the artist's character, his natural ability to sympathise with the oppressed people and to write truthfully.

None of this in any way detracts from the significance of pre-Marxist aesthetics as the theoretical source of Marxist-Leninist aesthetics. Yet it was Marx, Engels and Lenin who gave a radically new explanation of social life and art. The founders of scientific communism were the first to show that freedom of creativity must be seen as an indivisible union of two fundamental and interrelated aspects—the aesthetic-epistemological, conditioned by the demands of the objective laws governing the perception of reality, and the social, extending its roots into social practice. Neither may be correctly understood if divorced from the other. Hence the problem as a whole may be solved if it is viewed as an aspect of life itself. In other words, solution must be sought not only and not so much in the sphere of ideas as in the process of the revolutionary transformation of the whole of society on the basis of socialism and communism.

Indeed, if one proceeds from any other theory of freedom, then it will be easy to pass for it any kind of non-freedom. And this is what frequently happens. Pragmatist philosophers, for example, understand by freedom not one's consciousness of social necessity, but rather the obtaining of benefit for oneself, for the bourgeois class. And there is nothing surprising in the fact that it is they who provide the theoretical basis for the imperialist thesis regarding the "free world" of capitalist enterprise.

It is more complicated, however, in the case of the honest, talented artists, prepared to serve the people but mistaken in their estimate of the essence and purpose of art. There are many among them who sometimes see their "freedom" as the struggle against truth in art. They think they are aspiring to create a "new art" of the twentieth century, which, according to them, must of necessity be different from the "old" art. The logic of life is such that sooner or later the most talented of these people arrive at a correct reflection of reality, but by no means all of them succeed in making up for wasted time.

In all subjective treatments of freedom, the most important problem is not considered: what attitude does the artist, striving for personal creative freedom, take towards the interests of the people, the interests of the revolutionary class and the demands of genuine art?

Real freedom is possible only when the people are free from social inequality of any sort. Therefore full freedom of creativity is impossible to obtain, on the one hand, unless the principles of the depiction of life correspond to the objective laws of art, and on the other hand, without the revolutionary movement of the working class and the toiling masses, unless the artist participates, using his artistic means, in the active struggle for socialism and communism.

* * *

No fewer mutually exclusive points of view are involved in the approach to the problem of partisanship in literature and art. Each class follows its own interests, and when it conceives of itself as a class, its partisanship has a content peculiarly its own. Thus ideologists of different classes interpret the concept of partisanship differently. Moreover, while freedom of creativity finds defenders and supporters among all classes, partisanship is recognised only by the progressive classes, and defended most consistently only by the proletariat and its party.

As has already been pointed out, class antagonisms began to be felt in the epoch of ideological preparation for bourgeois revolutions, when the division of society into classes became obvious. Adam Smith and David Ricardo contributed a great deal to the discovery of classes, making current the socio-economic concept of "class", as did the ideologists of the first French bourgeois revolution, above all Diderot and Rousseau. In the period of the French Restoration, the existence of class struggle as a motive force in history was revealed in the works of Mignet, Thierry and Guizot.

But for a long time the term "partisanship" was not widely used. The term "party" was first used by Kant, who applied it to any "interested" art. It was only in the thirties and forties of the 19th century that the word "partisanship" acquired a class meaning.

In the beginning of the 1840s the first discussion of partisanship took place in the press between the German poets

Ferdinand Freiligrath and Georg Herwegh. The discussion was sparked off by Freiligrath's poem "From Spain" (1841), in which Freiligrath, who at that time believed in "pure", "disinterested" art, announced that "the poet stands on a higher tower than the party". Freiligrath's point of view boiled down to the fact that the poet was free from all socio-political interests and obligations whatsoever. Freiligrath was answered by the then very young Herwegh, who with his *Verses of a Living Man* had moved by that moment into the ranks of the famous progressive German poets. Herwegh produced a poem *The Party* which was a hymn to the revolutionary partisanship of the time.

> *Partei! Partei! Wer sollte sie nicht nehmen,*
> *Die noch die Mutter aller Siege war!*
> *Wie mag ein Dichter solch ein Wort verfemen,*
> *Ein Wort, das alles Herrliche gebar?*[1]

Thus Herwegh expressed his indignation with Freiligrath, and asked him:

> *Nur offen wie ein Mann: Für oder wider?*
> *Und die Parole: Sklave oder frei?*[2]

In this poem Herwegh spoke up openly and consciously against the feudal-absolutist society. He wrote that this society was "rotten all through" and "mortally sick".

> *Laßt, Dichter, laßt auch ihr den Kranken sterben*
> *Für unsres Volkes Zukunft nehmt Partei!*[3]

Summoning his literary colleagues into battle, Herwegh appreciated, however, that not all would follow him under the same banner. But this did not worry him. It would be much worse, the poet thought, if the artist did not wish to discover for himself whether he was "slave or free".

Not dispassionate to this quarrel was the young Marx, at that time editor of the *Rheinische Zeitung*. It was he who

---

[1] Georg Herwegh, *Der Freiheit eine Gasse*, Berlin, 1948, pp. 158-59.
Our Party, who would not embrace the cause
That to every victory led the way.
How could poets such a name abuse
Through which all joy has seen the light of day.
[2] *Decide for or against, bravely like a man,*
Then choose your password—slave or free?
[3] *You too should leave the sick to die, O poets all!*
Think of the people's future, answer the Party's call!

134

first published the poem *The Party* in his paper. Freiligrath's subsequent move to a revolutionary-democrat and then a proletarian position (1847-1849) was also effected under the influence of Marx. Meanwhile the argument centred around bourgeois partisanship, which in the Germany of the time reflected progressive moods.

At almost the same time as the first discussion of partisanship was taking place in the West, the concept was beginning to be used in Russian criticism. Partisanship was developing in Russian literature, and not only of a revolutionary nature, but of a reactionary kind, in the work of the "protectionists".

The concept of partisanship was first introduced into Russian criticism by Belinsky. Objecting to the supporters of "pure art", he wrote in "Contemporary Notes": "The pretence of not belonging to a party always coincides with the pretence of being alone able to see clearly the undisputed truth, which everyone else views through the dimmed glasses of partiality and bias."[1] The critic believed that such "unbiassed" people were simply indifferent, since, in his opinion, "only a genius can exist without belonging to a party". This last statement, however, did not imply any solidarity of Belinsky with Kant, who thought that genius was "disinterested" in questions of social struggle. In fact, Belinsky immediately added that the genius did not belong to a party simply because "he himself is a banner in whose shade a vast party soon forms". In other words, the genius is the greatest "party" man in art.

Both examples give no grounds, however, for believing that a scientific treatment of partisanship had appeared before Marxism. It was still not present even later, in the works of Chernyshevsky and Dobrolyubov, though these two took a big step forward in the foundation of partisanship. The important thing, however, is that the question was raised. But in what manner was it treated? With Herwegh it was only a poetically expressed political problem. Herwegh was no theoretician. Belinsky gave the problem a significantly wider and deeper treatment. But here the emphasis shifts to the other direction: in Belinsky's time the development of social thought in Russia took mainly liter-

---

[1] V. G. Belinsky, *Complete Works*, Vol. X, Academy of Sciences of the USSR, Moscow, 1956, p. 92, Russ. ed.

ary forms. It was a question of the analysis of the correspondence between various "partial" convictions and the demands of a realistic portrayal of life, in essence the objective laws of art, though Belinsky's analysis did not lead to this. The inadequacy of Belinsky's treatment of partisanship is obvious. By "partiality", or the status of belonging to a "party", he could not, of course, mean the artist's definite and conscious class position, since for him it meant generally any socio-aesthetic attitude in art. Such an understanding of the term "party" allows to include under this heading various literary tendencies, even very small artistic groups. Indeed, it was these that Belinsky had primarily in mind when he wrote about "partiality". In attacking the theory of "pure art", Belinsky considered the Slavophiles and "natural school" as "parties", without distinguishing the political side from the purely literary. In fact, very many of the representatives of such "parties" did not rise either then or later to the level of partisanship, to an open struggle for the interests of some definite class, and sometimes members of the same group sharply differed in their political views.

It is sufficient to recall the complicated ideological relations that existed between such varied representatives of the "natural school" as Belinsky, Herzen, Dostoyevsky, Goncharov and Turgenev.

It should, however, be emphasised that Belinsky's lack of clarity in the understanding of the class basis of partisanship, and the failure to distinguish between the social and literary sides of the question, which was generally a feature of literature and social thought at that time, did not result in a vulgar absorption of the aesthetic-epistemological nature of creativity by its social aspect. This offers abundant material for a study of both the political and aesthetic-epistemological aspects of partisanship. At this point it is interesting to note that divergence in political views by no means always prevented the artists from uniting together in literary "parties" or movements. This fact illustrates the contradictoriness of the outlooks of such artists, and their possibility of developing, through artistic discoveries, more correct and progressive views.

Chernyshevsky, Dobrolyubov and Saltykov-Shchedrin went significantly further than Belinsky in working out the class, political and also the epistemological and cognitive foundations of partisanship. They openly declared that they represented the "party of the people" in literature. This was not simply a reference to the fact that such a "party" comprised the "natural school" or the "Gogolian" movement, as Chernyshevsky called critical realism. This was a conscious and deeply founded political line in literature, an expression of Russian revolutionary-democratic (basically peasant) ideology. Their thoughts about the class and epistemological nature of art did not represent a harmonious system, nor did they give a socio-historical analysis of the actual relationship between freedom and partisanship of creativity. They did not go beyond their epoch and their country. But the development of literature proves the correctness of their idea that to serve the people honestly, literature must, first of all, be true to life.

The problem of the partisanship of creativity found its genuine, scientific solution on the basis of the Marxist discovery of the objective laws of all social development, which had been unknown to pre-Marxist aesthetics. Marx and Engels, and still more comprehensively Lenin, laid down that partisanship in ideology, and in particular in literature, represents the author's class position. It is impossible to live in a society and be free from that society; this circumstance often engenders a spontaneous expression of class interests, that is, an unconscious class sympathy. The distinctive feature of partisanship is the conscious, committed service of the author to his class, assuming the independent political participation of this class in the social struggle.

Regarding partisanship as the highest form of ideology, the founders of scientific communism revealed its specific manifestation in art, where it exists in artistic images, and demonstrated the dependence of the partisanship of various classes on concrete historical and national conditions, in which the class struggle is unfolding at every given moment, and in which one artist or another works. Lenin studied the new situation taking shape in the revolutionary movement in Russia and other countries at the end of the nineteenth and the beginning of the twentieth centuries, elaborated the scientific principles of party direction of the literature and art of the proletariat, and exploded the myth about the "non-interference" of the capitalist class and bourgeois parties in the process of artistic creation. Lenin was the first to pose and answer the question of communist partisanship as the highest manifestation of literature's devotion to the people during the period of transition from capitalism to socialism.

It has been admitted since ancient times that partisanship exists in literature and that in certain circumstances freedom of creativity may also exist. There is hardly anyone who would deny this, even among bourgeois and revisionist aestheticists. The whole trouble is that these categories are treated differently by ideologists of different classes. There is especially wide disagreement on the following points: is partisanship compatible with freedom of creativity? If so, what kind of partisanship is compatible with what kind of freedom and in what kind of society?

The variety of opinions is caused by the extreme lack of homogeneity of bourgeois social consciousness and by the existence of many freedoms, especially in the epoch of acute class struggle. However, since the concept of freedom relates to all spheres of everyday life (economics, politics, literature, art, etc.), disagreements about it are only natural, at least until its scientific definition is universally accepted. At the moment the society of the exploiters, as Abraham Lincoln pointed out in his time, enjoys the "freedom of the wolves", and this is what gives rise to disagreement. "The shepherd drives the wolf from the sheep's throat, for which the sheep thanks the shepherd as his liberator, while the wolf denounces him for the same act, as the destroyer of liberty."[1]

Lincoln used to fight the freedom of the wolf. It is typical that the National Association of Manufacturers in reply to the question: "Are the people free to abolish the private ownership of the means of production through their democratic system of government?", gave an "explanation" of the doctrine of the "free world", saying: "They are not, because that would destroy the freedom of the owners."[2] This is all quite clear, as in the case of "Southern Bourbons" who "still descant upon their freedom to keep the Negro people 'in their place', which includes for them the freedom of organised terror, discrimination and lynching".[3]

The question of freedom becomes confused when bour-

---

[1] Howard Selsam, *Socialism and Ethics*, London, 1947, p. 188.
[2] Ibid., p. 192.
[3] Ibid., p. 191.

geois ideologists begin to give it "profound" theoretical substantiations. Generalising these substantiations, Howard Selsam writes that freedom here often signifies "freedom from the coercion of anything material, the pure determination of actions and events by reason alone, the autonomy or freedom of ideas". Others consider that freedom exists "solely in the realm of spirit, with its conclusion that we are free only in our thought and feeling, but that all actions (being events in the world of space and time) are unfree...".[1]

Then there is the extreme individualistic conception of "freedom as the absence of all restraint, as the freedom of anyone to do whatever any idea, whim, fancy or caprice dictates".[2]

However paradoxical it may seem, the disagreement on the definition of freedom became widespread at the very time when its correct understanding was within reach, i.e., in the period of the formation of bourgeois consciousness. In contrast to the epoch of feudalism, when the question was never posed, everything seemed ordained by God and there was no need for discussion, the bourgeoisie entered the historical arena bearing the banner of the freedom of the individual and thought. This bourgeois freedom was itself a paradox. To the extent that it was free from feudal regimentation, hierarchy and serfdom, it was real freedom— a step forward for humanity towards liberation from the exploitation of one class by another. But to the extent that it was freedom for another, capitalist exploitation, bourgeois freedom was from its birthday in fact its own opposite— blind and elemental necessity. The true face of bourgeois freedom became evident quite soon. Men sought to determine the role of the individual in society, and a person began to be valued in terms of his accumulated wealth, regardless of his social status, and the most varied theories of individualism arose. The central figure in these theories became the isolated individual, placing himself above society, and taking the power of the wealth he had appropriated from society as his own power, the result of his own personal genius. This inevitably gave rise to the most egocentric views of freedom.

---

[1] Ibid., p. 192.
[2] Ibid.

The real reason for these changes lay in the rapidly growing division of social labour. There had never been, of course, such a thing as an individual unconnected with society and independent of it. But at the stage when new social forces are coming into being in the midst of feudalism, "social relationships", as Marx and Engels wrote, "take on an independent existence".[1] The "division within the life of each individual, insofar as it is personal, and insofar as it is determined by some branch of labour and the conditions pertaining to it" now becomes wider. This, however, should not be interpreted in the sense that the rentier or capitalist ceases to be a personality. Not at all. But now, as never before, "their personality is conditioned and determined by quite definite class relationships".[2] Therefore the difference between their personal lives and their lives as representatives of their class, "determined by some branch of labour", "appears only in their opposition to another class and, for themselves, only when they go bankrupt", that is, when it becomes obvious that they—unlike the feudalists—held their place in the ranks of the exploiters not legally, but simply by virtue of their wealth.

The individual's conditions of life acquire an accidental nature with the appearance of the class antagonism between the proletariat and the bourgeoisie.

"This accidental character is only engendered and developed by competition and the struggle of individuals among themselves. Thus, in imagination, individuals seem freer under the dominance of the bourgeoisie than before, because their conditions of life seem accidental; in reality, of course, they are less free, because they are subjected to the violence of things."[3]

Marx and Engels wrote this in their *German Ideology*. In later works they often returned to the analysis of freedom in a bourgeois society. But it is already clear from the above that, first, bourgeois freedoms are illusory, for the individual is compelled to act in a chaos of contingencies, and, second, these contingencies serve only to conceal the growing violence of things.

However, bourgeois theories of the absolute freedom of the individual are not ossified or static but are constantly

---

[1] Marx and Engels, *The German Ideology*, Moscow, 1968, p. 95.
[2] Ibid.
[3] Ibid.

changing, as do bourgeois freedoms themselves. Their social role depends directly on the process of capitalist development, the degree to which capitalism has advanced. Thus at the dawn of capitalism the demand for freedom of the individual was revolutionary as a demand for liberation from feudal restrictions; in the period of advanced capitalism, however, freedom of the individual lost its progressive significance. And when the proletariat appears as an independent class, and especially in conditions of imperialism, when the organisation and solidarity of the proletariat threaten the very existence of the capitalist system, the preaching of bourgeois individualism serves as "a principal theoretical justification of economic exploitation and thus a hindrance to every movement that aims at the improvement of the conditions of life for the overwhelming majority of individuals".[1] Every exploiter toys with the idea of "the liberty of the individual" in order to justify his illegally gained profits.

Such, however, is the essence of only those bourgeois theories that under the guise of the elevation of the individual and his freedom in fact justify the restriction and sometimes even total extinction of genuine freedom of the individual under capitalism. We shall return later to these theories. The bourgeoisie, however, also cultivates quite opposite points of view; superficially opposite, of course, for in essence they only supplement those mentioned above. Selsam sarcastically remarks that bourgeois ideologists "have never depended on one theory if two or more might do better". The subject under consideration is above all the "organic theory of society", first formulated by Hegel and subsequently revived by Bradley and Bosanquet in England and Gentile and Croce in Italy. According to this theory, society is an organic whole, the product of a historical evolution. Despite the wills and desires of individuals, it is rational. It is above human wills and desires, for the latter are subjective. Society is the embodiment of objective reason. "Who are you or who am I to criticise that which is the product of centuries of development?"[2] According to this theory, freedom of the individual consists not in the assertion of "self" but in the rejection of it, and in the acceptance,

---

[1] Howard Selsam, op. cit., pp. 130-31.
[2] Howard Selsam, op. cit., p. 131.

141

as one's own, of the laws, traditions and institutions of society, of which all men are part.

What remains of the bourgeois freedoms after this two-pronged attack on the individual? For the working people there is only a formal equality of political rights. But to the degree that they are only formal (and it cannot be otherwise in conditions of material inequality), even political freedoms in modern bourgeois society have in one way or another become the privilege of the capitalist class.

It is not difficult to see that the authors of the above interpretations of freedom can easily come to the conclusion that in no circumstances may freedom be compatible with partisanship. This is the motto, for instance, of contemporary bourgeois and revisionist aesthetics. The logic of our ideological opponents seems extremely simple: if partisanship means regimentation, and freedom—in their definition—tolerates no regimentation, then what possible combination can there be? This sophism is, however, far from innocent. It must be realised that the bourgeoisie is earnestly propagating another view, according to which bourgeois literature, and only bourgeois literature, is "non-party". And the combination of two such theories leads naturally to the conclusion that authentic freedom of creativity exists only in bourgeois art, because, we are told, it is free of partisanship. On the other hand, socialist art is ostensibly not free, because it is partisan.

* * *

Lenin attacked bourgeois theories of freedom and partisanship, proceeding in his arguments from the concrete historical situation in which the class struggle had grown in Russia and other countries at the turn of the century.

Lenin very acutely posed the question of the creative freedom of proletarian writers in the course of the first Russian revolution, when even many revolutionaries were unable to see this problem as being of prime importance. They thought it belonged to the distant future. Lenin's view of the leadership of the Party as a prime condition for the freedom of proletarian literature was especially unexpected.

Let us see what indispensable principles of the freedom of literary creativity were laid down by Lenin in his time, and what significance they have today.

Legality of the press was won in Russia in October 1905. So the next task, as formulated by Lenin in his article "Party Organisation and Party Literature", was that of creating a Social-Democratic press, free from censorship and victimisation by the government. This would ensure the liberation of the "literary activity" of the proletariat from interference by the bourgeois-landowner government.

Lenin wrote further that the Social-Democratic press must become free "also from capital, from careerism". This meant that proletarian literature must be free from the bourgeoisie materially, as well as politically.

Finally, Lenin pointed out that the Social-Democratic press must also be freed from "bourgeois-anarchist individualism".

The first two principles met with no opposition: the slavery of censorship and dependence on capital were a hindrance to everyone. But bourgeois-anarchic individualism, which was deeply rooted in the consciousness of the intelligentsia, was much harder to do away with. A long struggle lay ahead.

"Calm down, gentlemen!" Lenin wrote, addressing the "ardent supporters" of absolute freedom. "First of all, we are discussing party literature and its subordination to party control. . . . Secondly, we must say to you, bourgeois individualists, that your talk about absolute freedom is sheer hypocrisy."[1]

These Leninist principles are most subject to falsification by the defendants of individualism, who claim that they do not refer to artistic creativity.

Lenin, as we see, was really proposing the "subordination" of Party literature to Party control. This meant that eradication of bourgeois-anarchist individualism was primarily the task of the writers organisationally linked with the Party. But in his article "Party Organisation and Party Literature" Lenin meant not only party political literature but also artistic literature of Social-Democracy.

At the time of the first Russian revolution, Party literature had become extensive, Lenin stressed. But its leadership by Party organisations was inadequate. Many writers, committed to the Party, still continued to voice their opinions in the bourgeois press. As a result, ideological conces-

[1] See pp. 25, 26 of this book.

143

sions were made to bourgeois publishers. The Mensheviks, for example, sacrificed genuine freedom to the "individual independence" of the collective, and anarchist individualism affected the internal life of the Party.

Two principles collided. The Leninist principle was that the freedom of the writer is the conscious subjection of his activities to the interests of the Party and the people. The Menshevik principle was that freedom is the right of any author to do as he thinks fit.

Replying to the question as to what the freedom of proletarian literature should be, Lenin wrote: "Everyone is free to write and say whatever he likes, without any restrictions. But every voluntary association (including the party) is also free to expel members who use the name of the party to advocate anti-party views. Freedom of speech and the press must be absolute, but so must the freedom of association."[1] In these words lies the very essence of the dialectical relationship between creative freedom and partisanship.

Lenin pointed out that the criterion for determining Party members' actions—and this includes writers—is the Party Programme, its resolutions and its Rules, plus the total experience of international voluntary unions of the proletariat.

Lenin stressed that he was talking about freedom within the Party. But further, speaking of the necessity for strict discipline and solidarity, he also formulated the educational tasks among the "not completely Marxist" elements joining the Party. Since in conditions of legality a party becomes "a mass party all at once", it is inevitably joined by many inconsistent people, perhaps "even by some Christian elements, and even by some mystics". But that is not so terrible. "We have sound stomachs and we are rock-like Marxists. We shall digest those inconsistent elements."[2]

These statements contain indications of how to understand the freedom of the writer who is not a member of the Party. Lenin disclosed the very essence of the principles by which are guided the voluntary unions not affiliated to the Party but supporting its policies.

Communists support writers who criticise capitalism. For example, the pre-revolutionary *Pravda* (Truth), *Novaya Zhizn* (New Life), the Bolshevik *Proletary* (Proletarian) and

[1] See p. 25 of this book.
[2] See p. 26 of this book.

144

the Leninist *Zvezda* (Star) published realist works by writers who were not members of the Party. In such cases the single Leninist criterion was applied: whether the work was in the interests of the proletariat and the people.

This Leninist demand is consistently observed in the activity of the press and publishing houses of the USSR. We publish hundreds of works by foreign authors who give a correct depiction of bourgeois reality, though many of them advocate progressive ideas from a non-proletarian position. The names of Lion Feuchtwanger, Stefan Zweig, Ernest Hemingway, Graham Green, William Faulkner are well familiar to Soviet readers.

The creative organisations of the USSR are built on Leninist principles of freedom. This is understandable, for if a given group is to allow complete freedom of speech and the press to its members, then the members, in their turn, must allow that group the same freedom to evaluate their activities. Lenin stressed with utmost clarity that this applies to "every voluntary association". Thus the Union of Soviet Writers, when it has to keep to its Rules and break off relations with those who place themselves outside the ideological and political alliance of the writers, only asserts its right to freedom.

The bourgeoisie behaves differently. It also has its associations and unions, but it prefers material dependence to ideological unity, which becomes progressively less possible in an epoch of the decay of bourgeois consciousness.

This is why the above-mentioned Leninist proposition sounds so topical in reply to the advocates of self-will: "We must say to you, bourgeois individualists, that your talk about absolute freedom is sheer hypocrisy. There can be no real and effective 'freedom' in a society based on the power of money, a society in which the masses of working people live in poverty and a handful of rich men live like parasites."

Freedom is possible only within a society and not within an imaginary isolation from it. Under conditions when mere legality of the press had been gained in Russia, he saw this freedom in the necessity "to contrast this hypocritically free literature, which is in reality linked to the bourgeoisie, with a really free one that will be *openly* linked to the proletariat".[1]

---

[1] See p. 26 of this book.

Lenin gave in a few words the grandiose programme for the creation of a genuinely free proletarian literature, and called on the Party to set about realising this programme without delay. It was the urgency of the task that prompted the appearance of his famous article "Party Organisation and Party Literature". What is more, it appeared neither before nor after but precisely in November 1905, when it became legally possible to approach the people through a literature destined to become the prototype of the literature of victorious socialism.

This Leninist proposition is sometimes taken to mean that literature openly linked with the working class can be created only under socialism, and the following passage from Lenin's article is adduced as evidence: "It will be a free literature, because the idea of socialism and sympathy with the working people and not greed or careerism, will bring ever new forces to its ranks. It will be a free literature, because it will serve, not some satiated heroine, not the bored 'upper ten thousand' suffering from fatty degeneration, but the millions and tens of millions of working people—the flower of the country, its strength and its future. It will be a free literature, enriching the last word in the revolutionary thought of mankind with the experience and living work of the socialist proletariat. . . ."[1]

At first sight, Lenin does indeed seem to be referring only to the distant future (distant, that is, from 1905). "It will be a free literature," he repeats several times. Nevertheless it would be wrong to conclude therefrom that there can be no free literature in a bourgeois society.

It is, of course, true that a genuinely free literature can develop only under socialism and communism. It already exists in the USSR and other socialist countries. But it would be a mistake to see in Lenin's article only a view of the future, for that would be to underrate one of the most important aspects of the historical peculiarity of the 1905 revolution, which made it possible to pose the question of the creation of a free proletarian literature "within the framework of a bourgeois society", and would diminish the tremendous significance of Lenin's proposition for the Communist Parties of the capitalist countries.

Lenin ends his article with the words: "To work, then,

---

[1] See pp. 26-27 of this book.

comrades! We are faced with a new and difficult task. But it is a a noble and grateful one—to organise a broad, multiform and varied literature inseparably linked with the Social-Democratic working-class movement. All Social-Democratic literature must become Party literature. Every newspaper, journal, publishing house, etc., must immediately set about reorganising its work, leading up to a situation in which it will, in one form or another, be integrated into one Party organisation or another. Only then will 'Social-Democratic' literature really become worthy of that name; only then will it be able to fulfil its duty and, even within the framework of a bourgeois society, break out of bourgeois slavery and merge with the movement of the really advanced and thoroughly revolutionary class."[1]

Life has confirmed Lenin's magnificent perspicacity. The possibility and necessity of a struggle for a free proletarian literature under bourgeois legality, which he indicated, is an example of practical leadership for the Communist Parties in capitalist countries, where legality has been or can be won. In many bourgeois countries the Communist Parties overcome widespread restrictions and persecution by the forces of reaction, and openly publish their newspapers. Sometimes they even have publishing houses, which legally print Marxist-Leninist literature and works of socialist realism.

But it would be wrong to overlook some important circumstances. When Lenin wrote of the possibility of creating a free literature within the framework of a bourgeois society, he meant that it could be created only as the result of the heroic struggle of the proletariat against that society. Besides, though free from capital, it cannot, under the capitalist system, be free in the significantly wider sense in which we understand freedom of creativity under socialism.

Why is it that in a bourgeois society free proletarian literature is created in the course of struggle against that society? After all, the works of such masters of socialist realism as Martin Andersen Nexö, Paul Eluard, Jorge Amado, Pablo Neruda, Jack Lindsay, find open outlets in the press of several capitalist countries.

The point is that this fact does not depend on the bourgeoisie. The bourgeoisie would, of course, ban the works

---

[1] See p. 27 of this book.

of famous progressive writers, but is unable to do so because at the present time the alignment of class forces is not in its favour. In conditions of legality, socialist literature is usually issued by publishing houses not accountable to the bourgeoisie.

Hence the question of the freedom of literary creativity in a bourgeois society is not simple. The assertion, thoughtlessly repeated by so many people, that under capitalism all literature is dependent on the purse, has nothing to do with Lenin's demand for the creation of a free proletarian literature "within the framework of a bourgeois society". This assertion even fails to explain the fact that socialist realism evolved as a new artistic method in the works of Gorky before the October Revolution.

Lenin's propositions concerning the achievement of freedom by proletarian literature "within the framework of a bourgeois society" become especially clear when compared with his statements about writers who are really not free. When he talks of the dependence of literature on the purse-strings, etc., Lenin has in mind bourgeois writers who champion in their works the capitalist system, so dear to their hearts. "Bourgeois individualists"—these are whom Lenin is writing about. He shows how these bourgeois writers are enslaved, enslaved not only by the moneybag, but also by the fact they must serve the "satiated heroine" and the "upper ten thousand", and not the people.

Lenin demonstrated very convincingly that bourgeois literature proper cannot be free in any legal conditions, since by defending classes that are on the decline, it opposes the interests of the people, the interests of social progress. Its dependence on capital and class narrow-mindedness, its tendency to individualism and playing up to the tastes of a bourgeois public force bourgeois literature to give up a realistic depiction of life. But it is artistic truth, portrayed from the point of view of the people, that means genuine creative freedom.

The novelty of Lenin's treatment of creative freedom is especially clearly seen in these propositions. The great revolutionary leader proceeds from his central thesis that only he is free in art, science or any other sphere of social activity who fights unstintingly for the interests of the people. Since only the Communist Party is absolutely consistent in its struggle for the interests of the people, there arose the task of creating a free proletarian literature under its leadership. Hence it is easy to understand Lenin's opponents, who considered his proposition concerning creative freedom to be a "paradox". For centuries bourgeois ideologists have asserted that freedom means "freedom of the will" or "absolute freedom of action", incompatible with regimentation and control, the more so in artistic creativity, but now it transpires that it is they that are not free!

The originality of Lenin's formulation of the question consists in the fact that he views freedom not as the absence of all obstacles or restrictions (which from an objective point of view will always exist), and not simply as an end in itself, but as a unity of means and ends, a unity of rights and obligations, as the process of the struggle for freedom. There was a time when even individualism was to some extent a progressive trend; at the early stages in the development of bourgeois consciousness it served as a means of combating feudalism, which smothered all individual freedom. With the development and consolidation of capitalism, individualism turned into a kind of anti-humanism, and became antagonistic to the interests of the people.

In a socialist society which has ushered in new social relations, individualism gives place to collectivism, conscious discipline and the principle of "one for all and all for one". Political consciousness, firm ideological principles, social activity in the name of the working people, in fact all that constitutes communist partisanship, form the basic precondition and practical realisation of genuine freedom—freedom for the benefit of man building communism.

Lenin's concept of freedom helps also to elucidate the question of "inner freedom", "freedom of the individual will", which is the subject of endless arguments in bourgeois aesthetics. "Inner freedom" cannot be considered as freedom from society. Its manifestation is inevitably bound up with the author's outlook on the world, and his involvement in the struggle for the liberation of the people. Under capitalism such freedom is possible only for those who have understood the relationship between classes and have firmly sided with the proletariat, the people. No amount of persecution can shake their conviction that man's highest calling is to serve the people and to fight for their happiness. Such "inner freedom"—the only possible one under conditions of exploitation—is usually the prerogative of Communists.

Literature knows many men who were "inwardly free" even under severe social repression. In the period of cruellest reaction under Nicholas I, Belinsky wrote: "Freedom of creativity quite agrees with serving one's time; to do this one has no need to force oneself to write on certain subjects or to force one's fantasy. One has simply to be a citizen, a son of one's society and time, to identify with its interests, to combine one's efforts with its efforts. To do this one needs sympathy, love, a healthy, practical feeling for truth, which does not separate conviction from action, nor writing from life."

Without such "inner freedom", at the heart of which is a sacred love of the people and an unlimited devotion to the cause of their political and economic liberation, the great classical literature of the past would have been unthinkable.

The concept of freedom cannot be reduced simply to whether or not the press is legal at a given moment. Under capitalism, legality of the press is often made use of by scoundrels and careerists. The freedom of brave and courageous men consists precisely in a deep understanding of the historical meaning of social development, and of the impossibility of acting against the interests of the people. Whether or not this is difficult or dangerous is a secondary question.

It is a matter for regret that as a rule the attention of a certain section of our creative intelligentsia is focussed not so much on this genuinely heroic literature of the proletariat of capitalist countries, consciously serving the cause of socialism and enriching world culture by significant artistic discoveries, as on the works of bourgeois authors who are sometimes overtly anti-communist. Led on by the false theory of the "supra-class" character of art, certain Soviet writers, painters, musicians and other artists fail to observe the hypocrisy and cunning disguise in the external attributes of bourgeois "freedoms". Hence the naive talk about the "breadth" of the views of foreign authors, who, if you please, are "not instructed" to follow Freudianism, with its sick interest in the "stream of subconsciousness"; abstractionism, with its contempt for common sense; neo-realism, with its misunderstanding of the social perspectives of development; even pseudo-realism, with its plausibility of detail and basic falsity. Socialist realism, whose representatives portray reality from a consistent Marxist-Leninist point of view, is regarded by such lovers of "breadth" as "dull orthodoxy".

The desire for originality at any price induces politically immature writers to regard it as an end in itself, and leads them to believe that everything previously unknown to them must be new. So they "discover" anew the two hundred-year-old Kantian theory of "art for art's sake", Bergsonian intuitivism, which was discarded by the great writers at the beginning of the century, and various forms of decadence, defeated by our art in honest and open battle in the twenties. These "explorers" discard as "old" what in actual fact is the youngest and most innovatory form of art—socialist realism.

We must combat such errors vigorously, if only because they divert the artist away from the main line of development of Soviet art and limit his freedom of creativity gained for him by the Party, by the people.

Only a literature that has placed itself at the service of communist ideals makes no concessions in conditions of bourgeois legality. Its representatives are guided in their motives and actions not by self-interest or careerism, but by "the idea of socialism and the sympathy of the working people".

But, of course, under capitalism proletarian literature is free only within definite limits, principally in its ideological slant. Far from guaranteeing access to the people, bourgeois legality actually hinders this in all ways. The official press tries to place the progressive writers in political isolation.

It is only socialism that completely removes the obstacles to voicing ideas answering the interests of the people and the Party, and creates all conditions for the development of literature and the arts and their free accessibility to the people.

To Lenin, the chief of these conditions was cultural revolution. In conversation with Clara Zetkin, Lenin said that art belonged to the people. But to make it closer to the people, it was necessary to raise "the general educational and cultural standards".[1]

---

[1] Lenin, *On Literature and Art*, p. 251.

The cultural revolution raised the working masses out of spiritual slavery and ignorance and made the riches of culture available to them. In this accomplishment great credit is due to Soviet literature and the arts. Soviet writers, film and theatre workers, musicians and painters now have the entire Soviet people as their audience. Is that not proof of the complete freedom of creativity in the USSR?

In socialist society quite new relations between the artist and the state have been formed. "Revolution unleashes all forces fettered hitherto and drives them from their deep recesses of life to the surface," wrote Lenin. "Take for example the influence exerted by fashion and the caprices of the tsarist court as well as by the tastes and whims of the aristocracy and the bourgeoisie on the development of our painting, sculpture and architecture. In society based on private property, the artist produces for the market, needs customers. Our revolution freed artists from the yoke of these extremely prosaic conditions. It turned the state into their defender and client providing them with orders."[1]

This does not mean, of course, that the Soviet artist must violate his ideals. Far from it; insofar as the aims of the artist, supporting the working class, and the aims of the Soviet state, expressing the interests of the working people, are the same, the state sees in the artist's work the embodiment of the aesthetic ideals of socialism. Rather than limiting the artist's work, the patronage of the state makes it the property of the entire people.

The socialist revolution removes the gap between genuine art and the state. Thus the inspiration of Soviet art lies in the affirmation of reality, in the artistically perfect embodiment of socialist and communist transformations. Criticism of inadequacies serves as an affirmation of the policies and practice of the Communist Party, for no one combats inadequacies so consistently as the Party itself.

* * *

Having liquidated the contradiction between the state and genuine art, socialism has also liquidated the objective basis

---

[1] Lenin, *On Literature and Art,* pp. 249-50.

of the incompatibility of the artist's political views and aesthetic efforts. This affords the possibility of single-minded Party leadership of the entire development of literature and the arts in the USSR. Every artist in the land of socialism, as Lenin pointed out, has full right to work "freely", but this does not mean that he can neglect the interests of the people or the concrete sensual nature of art, substituting for it abstractions. Communists cannot "stand idly by and give chaos free rein to develop".[1]

In reply to those who made use of political freedom in order to reject realistic traditions and indulge in modernist and decadent experiments, Lenin said that in such a position "much is pure hypocrisy and of course unconscious deference to the art fashions ruling the West".[2] What art gives to a few hundred, even a few thousand of the populace at large is not the important thing; what is important is that art should be capable of uniting the "feelings, thoughts and will" of the masses, of elevating the masses, of stirring "to activity and developing the art instincts within them".[3] Socialist realism is such an art.

Communist partisanship is based on the artist's deep conviction of the Party's rightness, and reflects the noblest ideals of mankind. Only people for whom the Party has not become the focus of their life and creativity can resist such partisanship.

To be always with the people, with the Communist Party—this is the meaning of the work of writers, painters, composers and film and theatre workers.

Summoning them to portray what is positive in our life, the Party teaches them at the same time to reveal and condemn the imperfections that hinder the forward march of society. The question is, from what point of departure, and for what end does the artist do this? In order to affirm what is new and communist, or in order to refute it? It must be done for the affirmation of communist ideals—such is the demand of life, the object and purpose of the Party leadership of Soviet literature and art.

A Marxist-Leninist outlook is the only Party line following which the Soviet artist can clearly outline the decisive

[1] Ibid. p. 250.
[2] Ibid.
[3] Ibid. p. 251.

153

perspectives of our society's advance towards communism. These perspectives are a classless social system with single national ownership of the means of production, with complete social equality of all members of society, in which an all-round development of men is accompanied by a growth of productive forces on the basis of continually developing science and technology, where "all the springs of co-operative wealth will flow more abundantly, and the great principle 'From each according to his ability, to each according to his needs' will be implemented."[1]

Mankind knows no loftier aim than the building of communism. Therefore the task of the art that serves communism is to embody above all the positive features in the life of Soviet society, which has first set foot on the road to communism; the features that most fully express the essence of the epoch, the elevated moral composition of Soviet man, the beauty of his thoughts and deeds. We cannot be reconciled with the fact that even slander on Soviet reality is sometimes justified as "proceeding from good intentions", or by considerations of some sort of timeless "universal" truth. The highest form of truth is the truth of communism, and the loftiest humanism is the struggle for communism.

In combating formalism and abstractionism, the Party does not stick political labels on anyone. But it does reveal the ideological and moral damage done by the errors of various creative workers. It does this so that they might realise that their errors benefit our ideological opponents. And however hard it may seem, everyone in error must be brave enough to admit his errors and correct them. The humanism of the Party's policy lies in the fact that it is interested in the correct development of every single person, and regards his talent as the property of the people, as an important factor in the fight for communism.

One of the most characteristic features of Party guidance of Soviet literature and the arts, displayed especially clearly since the 20th, 22nd and 23rd congresses of the CPSU, is that the Party pays close attention not only to the political aspects of creative work, but also to the closely related problems of artistic techniques, and the aesthetic value of the artistic portrayal of life. Guided by Lenin's theory of knowledge, which also has a direct relevance to art, our

---

[1] *The Road to Communism,* p. 509.

154

Party concerns itself with the development and enriching of the realistic traditions, which are the most appropriate to art.

In this connection the question of freedom of creativity is now given a wider and deeper meaning. It is not simply the removal of obstacles lying outside the field of creativity—they have been long since removed, since under socialism there is genuine freedom for all who serve the people—but also the elimination of the authors' anarchical tendencies in creative work.

The Party shows the artist that a subjectivist attitude to the portrayal of reality is only apparently "total" freedom, and that in fact, insofar as it is a distortion of life, subjectivism deprives art of real freedom, which consists in the ability to show the truth of life.

Neither injunction nor unfounded criticism—for in cultural matters haste and peremptoriness are most harmful—but rather the action of the Party's ideas on the creative processes, friendly advice, deep understanding of the specific nature of art, the ability to detect errors in good time and to help the author to realise his mistake, the desire to support all things genuinely new and communist—these are the main features of the Party's guidance of the artistic process.

Party guidance is the most important precondition for the successful development of Soviet literature and the arts.

1967

Moisei Kagan

THE FORMATION AND DEVELOPMENT OF SOCIALIST ART

The Logic of the Formation of Socialist Art in the Era of Capitalism

Socialist art has been brought forth by *the historical process of the formation of a revolutionary proletariat* and its class awareness and psychology, and by its transformation from "a class in itself" into "a class for itself". In the 1840s Marxist scientific theory, which is the foundation of the outlook and ideals of the working class, was being worked out in Germany, and it is in no way surprising that parallel with this the "artistic ideology" of the socialist proletariat—its art—was also beginning to crystallise.

Defining the social significance of the rising of Silesian weavers in 1844, Marx wrote: "The Silesian rising *begins* with precisely what the French and English workers' risings *ended* with—namely, with the fact that it perceives the essence of the proletariat."[1] Marx regarded the *Song of the Silesian Weavers*, which came into being during the Silesian rising, as the direct result and manifestation of a high level of class consciousness among the progressive section of German workers, and as a "bold *call* to battle, in which ... the proletariat immediately, resolutely, unceremoniously and powerfully announces for everyone to hear that it is opposed to a society of private ownership".[2]

The working class had very little opportunity to make its way with its own hands, by its own efforts, into art. But it had another possibility—to exert a spiritual influence on the democratic strata of the artistic intelligentsia. It was pre-

---

[1] *Marx and Engels on Art*, Vol. I, p. 559, Russ. ed.
[2] Ibid.

cisely here, among the representatives of revolutionary romanticism and critical realism, and later, in the twentieth century, even among the Left expressionists, surrealists and futurists that the working class "enlisted" its poets and artists, helping them escape the captivity of petty-bourgeois ideology and enabling them to become, with varying degrees of success, the articulators of socialist awareness. When the outstanding German poet Heinrich Heine wrote his *Song of the Silesian Weavers*, Engels concluded that the author had "joined our ranks" and that in several of his poems Heine was "preaching socialism".[1] Marx saw the first shoots of revolutionary, socialist art in the poems of Herwegh and Freiligrath, and Engels called Georg Weerth "the first and *most significant* poet of the German proletariat", who went considerably further along the road than either Freiligrath or Heine.[2]

It is interesting that the founders of Marxism observed the first shoots of proletarian art not only in German literature but also in German painting. Engels wrote, for example, that one of Hübner's paintings "did far more for socialist agitation than a hundred pamphlets might have done". Another German painter, Charles Lessing, according to Engels, "became a convert to socialism".[3]

Correspondence of Marx and Engels with Ferdinand Lassalle, which contains an analysis of his tragedy *Franz von Sickingen*, and Engels' letters to Minna Kautsky and Margaret Harkness show that the founders of Marxism considered it perfectly logical and timely that these writers should try to create the first models of socialist art, and attributed their failures to purely individual peculiarities of their consciousness, the inconsistency of their world outlook and aesthetic principles.

Thus nineteenth century socialist art made its first steps, sometimes timid and contradictory, in Germany, and then in other European countries. This is evidenced, in particular, by the verses of the English worker Edward P. Mead, cited by Engels in his article "The Condition of the Working Class in England",[4] or the extremely popular novel of

---

[1] Marx and Engels, *Works*, Vol. 2, p. 521, Russ. ed.
[2] Ibid., Vol. 21, p. 5.
[3] Ibid., Vol. 2, pp. 519-20.
[4] Marx and Engels, *On Britain*, Moscow, 1962, pp. 220-21.

William Morris—*News from Nowhere*. Socialist art burgeoned richly in France, producing the poems and songs of the Communards, the summit of which was the immortal *Internationale* of Eugéne Pottier and Pierre Degeyter; the revolutionary sketches of Honoré Daumier and other artists and lastly the broad artistic movement in contemporary French culture, headed by Eluard, Stil, Fougeron, Taslitzky.... This powerful movement has affected to some degree the greatest exponents of French culture: France, Barbusse, Rolland, Léger and Picasso.

Development of socialist art in other capitalist countries of Europe and Asia, and North and South Americas produced such figures as Neruda and Nezval, Amado and Hikmet, Andersen Nexö and Pratolini, Guttuzo and Bidstrup, Fučik and Guillén, and made widely known the names of Brecht and Becker, Eisler and Busch, who represent socialist art in Germany.

It is also perfectly logical that the successes of socialist art in each country should be proportionate to the scope of the workers' and communist movement: in France they are immeasurably bigger than in Britain; in Italy they are more significant than in Japan; in Latin America they are more serious than in the USA. For this reason the first victories of socialist art in Russia were scored at the time of the revolution of 1905-07, which for Maxim Gorky was a most important landmark on his ideological-aesthetic path, making it possible for him to "bind himself very closely", as Lenin said, to the workers' movement.[1]

Proletarian art had made its way in Russia as long ago as the 1890s in the revolutionary verses and songs of Radin (who wrote *Step out boldly, comrades...*), Krzhizhanovsky (who wrote the Russian texts of *Warszawianka, Rage, o tyrants*, and *Red Banner*), Kots (who wrote the Russian text of the *Internationale*) and a whole series of other revolutionary poets; but it was Gorky that Lenin called "the greatest representative of *proletarian art*".[2] Gorky became the founder of socialist realism in literature because in the novel *Mother* and the play *The Enemies* he was able to find the ideological and artistic solution of the problems that had been beyond the modest abilities of Lassalle, Kautsky or

[1] Lenin, *Collected Works,* Vol. 16, p. 106.
[2] Ibid., p. 207.

Harkness, and even the very gifted Hauptmann and Zola, who displayed interest in the life and struggle of the working class in their works. Lunacharsky's statement that in Gorky the proletariat "became artistically aware of itself for the first time, as it had become philosophically and politically aware in Marx, Engels and Lenin" should certainly not be understood as suggesting—as some have thought—that Gorky was the first proletarian artist in the history of world art; what it means is that the great Russian writer was the first to present the proletariat's socialist understanding of the world as an independent aesthetic system of views on artistic creativity.

Thus in the course of the development of European artistic culture in the nineteenth and twentieth centuries a peculiarly proletarian aesthetic programme and a new method of artistic creativity for carrying it out have gradually taken shape.

How, then, did the socialist artistic method grow out of the specific ideological and aesthetic interests and ideals of the revolutionary proletariat? And how did Marxist science provide the theoretical basis for this process?

The Establishment of the Artistic Method and Theory of Socialist Realism

Let us begin from the most obvious: proletarian art regarded the world it reflected from a new point of view to which it had been elevated by the revolutionary struggle of the working class. To be precise, this was a socialist point of view (we have in mind the ideology of scientific, not utopian, socialism, of course). When Engels was defining the ideological essence of works portraying the world from the position of the revolutionary proletariat, he spoke directly of "the socialist problem novel" (letter to Minna Kautsky) and "a point-blank socialist novel"[1] (letter to Margaret Harkness). A few decades later Lenin called the ideological position of proletarian art communist partisanship.

A more complicated question is whether a definite aesthetic system is worked out in the consciousness of the working class, and if so, what is it?

---

[1] Marx and Engels, *Selected Correspondence*, Moscow, 1955, pp. 467, 479.

Revisionists have answered this question as follows: there is nothing definite in the aesthetic demands of the proletariat and socialist nations, nor can there be any. By guaranteeing complete freedom of artistic creativity, socialist ideology thereby accepts any principles of artistic interpretation of life—realist and romantic, symbolic and expressionist, surrealist and even abstractionist. In other words, socialist art is indeterminate in both style and method; it is only an ideological, and not an ideological-artistic movement. The influence this conception has on the artistic intelligentsia of capitalist and even socialist countries compels us to devote serious attention to the way this question was analysed by the founders of Marxism and to examine under this heading the real process of the formation and development of socialist art.

Marx and Engels' fundamental objections to Ferdinand Lassalle's tragedy *Franz von Sickingen* concerned not only the political and philosophical concepts, but the artistic principles at the root of it. Both Marx and Engels—independently of one another—saw the error of the idealisation of reality that Lassalle brought into his work, and they unanimously asserted that an organic element of socialist art must be "Shakespearisation", i.e., realism. "In accordance with *my* view of the drama," Engels explained, "one must not forget the realistic for the idealistic, Shakespeare for Schiller", for "the future of drama" is "the total blending of great ideological depth and the comprehended sense of history ... with Shakespearian liveliness and action", i.e., with realism.[1]

In another place Marx and Engels wrote that the leaders of the revolution must be painted in the harsh colours of Rembrandt, with all the truthfulness of life, and not with buskins on their feet and haloes around their heads, for in such pompous metamorphoses of Raphaelean portraits all the truth of the portrayal is lost. In a letter to Minna Kautsky, Engels once more disapproved of her tendency to idealise her heroes: Arnold was "much too worthy a man", he was "too good for this world"; "in Elsa there is still a certain individualisation, though verging on idealisation"; "...it will never do for an author to put his own hero on too high a pedestal".[2] In a letter to Margaret Harkness,

[1] Marx and Engels, *Selected Correspondence*, p. 142.
[2] Ibid., p. 467.

Engels criticised her story because it was "not quite realistic enough", with too untypical circumstances, and he cited as the greatest example of realism *La Comédie Humaine* of Balzac whose wealth of experience, in his opinion, was invaluable for the socialist novel.[1]

The aesthetic position of Lenin was analogous. In his articles on Lev Tolstoi and in innumerable other pronouncements on aesthetics Lenin insisted that proletarian art must follow the path of realism, the truthful reflection of life, and he strongly indicted all of idealisation of reality. The English artist Clare Sheridan, who made a sculptural portrait of Lenin and had conversations with him on artistic topics, has cited his words in her memoirs: "That is the fault of bourgeois art—it always beautifies."[2] Even in Gorky's novel *Mother*, which Lenin, unlike Plekhanov, valued highly, he saw, according to Maria Andreyeva, a basic fault—a certain idealisation of the revolutionary intelligentsia.[3]

Such are the grounds for asserting that the idea of an organic link between socialist outlook, or communist partisanship and realist aspirations in artistic creativity, i.e., the idea of socialist realism, was common to Marx, Engels and Lenin. The very formula "socialist realism", whoever invented it, is a concise summary of the ideas of the classics of Marxism-Leninism, who fulfilled the historic service of outlining the basic principles of the creative method of socialist art.

But what was the logic that convinced Marx, Engels and Lenin that, in its artistic perception of the world, socialist consciousness would demand a confluence with the realist and not with any other aesthetic stream? Did such a conviction proceed from their own personal tastes and aesthetic prejudices?

Obviously the reasons were very much deeper than that. Marx and Engels had a high opinion of the art of antiquity, and they admired Raphael and Schiller, but this did not prevent them from considering that the nascent proletarian art should employ the methods of Shakespeare and Rembrandt, and not those of Raphael and Schiller, and that the principles of reflection of life peculiar to the art of antiquity could not serve as a point of departure for socialist art.

---

[1] Ibid., pp. 478-79.
[2] Clare Sheridan, *Naked Truth*, New York, 1928, p. 190.
[3] *Reminiscences of Lenin*, Vol. I, Moscow, 1956, p. 326, Russ. ed.

Besides, we know from the authoritative evidence of Lunacharsky that "Vladimir Ilyich has never tried to impose his own aesthetic sympathies and antipathies as the guiding principles".[1] This is yet one more proof that for Lenin the struggle for a realist tendency in socialist art was a theory-based policy, not an expression of subjective aesthetic prejudices.

The necessity for realist principles in socialist art is based on the Marxist-Leninist world outlook, which has turned the idea of socialism from an utopian dream and abstract ideal into a science. Marx and Engels stressed that "communism is for us not a *state of affairs* which is to be established, an *ideal* to which reality will have to adjust itself. We call communism the *real* movement which abolishes the present state of things".[2]

This thought, formulated with amazing clarity, has direct bearing on aesthetics. Just as inevitably as petty-bourgeois ideology and, even more so, feudal utopian socialism impelled art to take the path of romantic *idealisation* of life (since the ideal had no roots in real life and therefore had to be invented on the principle "it never is like this, but it ought to be"), the ideology of scientific socialism demanded from art a strictly *realistic* approach to life, for this was the only condition that could enable art to understand the "real movement" from the old social state of affairs to the new. The socialist world outlook of the proletariat is organically opposed to any form of idealisation of reality and turns to realism as the only appropriate means of modelling life in artistic images.

But from this follows the second important aesthetic conclusion: those forms of realism that had been worked out by pre-socialist art were unsuitable to embody the socialist outlook, since neither the Renaissance nor the enlightened or critical realism of the nineteenth century was able to reflect the very process of the "real movement" of life, being restricted to a truthful recreation of the situation as it was in their time. The realist artists of the seventeenth, eighteenth and nineteenth centuries did not—nor could they—clearly see the future perspective of social development; they were unable to foresee how things would turn,

---

[1] Lenin, *On Culture and Art*, p. 527.
[2] Marx and Engels, *The German Ideology*, Moscow, 1968, p. 48.

or how tomorrow grows out of today, so that they had either to describe the facts of life as it was, ignoring the historical processes, or express the bitter and pessimistic conviction that the existing unhappy state of affairs could never be changed, or, finally, they could try to make sense of the tendencies of the development of life by enlisting the aid of utopian conceptions of a political, aesthetic or even religious nature, as had Gogol and Dickens, Tolstoi and Dostoyevsky, Chekhov and Ibsen. It is hardly surprising that in this last case the realist method would not work, would "skid", and even the most convinced realists were compelled to fly to various means of idealisation, creating far from realistic images of ideal landowners or capitalists, of Prince Myshkin or Platon Karatayev.

Only the scientific world outlook of the socialist proletariat could show the way out from such an impasse. By opening the artist's eyes to the true laws of social development, it demanded realism for its interpretation in art forms, and at the same time forced realism to modify and to adopt new, hitherto inaccessible means of moulding images of the dynamics of social existence and consciousness of men. It demanded the creation, in the words of Marx and Engels, not of the "present state of things" as such, but of the "real movement, which abolishes the present state of things". This is why Harkness' attempt to combine a socialist viewpoint with realism turned out to be superficial and mechanical, and not organic, as Engels explained. The English authoress' assimilation of critical realism enabled her to create characters "typical enough, as far as they go", and these limits were too narrow from the point of view of the new type of realism, socialist realism for which socio-historical circumstances are typical not because the working class is oppressed and suffering, but because it tries to overcome its suffering by active opposition to the oppressors, because it rises up in revolutionary struggle, becoming the major dynamic force of social development. "The rebellious reaction of the working class," wrote Engels, "against the oppressive medium which surrounds them, their attempts—convulsive half-conscious or conscious—at recovering their status of human beings, belong to history and must therefore lay claim to a place in the domain of realism."[1]

---

[1] Marx and Engels, *Selected Correspondence*, p. 479.

Such is the logic that explains the overwhelming tendency of the socialist outlook towards realism, and not to some other artistic trend; at the same time it explains the transformation of realism when it has been enriched by the socialist world outlook and appears as a new method of artistic creativity—the method of socialist realism. In the *Song of the Silesian Weavers* and the *Internationale*, in the poems of Georg Weerth and in the songs of the Russian revolutionaries this method appeared "in embryo", since the very nature of the song genre only made it possible to "outline" the idea of the revolutionary reshaping of the world. The method of socialist realism could unfurl and bring to light its concealed abilities to recreate the actual process of life only in those forms and genres of art which portray life in the forms of life itself: in narrative genres of literature, in drama, painting and drawing—above all, in the novel and the drama, since the static nature of the figurative arts does not make it possible for them to embody the dynamics of life. For this very reason the searchings of the German painters Hübner and Lessing, like the treatment of the revolutionary struggle of the working class by the great French artist Daumier or the notable Russian painter Kasatkin, did not reveal the potentialities of socialist realism so definitely and clearly as Gorky's novel *Mother* and his drama *The Enemies.*

Here Gorky achieved what Engels had prophetically proclaimed twenty years earlier. He gave an artistic affirmation of the "place in the domain of realism" of the revolutionary struggle of the proletariat. The superiority of Gorky over his great senior contemporaries Lev Tolstoi and Anton Chekhov was not that he was more gifted or that his criticism of capitalism went deeper; it was his artistic understanding of the basic social conflict of the epoch—the collision between the bourgeoisie and the proletariat. Gorky saw that it was not moral self-perfection nor revival of Christian morality, but the revolutionary struggle of the working class that was the only real course to destroy social evil. Moreover, Gorky was able to show that this course was not imposed on society by theoreticians, ideologists and politicians, but was dictated by the objective development of life itself, the irreconcilable nature of class antagonism and the growth of proletarian awareness. The fate of Pavel Vlasov and Nilovna, who rose from ignorance and passivity to revolutionary heroism, reveals the regularity of social development which was—and still remains—inaccessible to critical realism. That is why Gorky's work was so highly rated by Lenin.

In working out the aesthetic programme of proletarian art, Lenin proceeded from the same premises as Marx and Engels and came, naturally enough, to the same conclusions. For Lenin the acknowledgement of the necessity for a realist direction in socialist art was closely linked with his general understanding of truth in the spiritual life of the working class and in the activities of the Bolshevik Party and the Soviet Government. It is no accident that the central Party newspaper fostered by Lenin is called *Pravda* (Truth), and that this word remained in the title despite the severity of the censorship. And after the victory of the socialist revolution in Russia, Lenin never tired of repeating in speeches and articles that *truth* was essential in the Party's work of propaganda and agitation, and how harmful to the interests of the revolution and the building of socialism was *any form of idealisation* of the real state of things, *embellishment* of truth, dream-building, wishful thinking, or even timid, fearful, half-hearted *half-truth*.

Fully aware that the enemies of the revolution might make use of Soviet self-criticism to serve their own interests, Lenin said: "Let them! We shall benefit far more from the straightforward and candid truth, because we are sure that although this truth is harsh, nevertheless, if it is clearly heard, every class-conscious worker, every working peasant, will draw the only correct conclusion that can be drawn from it."[1]

The Lenin concept of truth as the highest political, pedagogic and aesthetic value is beautifully expressed by Alexander Tvardovsky:

> Life will lose its whole meaning
> Do you know without what?
> Truth that makes the life worth living,
> Truth that goes to the heart!
> Truth and only truth for me,
> Bitter as it wants to be.

Distortions of the principles of socialist realism that have taken place in the past are in many ways due to a departure from Lenin's principles on this point. The banner of "socialist realism" was used by authors whose works were far

---

[1] Lenin, *Collected Works*, Vol. 29, p. 256.

removed from any sort of realism. Since the 20th Congress of the CPSU these deviations have been decisively corrected and there has been a return to the truly Marxist, truly Leninist understanding of the necessity for the fullest, deepest and most uncompromising truthfulness in the art of socialist realism, whether it is depicting the country's revolutionary past, the tragic days of the Great Patriotic War, or the difficulties of the building of socialism in pre-war and post-war years. This process has already brought our art a number of major achievements in literature, the scenic arts and the cinema.

Neo-classicist tendencies to idealisation, however, are still making themselves known in theory and in practice. When certain theoreticians and critics replace the concept of the "positive hero", "heroic character" or "elevated image" by that of "ideal hero" and try to prove the correctness of and even necessity for idealisation of our life together with showing its typical aspects, they are basically proceeding from a metaphysical conception of the relationship between the real and the ideal, and at the same time they doubt the educative potential of realism as the art of the truth of life.

It goes without saying that to the extent that the communist ideal is realised in the character and actions of our contemporaries, i.e., becomes actual fact, it can and must be embodied in socialist art. But even in this case socialist art is reproducing real life, and the artistic technique is that of typifying, not idealising. Gorky's Pavel Vlasov and Nikolai Ostrovsky's Pavka Korchagin, the Commissar in Vishnevsky's *Optimistic Tragedy* and Sergei in Arbuzov's *Irkutsk Story*, the hero in the film trilogy about Maxim by Kozintsev and Trauberg and Alyosha Skvortsov in Chukhrai's *Ballad of a Soldier*—these are all typical heroes of our time, not ideal figures in a classical or romantic style. When the real is replaced by the ideal and when the artist tries to portray the ideal itself, instead of reflecting the socio-historical process of realising this ideal, nothing remains of the method of socialist realism but the name, and this gives reason to opponents of socialist art to speak of the incompatibility of realism and socialist world outlook.

Here, for example, is how one of the foremost representatives of modern existentialism, Albert Camus, takes issue with us. In his speech at Upsala University (Sweden) on December 14, 1957, Camus asserted that the basic premise of socialist realism is "the impossibility of portraying reality without making certain selections". True, Camus acknowledges that some sort of selection of life's material is always necessary in art, but he believes that the theory of socialist realism found its "principle of selection" "not in the reality that we know, but in the reality that will come in the future. In order to recreate what exists now, it is necessary to sketch what is to come. In other words, the subject of socialist realism is precisely what is not yet real. What a superb contradiction! ... In the final analysis such an art becomes socialist to the extent to which it ceases to be realist."

Such an interpretation of the method of socialist realism has, of course, nothing in common with its actual principles. Socialist realism does not recreate "what is to come" but precisely "what is"; "what is", however, is regarded not from a static point of view, but in the light of "what is to come". In the metaphysical reasoning of Camus there is no connection between the real and the ideal, which "is not yet real". In the dialectic thinking of the masters of socialist realism such a link does exist, and it serves as a model for the images created, for the artist sees how the ideal becomes the real. This enables socialist realism to go further than critical realism, using the same instrument of typification that the critical realists used.

This accounts for the dual attitude of socialist realism towards critical realism. Their common realist nature and their common democratic ideology make critical realism the main point of departure for socialist realism and its ally in the struggle against bourgeois society and decadent art. But as soon as the bourgeois world crumbles under the blows of the socialist revolution, the coexistence of the socialist and critical realism in the art of a socialist society becomes impossible. For critical realism is critical precisely because it denies the soundness and poetry of the existing social relations. Such a position, sincere and progressive in a bourgeois society, would be false and reactionary in a socialist society, the first harmonious and fair social system. Hence in the new historical conditions realism cannot develop in the two or more forms which it inevitably takes in a bourgeois society (critical realism, neo-realism, socialist realism). From this time onward socialist realism becomes the only form of realism and takes upon itself responsibility for the critical reflection of all that is abnormal and vulgar in a new society, or that survives from the old society and hinders the triumph of the communist ideal. Thus the critical aspect is organically essential to the art of socialist realism.

It may be understood from the above why all potentialities of socialist realism as a method of artistic creativity are not revealed in the first stage of its development, in the culture of a capitalist society, but only in its second stage, after the victory of socialist revolution, in the period of construction of a socialist society.

Regularities of the Development of Socialist Art in the Period of Transition from Capitalism to Socialism

The same logic that called the socialist art into existence in bourgeois culture also determined its modest role in this culture. When Lenin spoke of the "two cultures" in each national culture, he emphasised that the socialist culture existed only as "elements", whereas the bourgeois culture existed "in the form not merely of 'elements', but of the *dominant* culture".[1] This fully applies to art and explains why under capitalism socialist realism has enrolled only a few artists, and not only yields pride of place to bourgeois art, but also to the democratic art of critical realism. The method of socialist realism demands from the artist, in addition to talent and mastery, such a sum of ideological, psychological and moral qualities—consistency of socialist outlook, selflessness, disinterestedness, unity of aesthetic and political principles—as is far from typical of the artistic intelligentsia of a bourgeois society. And as long as this society exists and exerts a decisive influence on the artistic intelligentsia, socialist art cannot develop widely or become the leading trend.

But when the revolution destroys the bourgeois dominion and gives the power to the working class and working peasants, socialist realism begins to win a *dominant* position in the artistic development of the country. This is guaranteed not by any outside factors, such as the support of the

---

[1] Lenin, *Collected Works*, Vol. 20, p. 24.

government or ruling party, but chiefly by the operation of the objective law of correspondence of social consciousness to the character of social being. In a social system in which the working class rules, its dominance in spiritual life is inevitable.

Of course, the affirmation of socialist consciousness as the ruling system of views and aesthetic principles is not something that is achieved easily, in a flash. It is a long and difficult process of the gradual penetration of new ideals into the minds of people who have grown up in a bourgeois society and hence acquired far from communist conceptions and frame of mind. But no matter how complex and lengthy the process may be, the best representatives of the old artistic intelligentsia sooner or later cross over to socialist aesthetics. Such was the history of Alexander Blok and Valery Bryusov, Alexei Tolstoi and Ilya Ehrenburg, Sergei Prokofiev and Leonid Sobinov, Mikhail Nesterov and Boris Kustodiyev, Alexander Matveyev and Sergei Konenkov, Kuzma Petrov-Vodkin and Pyotr Konchalovsky, Konstantin Stanislavsky and Vladimir Nemirovich-Danchenko. As regards the new generations of artistic intelligentsia, who have grown up under a socialist system, their socialist consciousness is formed naturally and organically under the direct influence of the new system of social being. In the Soviet Union the predominance of communist ideas and the related method of socialist realism became a reality as long ago as the thirties. The First Congress of Soviet Writers in 1934 gave quite convincing proof of this.

An analogous situation may be seen in the artistic development of other countries that began the construction of socialism after the Second World War. In these, socialist aesthetics has been gaining positions of dominance with the greatest difficulty, but the general direction of the process leaves no room for doubt.

This is the basic regularity of socialist realism at this stage of the development of art. However, in the period of transition from capitalism to socialism other regularities in the evolution of socialist art come to light. In the first place, there is the logical and gradual widening of the sphere of action of the new method of artistic creation in art; in the second place, a similar logical and gradual extension of the life content in socialist art, and hence the evolution of the method of socialist realism itself; and in the third place, there is a logical and gradual accumulation of artistic forms and styles by the socialist art. Let us look briefly at each of these three.

The first sparks of socialist creativity within bourgeois civilisation sprang into life in all places—Germany, France, Russia and Cuba—primarily in songs and poems. We might recall again the songs of the Silesian uprising, the revolutionary songs of the Russian workers, the *Internationale,* the works of Hans Eisler, the songs of Robeson and the Cuban revolutionaries' *March of July 26.* How can this be explained? Evidently two reasons were at work: on the one hand, a marching song is easy to "pick up" to express the pathos of the revolutionary struggle, inspiring enormous masses of people and having a high emotional charge; on the other hand, as distinct from any other form of artistic creation, a popular song is designed not for aesthetic contemplation, but for independent performance in the very course of revolutionary activity—at the barricades, on May Day parades, at conferences and meetings—and therefore it is needed by the revolutionary movement more than other artistic genres.

It is no accident, of course, that socialist art in all countries of the world further develop in the narrative literary genres. The novel and novelette, which afforded the greatest possibilities to critical realism, corresponded even more to socialist realism's task of portraying the struggle of the proletariat against the bourgeoisie and the process of historical development of society and human consciousness. After its first experiments in the poetic-song genres socialist realism spread to the novel and the novelette; we may cite the works of Gorky, Barbusse, Andersen Nexö, Amado and Fučik. And only on rare occassions at this stage of historical development did it break into the theatre of the visual arts.

Entering into a new phase in the period of transition from capitalism to socialism, socialist realism retains its attachment to literature and continues to gain its most signal victories precisely in that field. It is hardly necessary to list the dozens of Soviet authors and writers of other socialist countries who personify the success of socialist realism, but we must make special mention of the fact that a detailed aesthetic programme of socialist realism was first formulated precisely for literature at the Writers' Congress in 1934, and later it began to spread to other arts. At all events, problems of the theory of socialist art have been worked out in the vast majority of cases on the basis of literature. This accounts sometimes for the fact that theoretical problems are treated on a level on which poetics "works", which is sometimes below that appropriate to aesthetics.

The literature-centred and novel-centred trend in the theory of socialist realism is all the less justified since in the twenties and thirties, with literature retaining its leading role, there was an increasingly active penetration of socialist realism into the theatre and cinema, painting and music, sculpture and architecture, and, within each branch of art, into the different genres: into lyric poetry and tales, portrait painting and landscapes, symphony and opera. Lenin fully appreciated the significance of the cinema in the beginning of the twenties: "You must bear firmly in mind," he said to Lunacharsky, "that the cinema for us is the most important of all the arts."[1] According to Vasily Kachalov, a well-known Russian actor, when Gorky once said to Lenin that the young Soviet theatre "needed only heroics", Lenin retorted that it also needs lyricism, it needs Chekhov, and the truth of life.[2]

Thus the steady widening of the aspects and genres in which socialist realism operates should be seen as an objective regularity of its development, conditioned by its becoming the creative method predominant in the art and culture of the society, and hence striving to establish itself everywhere, overcoming the uneven development of the various genres and types of art inherited by the young socialist culture.

Another logical process characteristic of this stage of the development of socialist art is that the creative method at its basis must assimilate new material from life, hitherto unknown to it. When proletarian art was making its first steps in the capitalist society, it had a very limited and sharply defined choice of themes. Strictly speaking, it was not even a choice but one single thematic line—the revolutionary struggle of the working class. This limited content of socialist art was inevitable and natural in those conditions, for the proletariat affirmed itself spiritually precisely

---

[1] Lenin, *On Culture and Art*, p. 529.
[2] See p. 31 of this book.

171

by proclaiming the necessity for a revolutionary transformation of the world and getting ready to lead the socialist revolution. So the themes of labour or love, or feats of arms, or community with nature, or life and death, taken on their own, outside their relationship to the theme of revolution provided no opportunity for the socialist world outlook to reveal its distinctive features or stand out from the general democratic perception of the world that lay at the basis of critical realism and neo-realism. Hence mere portrayal of the life of the proletariat could in no way qualify as a criterion of socialist realism; witness the works of Meunier and Courbet, who did not reach beyond the bounds of critical realism; the works of Zola and Hauptmann, who progressed from critical realism to naturalism; or those models of neo-realism—the plays of Eduardo de Filippo, and de Sica's film *Bicycle Thieves.*

The state of affairs changes radically as soon as the working class attains the ruling position and has the opportunity to reveal its role in the transformation of society, no longer destructive-revolutionary, but positive and creative. So in the early years after the revolution a new, grandiose theme, that of freed labour entered Soviet art, and its importance increased rapidly with the movement of society towards socialism. As early as the twenties Gorky had grounds for asserting that "the most significant contemporary theme is labour", and ten years later, in his speech at the First Writers' Congress, he said: "As the basic hero of our books we must take labour, i.e., man organised by the processes of labour.... We must learn to see labour as a creative process."

As these new themes were being assimilated by Soviet art, new and hitherto unknown creative possibilities were also revealed in its method, for now the point was not just the recording of new technical and technological qualities of material production, but the embodiment in images of the beauty and spiritual grandeur of the free labour of the people, of labour as a "humanising" force, forming and reshaping the entire structure of man's thoughts and feelings. The old forms of realism—those used by Repin and Kasatkin, Meunier and Zola to portray the tragedy of forced labour—could not serve socialist realism, which required, as Gorky said, "new forms" to embody "the proud elation" of men's free labour.

172

The theme of labour was followed by the great variety of themes evoked by people's many-sided activities in the socialist society. The historical process of reshaping social relations affected every sphere of man's life and consciousness—his personal life, habits and customs, relationship with nature, understanding of the past and vision of the future. Socialist realism could not stand aside from all these processes. It had to try its strength in all aspects and genres of art, since it was only with their help that it could comprehend and reflect in images the entire rich system of new socio-historical links between the world and man, the collective and the individual, fathers and sons, man and woman, nature and human society, the world of things and the world of men, the present and the past, the present and the future.

The socialist realist method was gaining firmer footing in the historical and science-fiction novel, the lyric poetry, in landscape and still-life painting, the drama of everyday life and the philosophico-ethical play. The socialist ideology of art expanded to the scale of socialist humanism.

The depiction of the revolutionary development of society remains, of course, an essential political and aesthetic task, accessible only to socialist realism. But it now has the opportunity to embody the ideas of socialist humanism not only when depicting revolutionary events, class conflicts and heroism of the Civil War or the Great Patriotic War, but when studying relations between people at work, in everyday living, and in the most intimate spheres of life. Socialist humanism affirms genuinely human relations in society, between man and nature, and between man and inanimate things; and it condemns, reveals and annihilates aesthetically all that is egoistical, vulgar and banal. Such a socialist affirmation of life, knowing no bounds of genre or theme, becomes the criterion of socialist realism. A truthful recreation of life measured by the socialist ideal—this is the definition of socialist realism, broad and precise enough as applied to *all spheres* of artistic creativity, not exclusively to literature and drama.

With this is linked the third regularity of the development of socialist art in the period of transition from capitalism to socialism—the continued enrichment of its forms and styles. This process is conditioned, on the one hand, by the broadening of the thematic field of artistic cognition, since the peculiarities of the objects being portrayed compel realism to seek the new most appropriate artistic forms; and on the other hand, by the fact that as the socialist roots in real life develop and grow deeper, so, too, does human individuality grow and increasingly assert itself. Because of this, socialist art subordinates itself to the same dialectic of a single creative method and a variety of styles that we discovered in critical realism. Indeed, an analysis of Soviet art of the twenties and thirties shows its burgeoning in a rich variety of styles. Attempts to canonise one single stylistic branch and cut all the others away from the main trunk of Soviet art only succeeded in distorting for a while the objective laws of the development of socialist art. The 20th Congress of the CPSU, and the new Programme adopted by the Communist Party at its 22nd Congress assured Soviet art of a speedy return to the normal variety of styles.

Of course, this process is not proceeding equally successfully in all the arts. In sculpture and painting, for example, it is developing—for a number of reasons—with greater difficulty than in literature, the theatre or the cinema. It is, nevertheless, beyond question that variety of styles is a basic law of socialist realism.

Such are the main peculiarities that characterise socialist art in the second stage of its development. The third stage, which is conditioned by the movement of Soviet society towards communism, is only just beginning in our time. It is therefore extremely difficult to discuss it in categorical terms. Yet several processes are already well enough defined for us to make judgements concerning the future prospects of the artistic development of mankind in the communist era.

The Building of Communism and the Prospects of Art

The major achievements gained by art in the period of transition from capitalism to socialism must be consolidated and added to on the way to communism. To summarise what has already been said, we can distinguish the following basic aspects of the further development of art in a socialist society.

First of all there can be no doubt that the social significance of art and its role in people's lives will continue to grow. The talk of a crisis in artistic thinking, which, allegedly, cannot withstand competition from scientific thought and technical activities, has no serious theoretical foundation whatsoever. The antagonism between "physics and lyrics" is as imaginary and far-fetched as the antimony of "philosophy and poetry" in Hegel's aesthetics, or that of "science and art" in Pisarev's, or of "technique and artistry" in Ruskin's. Such theoretical aberrations are based either on the erroneous concept that the conflicts engendered by a certain stage in the development of bourgeois civilisation, have an absolute character, or on the false aesthetic premise—"Art and science are different forms of perception of the same object"—from which it inevitably follows that scientific progress is fatal to art. An artistic perception of the world is not a substitute for scientific-theoretical thinking, for art has its specific subject of perception and its own objectives; that is why a historical conflict between art and science is impossible. This means that scientific progress is no threat to the artistic development of mankind, and there is no need for the restoration of the mythical-religious structure of social consciousness suggested by Schelling and repeated in our own times by Ransome. Myth-based thinking really did condition the blossoming of art in the early stage of its history, but the highest stage of artistic perception of the world will rest on a sober, scientific-materialist understanding of the dialectic of truth and fiction, and on a recognition that the creation of images of reality is an important and irreplaceable means of a purposeful and all-round formation of the spiritual life of man.

Furthermore, it may be asserted that the social value of art will increase as the relations between society and individual change from those of compulsion to those of education. Withering away of political and juridical institutions—not to mention religious—and the inevitable transformation of ethical criteria into aesthetic ones (let us recall Gorky's prophetic words: "Aesthetics is the ethics of the future") will make art the chief and special instrument for shaping the spiritual life of the individual as required by social practice constantly striving towards perfection.

Such a deduction is not utopian or speculative. It rests on an analysis and a theoretical generalisation of the processes that are unfolding ever more clearly in socialist society, and give the Marxist-Leninist aesthetic theory every reason to reflect the age-old ideas concerning the antagonism between technology and art, and the apparently inevitable ousting of artistic creation by the technical. In fact a synthesis of technical and artistic activity may be widely observed nowadays in so-called designing. This indicates that, because of its functional and psychological one-sidedness, purely technical activity cannot satisfy the harmoniously developing personality, seeking self-assertion in creative activity and in the process of consumption of what society has created for it.

Thus the first prospect for the artistic development of mankind in the period of movement towards communism is a consistent growth in the social significance of art, which will continue to enrich human life more fully, creating a milieu that will affect people constantly wherever they are, at home or at work, engaged in social activity or having their leisure time. From this inevitably follows the second prospect—a balanced combination, within the aesthetic experience of each individual, of enjoyment and creation of artistic values.

Here communist culture must achieve the harmony of artistic creativity and aesthetic enjoyment peculiar to antiquity, though at a level immeasurably higher. We see more and more amateur artists appearing in the traditional spheres of creative activity; more and more people taking interest in the work of amateur photo and cinema clubs; the growing application of art principles in the work of engineers, technicians and designers; and finally, increasing attention to the artistic-creative development of the rising generations. All this is sure to bring mankind to such a level of artistic development that enjoyment of works of art created by others would no longer satisfy an individual and he would be eager to try his own artistic-creative abilities. It is this way that will provide the fullest, most consistent and most complete solution of the eternal problem of the accessibility of art to the people.

The third perspective of the artistic development of mankind concerns the content of art, its forms and styles, and the principles of its method. Here we must not guess at what will be the art of the communist era, we must try to understand the laws governing the artistic processes already at work in socialist society. Such an approach enables us to assert that art will continue to develop on the dialectical basis of unity and variety of form. The organic unity of thought, feelings, views and ideals expressed in communist art must become even deeper, for such a unity is the product of the solidarity of free workers, drawn together by common interests and aspirations. At the same time, communist art must become increasingly richer and varied in form, for each work of art will manifest the unique, free and full-blooded development of the artist, who interprets and expresses in his own individual manner what is common to the entire people, to the whole of mankind. This means that the dialectical unity of method and variety of styles, which characterises the whole history of realism, and is especially fully revealed in socialist realism, will remain the law of development of communist art.

Whether this method will retain the name of socialist realism or be called communist realism is, of course, of no importance. The important thing is that it should retain and deepen its realist nature, for communist mankind, no less than we do today, will need a true understanding of the historically concrete and constantly self-perfecting links between nature and man, and between society and individual, unclouded by illusion, self-deception and idealisation of reality. And this by no means excludes the fact that the realist method of communist art will be constantly enriched with new means, techniques and forms of representing life in images so as not to fall behind social development. Thus the dialectic of unity and multiformity will be seen to be connected with another aspect of the development of communist art—the unity of the permanent and the changing, the lasting and the self-renewing. In other words, innovation must be the constant motive force of artistic development, but this innovation will never cause realism to change its positions or lead to its replacement by any other aesthetic system, for the principle of constant self-renewal is rooted in its very nature.

All these and similar processes—within whatever modest limits they may have so far appeared, and whatever the obstacles they may have met with along the way—are natural, irresistible and logical, for each field of artistic creativity has unique perceptive possibilities and a unique poetic content, and the full and multisided spiritual life of the individual produces a demand for the widest possible aesthetic horizons. The all-round development of the personality implies its all-round artistic development, and communist culture is summoned by history to guarantee such an opportunity to all men.

Of course, this should not be taken to mean that man is deprived of any artistic predisposition and loses the right to give his preference to any one genre of art as opposed to another. Rather the opposite is the case: specific aesthetic interests will always remain a means of expressing one's individuality, since owing to his peculiar traits of character, temperament, bent of mind, age, experience, etc., one man will feel more interested in and responsive to a lyrical art form, and another to an epic; one man will be more attracted by prose, another by poetry; one will be more sensitive to words, another to colour, a third to sounds. But it is one thing to have a wide range of aesthetic interests and needs with a certain preference for some one form of art and it is quite a different thing to know and love only one type of artistic value and to know only one door into the world of art. In order to fling wide before mankind all the doors into the world of art and let each man freely develop his aesthetic preferences, the culture of communist society must guarantee equal opportunities for all fields of artistic creativity.

Such, evidently, are the basic prospects of socialist art, which have all found their reflection in the new Programme adopted by the Communist Party at its 22nd Congress. This means that foreseeing the course of artistic development has a very great practical significance and not merely an abstract-theoretical one, for we are concerned to know what processes in the contemporary artistic life of socialist society we must support in all ways in order to facilitate and expedite the development of communist culture. By giving us such knowledge, Marxist-Leninist aesthetics reveals its ability to serve as a guide to action, thereby fulfilling the task formulated by Marx—not only of explaining the world, but of remaking it.

1966

Dmitry Sarabyanov

ON THE QUESTION OF THE CREATIVE MULTIFORMITY
OF SOVIET ART

The problem of the multiformity of Soviet art is one of those controversial topics around which heated arguments have frequently broken out and continue to do so. The opponents of socialist realism have often put forward as their main argument the idea that the principles of socialist realism hinder the development of the artist's individuality and erase the differences between masters by limiting their freedom of creativity.

There is no need to go into detail about what these critics understand by freedom of creativity. To them it means complete subjective arbitrariness, a neglect of the laws that link art and life, and a total disregard of the genuine interests of society and the people.

It is not difficult to see what such freedom of creativity leads to in practice, if one recalls contemporary abstract art in its various manifestations, *tâchisme* for one. Can the representatives of this new-fangled artistic stream boast of multiformity of artistic manner, wealth and abundance of artistic means, multiplicity of themes and motifs? One cannot but agree that such art is faceless and monotonous. It shows yet again that in a society in which artistic life is governed by fashion, and the quests of the majority of artists by a desire to suit the tastes of a narrow circle of originality-seeking "connoisseurs", freedom of creativity and originality are only illusory.

The Soviet artist is quite aware of his dependence on the interests of the society in which he lives and on the people whose aesthetic needs he is to satisfy. Artistic freedom in socialist society means that each artist, depending on his personal inclinations and the peculiarities of his talent, selects the genre or branch of art, the themes and images to which his creative individuality leads him, but resolves them from the position of the only correct aesthetic ideal of communism, common to all the arts.

Representatives of bourgeois culture and modern revisionists, looking assiduously for evidence of the weakness of Soviet culture, do not wish to notice the real multiformity of our art. They would like Soviet art to be deprived of that unity that now distinguishes it. They would also like Soviet art to have such "trends" as surrealism or abstractionism. Incidentally, it is quite clear that in Soviet art there is only one trend, and this is firmly bound to the method of socialist realism for a long time to come. This trend is determined primarily by the spiritual requirements and aesthetic tastes of the people. This constant link with the life of the people stimulates its progress. This trend has the power to give back to the people the cultural riches they had for centuries been deprived of in the exploiting society, and to satisfy the interests of the people, which grow from year to year and thereby constantly pose new problems to the artist. Other trends and other methods do not find fertile soil on which to develop in Soviet society.

In this lies the force of Soviet art, which serves the interests of the people, the highest expression of which is the policy of the Party.

The question of the multiformity of Soviet art is also very topical, because until recently certain Soviet cultural figures were trying to reduce every one genre of art to the work of one group of masters and thus restrict the multiformity of Soviet culture. This tendency was particularly obvious at the end of the forties and beginning of the fifties; it was a direct or indirect consequence of the cult of personality, which made itself felt in various ideological fields. This tendency, which managed to become fairly strong, facilitated the spread of that distorted conception of socialist realism on which bourgeois and revisionist critics of Soviet art base their speculations.

The mistaken point of view that led to this one-sided interpretation of socialist realism has now been largely dispelled in Soviet study of art. A great part was played in this by the decision of the Central Committee of the

CPSU of May 28, 1958, "On the Correction of Errors in the Evaluation of the Operas *The Great Friendship, Bogdan Khmelnitsky* and *With All My Heart.*" One more evidence of the Party's correct line in ideological questions, this decision was directed against one-sided evaluations in Soviet music, but its significance goes far beyond the limits of music alone.

Until recently, other branches of Soviet art, such as the visual arts, also suffered from tendencies similar to those censured in the last CC decision. Insufficient recognition had been given to such great masters as Saryan and Konchalovsky in painting; Konenkov and Lebedeva in sculpture; Favorsky and Kravchenko in graphics. These artists, who at an early stage of their development showed formalist tendencies but later overcame them, were frequently regarded as inferior or defective. The decision of the CC CPSU of May 28 restored full justice with regard to these genuinely realist artists and the contribution they have made to Soviet art.

The problem of the multiformity of Soviet art has many varied aspects. One of them concerns variety of national styles.

A comparison of the arts of the various nationalities in the Soviet Union shows the national individuality of each of them. From its very first steps, Soviet art has developed as a multinational art, in which common aims and content combine with national traits and traditions. These traditions have determined the originality of each national stream within the various fields of culture. In some cases, for instance, in Armenian and Georgian painting and theatre, these traditions had already existed for centuries and were in an advanced stage of development. They provided a solid basis for the fruitful development of the new method. In other cases, national traditions were created anew in various fields of art after the revolution, with the help of fraternal nationalities. These new traditions reflect the radical change wrought by socialism in the national awareness of the peoples.

In a socialist society, the culture of each nation preserves its individuality. Culture is accessible to millions of people, who constitute a nation and are the bearers of its specific traits. But this does not mean that national culture is restricted within definite, narrow limits, is indifferent to the cultural achievements of other nations and not profiting from them in its own development. On the contrary, there is always an indisputable community between the cultures of socialist nations, since the content of all of these cultures is directly linked with socialist reality. As socialist relations have developed and become more firmly established, the national form has also changed, and this has led to the growing community of nations struggling together to build a new society. The community of national cultures has never contradicted the individuality of each of them. This dialectic unity of the common and the individual is an important characteristic of the development of national cultures under socialism.

The national multiformity of Soviet culture is the result of the nationalities policy of the Communist Party, the result of respect for the culture of each nation and for the individuality of each people.

This article is not intended as a detailed analysis of the national multiformity of Soviet art. This problem deserves a special study. We shall be discussing the multiformity that springs not from differences of national tradition, but from the individual inclinations of the artists, the varied needs of the people, the variety of life itself, and the various traditions within one national culture. Moreover, we shall not be touching on the very important theoretical question of the various streams and styles within Soviet art, though this question has a direct bearing on the problem of artistic multiformity. The problem is also interesting in its own right, the more so as the question of style in Soviet art is not yet sufficiently studied.

Soviet art certainly did not arrive at once at an organic combination of common aims and individual manifestation of these common tendencies in the work of different masters. At various periods of its history, the multiformity of Soviet art has borne a specific character.

Alongside art that was not basically different from pre-revolutionary art, and the bourgeois-anarchist tendencies typical of the early twentieth century art, the first years of the revolution saw the appearance of certain works that already held the germ of the Soviet art of the future.

This general trend of Soviet art, whose typical features are new ideological meaning and devotion to the people, has incorporated all that was best in the various schools and groups that existed in the period when Soviet art was finding its feet.

An analysis of the achievements of Soviet artistic culture in the thirties through fifties, i.e., in the period when the principles of socialist realism took shape in theory and found their reflection in practice, demonstrates that the unity of Soviet art is based not on community of formal or stylistic traits, but on community of method and principles.

Different artists follow different traditions. For instance, Boris Ioganson proceeds from the heritage left by the *peredvizhniki*[1] and, in the main, by Repin. Arkady Plastov shows preference for the traditions of some early twentieth century Russian masters. The composer Sergei Prokofiev undoubtedly learned from the outstanding German musicians of the eighteenth century, and Aram Khachaturyan aspires in many ways to continue the tradition of Chaikovsky and Rakhmaninov, Russian classics of the symphony and piano music. Of course, for each of these masters the heritage is only a sort of springboard for the solution of modern problems. But it sometimes determines the style, manner and totality of techniques used by a given master.

Soviet painters, composers, architects and theatre and film actors have their own individual destinies and sources of inspiration. Each favours definite traditions and has gone through some one artistic school, and his choice in this matter is determined by the specificity of his talent and by his inclination towards certain genres, themes or motifs.

Soviet art of the past quarter-century presents an extremely varied picture with regard to genre, tradition and manner.

Alongside those masters of the stage who follow Stanislavsky's system, we might name such producers as Nikolai Okhlopkov and Valentin Pluchek whose quests for novelty are fed by quite other sources. The greatest Soviet masters of the symphony, opera and chamber music, such as Prokofiev, Shostakovich, Myaskovsky, Khachaturyan and Kabalevsky are so individual that they cannot be united under a single style. In painting, in addition to Ioganson and Plastov, whom we have already mentioned, we might name Nesterov, S. Gerasimov, Saryan, Konchalovsky, Grabar, Deineka, Nissky, Yablonskaya and Chuikov—which is sufficiently full a representation of the multiformity of artistic styles of Soviet

---

[1] *Peredvizhniki*, sometimes known in English as "Wanderers"—*Tr.*

painters. Among sculptors we might name Mukhina, Konenkov, Lebedeva, Tomsky, Nikogosyan, Anikushin and Kibalnikov; and among graphic artists—Favorsky, Shmarinov, Kibrik, G. Vereisky, the Kukryniksy, Prorokov and Soifertis. The work of any one of these artists proves that every branch of art can boast of a lot of bright individualities following varied traditions and having their own inclinations and manners.

What are the roots of this multiformity?

First of all we must remember that in earlier times, too, in the period of blossoming of world art, its multiformity reflected the variety of life itself. When art was confronted with great social problems it never confined itself to only one side of life but was able to look into the soul of the time. The Italian Renaissance, though united by a definitely expressed common style, knew the lofty sovereignty of Raphael and the wise simplicity of Leonardo, the titanic force of Michelangelo and the passion of Titian. All these great masters differed not simply by their inclinations and talents, but in that they expressed different aspects of a multifaceted life.

In a socialist society this multiform objective reality is the major object of artistic perception. Soviet artists like all realist artists, do not see the aim of creativity as self-expression, but as the embodiment of certain aspects of reality and penetration into its very essence. This does not exclude and even presupposes the artist's individual approach to the object of his study. But the basis of the artist's creativity, if his method is socialist realism, lies in reality itself. This reality has many sides and facets. The essential in it, that which must be the object of aesthetic interpretation, seems to be found in various spheres of life. It may be revealed only by artists working in various genres, devoted to different themes, and seeking their interests in varied spheres of contemporary or past history.

Another important feature which accounts for the variety of artistic individualities is the variety of needs in socialist society which is quite different from that in capitalist society. Since in socialist society there are no antagonistic classes, the aesthetic interests of the members of that society do not clash. Soviet people have a common interest in an art that is humane, noble, realistic, educative and inspiring. It would be wrong to think that artistic interests in a socialist society have class distinctions, and that, say, collective farmers are interested in one kind of art and the working class in quite another. The variety of aesthetic interests is determined first of all by the all-round development of man under socialism, the development of his spiritual world and his individual tastes.

This characteristic of the life of socialist society not merely dictates the variety of demands, but also prompts many and varied roads for artists to follow in their quests. The socialist revolution created the necessary conditions for the spiritual growth of man. Though not smooth or devoid of contradictions and difficulties, this process has led to the blooming of various talents and has conditioned the successes of Soviet art during the many years of its existence.

Taking examples from Soviet painting, we shall try to show that the multiformity of Soviet art is not only an actual fact, which cannot be ignored in solving the theoretical problems of art of socialist realism, but also an essential precondition of its development.

To return to our examples: certain of Ioganson's pictures, painted in the thirties, such as *The Interrogation of the Communists* and *In an Old Urals Factory,* have become, as it were, Soviet classics. In these pictures a great deal is inherited from the *peredvizhniki* and, above all, from Repin. We may call to mind Repin's *Refusal to Confess* or *Arrest of a Propagandist*—pictures based on contrasts, dramatic collisions of the characters, in which a conflict is depicted by the direct confrontation of two opposing forces. Repin's true, active realism serves Ioganson as a point of departure. But he does not simply revive Repin's tradition; he develops it. This naturally does not mean that Ioganson is superior to Repin in techniques, depth of penetration, or force of presentation. Progress in art does not always mean that works in any one period are greater in artistic qualities than works of preceding periods. The progress is achieved by further revealing new sides of life and finding new content, new forms and new techniques of expression in art.

Ioganson interprets historical events of the distant or not so distant past from the point of view of today. The victory of the revolution and the successes of socialism permit the artist to express in a particularly graphic way the strength of the revolutionary heroism of the people he portrays, their faith in victory and capacity to sacrifice their lives unhesitatingly. Ioganson is able to give his compositions a monumental ring because of the deep social generalisations of his images, the laconicism and simplicity of his means of expression.

These traditions of painting on historical or contemporary themes have been continued by Sergei Gerasimov in his wartime canvas, *The Mother of a Partisan*, and by many other artists, whose contribution may be less significant, but still important for the history of painting.

If the question is put, whether this line in Soviet art is merely an echo of the art of the *peredvizhniki*, or whether it has its roots in contemporary life, one can only reply as follows: this line is called to life by reality itself, but it rests on a great and old national artistic tradition. Indeed, is it not true that the heroism portrayed in *The Interrogation of the Communists*, or the images which reveal high moral qualities of the fighters, the self-sacrificing heroes, inspired with a new faith and new ideas, came about with the epoch of the revolution and the building of socialism, which demanded sacrifice and the utmost straining of forces? After all, Ioganson's pictures are not just historical illustrations but an embodiment of the ideal which the people look up to. It is this that makes his pictures partisan and national, and these are the basic qualities that characterise art of socialist realism.

It is natural that the most vivid works in Soviet historical painting are those that portray the collision of antagonistic historical forces and the triumph of progressive forces. It is no less natural that artists turn to the traditions of Repin as most vital for a solution of the problems posed by reality itself.

The works of Ioganson and certain other similar masters represent only one of the many aspects of Soviet painting. One has only to turn to the work of other artists, such as Plastov or Chuikov, to see that their art is just as vital, just as closely linked with Soviet reality and just as deeply rooted in the popular conception of beauty, although these three artists differ not only in the sources of their creativity, but in the results they produce. The individuality of each of these masters is unhindered by what unites them: the single method of socialist realism they employ, the common ultimate aims of their art, subordinated to the task of educating the people, and their devotion to Party and people. By virtue of the circumstances of life and art, and of individuality of talent, these common principles and tendencies have been realised in completely different ways.

Plastov, like Ioganson, is a master painter. But Plastov deals with contemporary subjects. He has spent his entire life in the country. All his works are dedicated to the peasants. The countryside has provided and continues to provide the material for his work. For many years the artist has been observing the people who not infrequently become the heroes of his works and acquire in them a new, transformed existence. In Plastov's pictures the popular conceptions of the beauty of life and man find vivid poetic expression.

Poetry is the basic trait of Plastov's canvases. It is the poetry of work or leisure, the poetry of the peasants' everyday life for which this talented master has such acute feeling.

Looking at Plastov's pictures one has the impression that the artist has become one with the rural milieu that is the object of his art. When Plastov depicts a jolly peasant festival—the harvest festival or a crowded fair permeated with infectious gaiety, or scenes from everyday life—his canvas is alive with people like himself, people who know the worth of labour, who have acquired worldly wisdom through gladness and sorrow, happiness and want that fell to their lot.

But it is not a matter simply of a deep understanding of the peasant character and of knowledge of rural life. Plastov expresses in his works the fundamental aspects of the artistic ideal of the people. In his canvases, particularly those depicting peasant festivals, there are bold colour combinations and his stroke is as confident and inaffected as the people he paints. Love of life and optimism distinguish Plastov's works.

Two of Plastov's post-war pictures, *The Threshing Time* and *The Tractor Drivers Supper*, are particularly good examples of this. Plastov's men are absorbed in what they are doing; they can hardly spare a moment to eat their evening meal or have a drink of cold water. Their work awaits them. They find pleasure in it; its all-consuming rhythm seizes them and enables them to feel their strength.

In such of Plastov's paintings the real hero is free and creative work. This is the new element brought to Soviet art by reality itself, and introduced by Plastov into the peasant genre. This is what makes him different from the masters of the late nineteenth and the early twentieth centuries from whom he learnt. Plastov has been able to preserve their lyricism, and at the same time he has elevated his pictures, depicting the most simple and everyday aspects of peasant life, to the level of broad generalisation, revealing through the particular what is general and important in the life of Soviet people.

Plastov's manner is quite his own, and it distinguishes him not only from the old masters of the peasant theme, but also from his contemporaries. He does not attempt to embrace all aspects of peasant life. He has his favourite themes. Plastov's own life has given him a deep understanding of the peasant labour and a true feeling for nature and understanding of its relationship with man so close to it. Plastov has a special talent for conveying the picturesque brilliance and wealth of folk customs, costumes and characters, the beauty of the land, the richness and fullness of life. All this determines his special place in Soviet painting.

Similar in many ways to Plastov is another outstanding Soviet painter, Semyon Chuikov. Like Plastov, Chuikov has favourite themes and images and has a clearly expressed poetic bent. His art is linked with Kirghizia.

Chuikov is somewhat more contemplative than Plastov. There is more lyricism in him, bright and sunny. He reveals beauty in his characters' every movement and gesture, full of natural grace and proud dignity. The people in Chuikov's pictures are busy with everyday things—carrying hay, resting by the haystacks, returning home from work, or bathing their children in cool mountain streams. There is nothing out of the ordinary in any of these activities, but through them the observer gains a deeper feeling for the beauty of everyday life.

Plastov and Chuikov go their own ways in revealing the beautiful in life. It results from their different individualities and from a difference in their approach to the tasks they set themselves. Plastov's characters are not only the vehicles for expressing the beauty that the artist finds in life, but also people who perceive this beauty as he does himself. Chuikov's characters seem to be unaware of their beauty. The inner energy of Plastov's characters seems to blend with the artist's own temperament. In Chuikov's pictures, people and nature are attractive for their calm grandeur. Hence the artist's constant interest in plastic expressiveness, which he finds in the simplest and most uncontrived things. Hence those techniques of composition, which allow him to discover the plastic perfection of the human body and the harmony of man and nature. It is not in combinations of contrasting colours that Chuikov seeks the picturesque richness of the world. He favours a carefully blended combination of finely graded tints, which corresponds so well with his lofty conception of the serene and stately beauty of the world.

Like Plastov, Chuikov is one of the outstanding representatives of the new qualities in Soviet art. He extols the life of free Soviet man; he reveals the new in life and in the attitude to life that has been brought by socialism and become everyday for Soviet people; he imbues everything that his art touches upon with his own sincere joy at the beauty of the new life. Pictures such as those painted by Chuikov and Plastov can be created only by artists who passionately love the people and nature to which their works are dedicated.

Almost every major Soviet painter is himself an important facet of the whole of Soviet art. And it is no accident that in thematic painting we have not only the dramatic quality of Ioganson, the poetry of Plastov and the lyricism of Chuikov, but a keen feeling of the new rhythm of life, the leitmotif of the common mood of the times embodied in the pictures of Deineka.

Deineka is by no means unique in Soviet art. Similar, up to a point, to Deineka's creative principles are Yuri Pimenov in genre-painting, Georgi Nissky in landscape painting, and Andrei Goncharov in graphics. This is an original group of artists, many of whom belonged in the twenties to the Studio Arts Society (SAS). For them the most important problem was that of innovation in art. A feeling for the new, an acute vision of the world and an ability to see the eloquent signs of the time—all these are peculiar to the work of Deineka and the artists near to him.

The subjects of Deineka's paintings are taken from the life of the workers, from science and sport. His characters are workers and peasants, builders, sportsmen and airmen. The clothes they wear, the modern surroundings in which they are painted and other details illustrate what life is in the Land of Soviets.

In the twenties, alongside the heroes of the Civil War, Deineka introduces miners and textile workers into his pictures. In the thirties, the onward march of the young country brimming with strength and energy suggests new heroes—those who are achieving the targets of the five-year plans, sportsmen and parachute jumpers. Children dreaming of flying (*Airmen of the Future*) seem to embody the future and to personify the new generation that would enter life a few years later. During the war years Deineka paints sailors defending Sevastopol and peasants driven into captivity and storing up their wrath in order to hurl their challenge into the face of the hated invaders. After the war Deineka joins those who were restoring industry (*The Donetsk Coal Basin*) and pushing forward building throughout the land, who went on living and working (*Building Sites Near Moscow, By the Sea, The Tractor Driver*).

Deineka is abreast of the times in his work and this feeling of modernity is typical of the artist. It is implicit in his very style, in the bold composition, the somewhat simplified, austere but expressive combinations of colour, the tectonic rhythm and ability to convey movement, whether the flight of an aircraft, the legendary Nikitka's leap from the belltower, the sportswomen's sprint or the descent of a fascist air ace from his plane shot down in flames.

These stylistic peculiarities are Deineka's deeply individual traits. If one compares his works with those of the artists who at one time belonged to the same group and even later adhered to identical artistic principles, it is not difficult to find a difference between them.

For example, Pimenov, like Deineka, also tries to reveal what is new in the reality around him. He is interested in the new man, his internal and external make-up. But as distinct from Deineka, Pimenov prefers a lyrical theme. The image of the young working woman, the city girl, attracts this artist in his attempt to achieve the integrity of motion, sharpness of perception and gentleness of image. Therefore his work is typified by light, transparent shades of colour and brightness of tone, and the rhythm of his sketching is always calmer and more static than that of Deineka.

Similar comparisons could be made between the other artists from the SAS group. They would only affirm our claim that within any one group having a similar method and style, the artists greatly differ, owing to their individual, peculiar talents.

Art abhors repetition. Just as there are no two people in the world who exactly resemble each other in looks, thoughts or emotions, so there cannot be two identical artists. For the creative work of an artist embodies his mental make-up, his concept of the world and the feelings and emotions unique to him alone.

Therefore every artist leaves in the art of his time his own trace, however small it may be. This is an essential condition of genuine artistic creation, and in a socialist society this condition is not merely preserved—it is a law of development of socialist art.

The creative multiformity of art acquires the character of a law for a number of reasons. In a socialist society the artist frees himself more and more consistently and irrevocably from the tyranny of fashion; his aspirations become more and more identified with the demands of socialist society; the wide range of aesthetic requirements allows most varied and individual talents to strike a chord in the hearts of those for whom they create their works. Individual talent is liberated from the artificial obstacles that hold back its development. Socialist society, however, makes definite demands on the artist. Several of these have a direct bearing on our problem. In recent years a particularly great deal has been said about the fact that the artist must resolve his chosen theme not only by fathoming its meaning and studying all the relevant aspects of life, but also by expressing his own outlook and feelings, and finding the unique expressive means for his theme. Clarity of the artist's personal attitude to the object of his aesthetic perception is an important condition of the integrity of a work of art. This requirement, when addressed not to one definite artist but to art as a whole, becomes a demand for multiformity.

That is only one aspect of the matter. The other depends on the socialist nature of society, and is included in it. The development of socialist relations cannot take place unless the necessary conditions are created for the all-round development of man, for the broadening and deepening of his aesthetic requirements. But these latter will be satisfied only if every form of art is given full scope for its development. Therefore the blooming of varied creative individualities within the confines of a common method becomes a law.

This law governs other genres of Soviet painting, too. Let us take Soviet portrait painting, for example. Here we have a number of artists, distinguished from each other by their perception of man, the plastic manner of their painting, and the traditions they follow. We might name Mikhail Nesterov, Pavel Korin, Nikolai Ulyanov, Igor Grabar and Alexander Gerasimov. These painters have followed quite different paths. Looking at the portraits created by them, you will have no difficulty in telling one artist from another, for each has his own style, his own favourite themes and motifs.

The remarkable portraitist of the thirties and early forties, Nesterov, is closely connected with traditions of the Russian realists of the second half of the nineteenth century. This, above all, is seen in his portraits painted during the Soviet period, when the aging artist gave up his experiments in religious themes, which had so attracted him in the pre-revolutionary years, and turned to the genre of portraiture. The realistic full-blooded images, the portrayal of man in motion—externally or internally, and the "pictorial" nature of his portraits are all typical of Nesterov's paintings and are part of the old Russian tradition of painting. But Nesterov also brings in basically new features; he paints his models dynamically, catching them in the moment of some creative activity. Similar to him are Shadr, Mukhina, Pavlov and Yudin, though in the latter's portraits there is no direct portrayal of the creative process.

The Nesterov line in Soviet painting is continued at present by Korin. Nesterov is strict and restrained in his characterisation and style, Korin's manner is even a little "ascetic". But he is similar to Nesterov in his desire to reveal man's powerful, active nature and to display the iron will and inner purposiveness of Soviet man.

Another trend in portrait painting is represented by Ulyanov who continues the tradition of his teacher, Valentin Serov. He is trying to reveal the artistic side in his characters and the source of their inspiration. A whole series of beautiful, lyrical portraits, which number among the greatest works in Soviet portraiture, has been created by Igor Grabar.

The variety of manner is no less evident in landscape

painting. Nature is so rich and variegated, that each artist has an opportunity to choose his own favourite motif. Very evident in landscape painting are national peculiarities and individual vision. Martiros Saryan and Ural Tansykbayev, Nikolai Romadin and Edouard Kalnyn are masters who all hymn the praise of the natural scene in the places they come from. But the point is not just that nature itself differs in various areas or republics, such as Armenia, Russia or the Ukraine; the point is that the natural scene in the artist's native country helps to shape his concept of beauty.

However, even within one national school, landscape painting is a genre in which each artist has the opportunity to display his own understanding of nature, his own feeling for the world and his own artistic vision.

Romadin's lyrical landscapes; the fine visual poetry of Sergei Gerasimov's canvases; the romantic and heroic pictures of northern nature created by Meshkov; the boldly composed living landscapes of Nissky, depicting the crowded life of seaports, railway stations and arterial roads; the elation of Chuikov's pictures of mountain scenery; Krymov's rather contemplative canvases with their faultless chiaroscuro —this is by no means a full list of the various artistic styles in modern landscape painting.

The sources and traditions that nourish Soviet landscape painting are very varied. Some artists draw on a legacy of the *peredvizhniki*, others turn to the masters in the Union of Russian Painters; some make use of the traditions of the impressionists and interpret them in a way more relevant to the tasks of Soviet art; for some of the artists mentioned the main problem is to create new forms of landscape painting, to find new motifs and portray nature transformed by our contemporaries. But whichever of these painters you take as an example, he will have introduced into landscape painting some feature that will have become an organic element of the genre as a whole. We are in joyous harmony with the colourful glitter of nature, its movement, its eternal change and sudden impulses. At the same time, we are not alien to lyrical contemplation of nature and to extolling it in a poetic way. The feelings expressed by the landscape painters move us, disturb us, arouse our admiration and love for our native land, for the earth that gave us birth and with which our destinies are linked.

The educative and informative function of Soviet art is

fulfilled by and large in painting based on topical subjects from present or past times. A special role is naturally played by contemporary themes. The most useful form of art, from the point of view of the Soviet people, is that which impinges directly on life and is devoted to the most vital and burning issues of the day. However, this must not lead to the denial of other genres which have every right to exist and develop successfully.

It would be basically wrong to underrate the role of landscape and still life simply because in these genres the painter is not relating something about man or about some important event. For a landscape or a still life, which depict the objects surrounding man, serves the artist as a means for revealing his inner world, his outlook on the external world and his attitude to that which surrounds him. This attitude can be read in the composition, the combination of colours, in the choice of motif from nature or of a group of objects, and in many other details.

Many of the outstanding Soviet painters, who belong largely to the older generation of artists, have devoted themselves to still life, landscape or portraiture and rarely turned to historical or genre painting. They include Konchalovsky, Mashkov, Lentulov, Saryan and Kuznetsov.

When one examines the still life paintings created by these quite different masters, one realises that a certain feature is common to all of them. They are all able to express, in a still life, their own philosophies and views on the world. Mashkov and Konchalovsky reflect the picturesque strength and firmness of the objects. Mashkov's still life seems more generalised, sometimes symbolic; Konchalovsky's is more concrete and personal. But both affirm life, its joy and beauty. The observer cannot but share the feelings of the artist, he experiences an aesthetic pleasure at perceiving the beauty of things around him and the harmony of the world expressed in concrete objects.

Whatever Saryan touches with his brush—a still life of flowers and fruit or a landscape, usually with mountain peaks in the distance, or a portrait—the artist always succeeds in conveying the freshness of nature, and the happiness of never aging youth.

As we have seen, the masters of the older generation belonging to one genre set themselves quite different objectives. But these masters are united by more than their genre;

they express ideas and sentiments kindred to Soviet man and create works that give man aesthetic pleasure.

We have been dealing primarily with artists of the older or middle generations. If we turn to our youth, which is beginning more and more to determine the modern tendencies in art, we shall easily see the same variety of quests, theme, image and manner.

Some of them, such as Korzhev, for example, prefer the narrative form, developing successfully the artistic traditions of the *peredvizhniki*. Others, like Stozharov or Tutunov, aim to express the poetry of the Russian countryside and its landscape, finding inimitable beauty in the northern night or in peasant houses, with windows gleaming in the rays of the sunset; or in a colour-rich collective-farm market; or in Russian architectural monuments of the seventeenth century. Such canvases bring to life the traditions of the Union of Russian Painters. Still another group of painters are searching for laconic means of expression, bold rhythm and poignancy in portraying nature. They are attracted by themes from industry and sport. This group includes, among others, Nikich, Salakhov, Ossovsky, Andronov and Nikonov.

The list does not end here, but the above-mentioned names are sufficient to reveal the variety of aims and individual manner among young Soviet painters. And though in the works of the younger painters in particular one feels an increasing tendency to adhere to one style of painting, it is obvious that such adherence cannot be an obstacle to the development of artistic individuality.

We have taken examples from painting in order to substantiate the guiding thesis of this article. There is still much to be said on the problem of multiformity in Soviet art. We have limited ourselves to posing a number of questions, emphasising one point, maybe not new but vital for the defence of the principles of socialist realism: the multiformity of Soviet art is an actual fact, which is not open to doubt and which must be taken into account in an analysis of the problems of art of socialist realism. This multiformity relies on one method—socialist realism.

1960

Semyon Freilikh

SOCIALIST REALISM IN THE ART OF CINEMA

Fragments from the book
Films and Years

In order to put one's finger on the pulse of socialist realism one must renounce the dogmatic conception of it as a completed phenomenon, compounded once and forever and existing in an immutable form. This is precisely the view that feeds the ideas of bourgeois art critics, convinced that socialist realism is something that exists outside the practice of art, independently of it, is grafted on to the practice and dictated by orders and decrees.

In any case, socialist realism arose long before it was ever formulated. It was not born in theoreticians' articles but in the paintings, sculptures, poetry, prose-works and films of the new, revolutionary art. The new method arose as a demand of the times and went through a number of stages of development before its basic principles and leading features became clear. Therefore we cannot make judgements as to whether or not a work created at an earlier period belongs to socialist realism as it is understood today. If we ignore the significance of a work for its own period, we cannot define its role in the present either; and this means we cannot define its role in the history of art as a whole.

Even with regard to the place of *Battleship "Potemkin"* (1925) in the history of cinema of socialist realism, there are certain opinions with which we beg to differ.

In his *Essay on the History of Cinema in the USSR,* the first fundamental research of its type, Professor N. Lebedev unexpectedly concludes his chapter on *Battleship "Potem-*

kin", which gives a basically correct definition of the style of the film, with the following:

"This was not yet the style of socialist realism. It lacked, firstly, depth of socialist consciousness, which even our most progressive masters of cinema had not yet been mature enough to attain; and secondly, a general popular character, and comprehensibility of content and form that would be understandable and absorbing for both a culturally advanced audience and the many millions of the ordinary cinema-goers.

"The style of *Battleship 'Potemkin'* was on the way to socialist realism but had not yet reached it. Before it could scale the heights of this style, Soviet cinema art had still to travel a long and complicated path."[1]

Leaving aside the question of the accessibility of *Battleship* to the many millions of ordinary spectators (its success both in the USSR and in other countries easily controverts this idea), we shall consider the assertion that "This was not yet the style of socialist realism". Is this actually the case? After all, if the style was not to be found in *Battleship*, then where, one might ask, was it to be found? Perhaps the method of socialist realism was indeed formulated first by Gorky and Zhdanov and then began to be grafted on to art? But this is not true, and the historian of the cinema did not, of course, think that it was. His incorrect conclusions result from the fact that in assessing the film he used today's understanding of socialist realism, and was influenced by the achievements of cinema in the period of sound films.

The peak of socialist realism is not beyond art. Each stage has its own peaks. The idea that *Battleship* was only on the way to socialist realism is basically wrong, because it was *Battleship* that blazed the trail. For its time it was itself a peak reached by virtue of its historical truth and the producer's mastery and political awareness. Another thing that was wrong to say is that even the "most progressive masters of cinema had not yet been mature enough". Mature enough for what, we might ask? For seeing the heights that we ourselves have espied only in the modern period? But could they have seen them? Would it not be more correct to put the question in a different way and to

---

[1] N. A. Lebedev, *Essay on the History of Cinema in the USSR*, Moscow, Gospolitizdat, 1947, p. 139, Russ. ed.

study to what degree they had in fact "matured" if they were able to show the revolution in such a way that not only has the Russian proletariat taken this picture into its armoury (i.e., apperceived its revolution and itself from the picture), but so has the proletariat of other countries. (There is abundant evidence of the revolutionary effect this film produced in other countries, and this is also supported by the pronouncements of progressive figures in world culture concerning the artistic standard of the work.)

Lebedev's judgements, which we are now questioning, arose to a large extent from an imprecise analysis of the picture. He wrote that in *Battleship* there are no "individual heroes" and that this turned the people into "a faceless mass". This displays a weak study of the method and the creative tasks of the maker of the film, Sergei Eisenstein, who was able through generalised portraits to grasp the character of the people, who are far from being faceless in the film, or else we would not have been disturbed about their fate.

We might not have referred to the assessment of *Battleship* given in this indisputably valuable essay, which has already become a bibliographic rarity, if it were not for the fact that this assessment has now become traditional. How many times have we since heard the reproach that the film is "devoid of bright, human characters".

One should judge a film not by what it lacks but by what it possesses. We should then find that in *Battleship* there is the first portrayal of a new psychological type, born of the revolution, and because of this the film began a new line in cinema art. The next step in the same direction was made by Vsevolod Pudovkin in the film *Mother* (1926). Both these films were peaks of achievement in the cinema art of the twenties.

Thus the concept that there is a standard of "hundred per cent" socialist realism, and attempts to measure various artistic works against this standard lead us into error. An outstanding work, as we have seen in this case, does not fit in with this sort of socialist realism, though it is from this film that socialist realism begins in the cinema.

But it is incorrect, on the other hand, to see in a work precisely this "hundred per cent" expression of socialist realism.

As we shall presently try to show, the film *Chapayev*

(1934) opens up new horizons to socialist realism. But it would be a mistake to think that *Chapayev* exhausted all the possibilities of the method. If this were true, art would have had no stimulus to develop. But this is not the case. In his portrayal of the Civil War in *Shchors* (1939), Alexander Dovzhenko followed his own path and opened up possibilities that were hidden in the romantic side of socialist art. *Chapayev* taught new ways of typifying reality. But its techniques should not be regarded as the one and only model to follow. When the Vasilyevs[1] were piecing together their film, they were right in cutting the scene in which the still raw Furmanov flees the battlefield at Slomikhinskaya. The producers were telling the story of Chapayev who gradually changed under Furmanov's influence, and not the story of Furmanov himself. But we should be wrong to elevate this concrete example of choice of material and typification into an obligatory law of cinema art. It would be wrong to think that since the cinema has a special power of concentration and demonstrativeness, the positive hero cannot behave in certain ways. This judgement, when translated into practical work, produces most grievous results, since by smoothing away any contradiction within the hero we rob him of individuality and life.

The principles of socialist realism are revealed in such films as *Battleship "Potemkin"* and *Chapayev*, and these in turn prepare the ground for the discovery of new ways of portraying life. The method of socialist realism, which has at its basis a revolutionary outlook, bold in its attitude to reality, cannot become the slave of its own achievements. Ever developing reality demands from Soviet art a constant enrichment of its method.

The prerequisites for the appearance of socialist realism are, in all cases, the achievement of a high level of realism by art and the artist's socialist awareness. However, historically concrete analysis shows that when these conditions are present, socialist realism manifests itself in different ways in the work of individual artists, in a given branch of art, or in the literature and art of a given country.

In Russia the first green shoots of art of socialist realism were already apparent in capitalist society, as witnessed in the literary works of Maxim Gorky and in several of the

---

[1] Sergei and Georgi Vasilyev.—*Tr.*

paintings of Abram Arkhipov and Sergei Ivanov. But it would be difficult to generalise from these examples, and look for elements of socialist realism in the pre-revolutionary Russian cinema, even in the most progressive pictures. There were no such elements in the cinema, nor could there be, although the first two Russian revolutions had already presented art with new problems. These problems could not be treated by the cinema, because it was in the hands of bourgeois entrepreneurs. Only when it was taken over by the proletariat could the cinema deal with these problems, and how efficiently! It took the cinema some seven or eight years to score its first victories—*Battleship "Potemkin"* and *Mother*.

The openly tendentious nature of these films was the source of their historical concreteness and artistic perfection. Sergei Eisenstein and Vsevolod Pudovkin put their trust in history, and it raised them to the crest of its wave.

2

But it is precisely for its tendentious side that Soviet cinema is frequently criticised, the pet "argument" being that partisanship restricts the artist's horizon and prevents him from being objective and historically concrete.

Of course, tendentiousness may be of various sorts. If it reflects the requirements of the objective developments of human society, then it makes the artist free. It is such tendentiousness (this must not be confused with time-serving which some people very often choose to make up for the lack of revolutionary fervour and talent, and compromise thereby the ideas of socialist realism) and such partisanship that enable the artist to stand firmly on position of historicism, to study the contradictory process of development and to see the essence of these contradictions. The latter moment is especially vital for the proletariat, since it will obtain freedom only in boldly overcoming these contradictions. Such partisanship helps to reveal the truth, which in art is the basis of artistry, and in the study of art is the basis of science and historicism.

First, let us turn to creative practice.

We have been talking of the artistic perfection of *Battleship "Potemkin"*. But this was possible only because the film brilliantly expressed the tendency of the new life. Moreover, art does not illustrate a tendency or an idea; it is a form in which they exist. And since this idea is *truth,* we watch the film as we would watch objective reality, and the film grips us.

Lion Feuchtwanger, in his novel *Success,* devotes a whole chapter to *Battleship "Potemkin"* (which in the novel is called *Battleship "Orlov"*). He vividly describes the film's effect on a former Bavarian Minister of Justice, Klenk, a man to whom its ideas are absolutely alien.

Let us recall the beginning of the chapter:

"While the other Berlin cinemas were either closed at that hour or playing to insignificantly small audiences, here the entrance was blocked by innumerable cars. Police. Onlookers. The film *Battleship "Orlov"* had already been shown thirty-six times, with four houses per day. Thirty-six thousand Berliners had already seen it. And still the people were excited, as though they were about to see something that the whole world had been waiting for.

"Klenk, who was a head taller than those sitting around him, had no thought of succumbing to the general excitement. He had read that the film had no plot, no women and no theme. Entertainment had been replaced by tendentiousness. Since he was in Berlin he ought, of course, to see such a thing, but he would not be hooked by the cinemamongers who dealt in sensation."[1]

And so, armed with scepticism, Klenk began to watch the film, having already decided to resist it. And yet the film began to interest him in its way. He began to be worried that the officers seemed to be blind to the seriousness of the situation; the sailors were really mad at being given maggoty meat for their meals. They ought to have taken firm measures, Klenk thought, recalling that they—the Germans—had also felt the approach of the storm during the last year of the war and had been too late to act. He thought, too, that the film ought to have been banned, but he had nevertheless lost sympathy with the officers. The ringleaders of the revolt were isolated now, covered with a tarpaulin and about to be shot. The rifles were already levelled at them. The hall was as tense as the sailors on the screen

---

[1] Lion Feuchtwanger, *Success* (in Russian translation), Moscow, 1958, pp. 514, 518.

awaiting the command—"Fire!" But at the last moment one of the sailors shouted something, and the rifles did not fire. And it was not only the people on the screen that were seized with rapture; so were those in the hall. And Klenk saw that *it* was beginning, that *it* had come. It would be senseless to ban this. It existed, it breathed in the air—a new and different world.

The film captivated Klenk, and again he began to resist it. He grew angry that the forces did not appear that ought to have restored order, both here, on board the ship, and on shore among the populace who had joined the mutinous battleship. Gigantic ships appeared, with their guns levelled at the free battleship. Then the doomed ship began to signal: "Do not fire, brothers!" It slowly approached its pursuers, signalling to them: "Do not fire!" The people in front of the screen breathed heavily, and the tension was almost unbearable. "Do not fire!"—hoped and prayed and willed with all their might the eight hundred spectators in the Berlin cinema. But was Minister Klenk a gentle and peaceable man? Hardly. He would really have laughed if he had thought anyone could suppose such a thing. He was a tough, wild, bellicose man, not prone to any sort of tenderness. So what were his thoughts as the mutinous battleship sailed to meet the levelled cannon? With all the force of his heart he also entreated: "Do not fire!"

An unheard-of joy filled his heart as the circle of pursuers let the battleship through and it sailed off unharmed for a neutral port. At the end of the chapter we read:

"Making his way out of the darkness and gloom of the cinema into the lighted and broad street, Klenk experienced an unfamiliar feeling of depression. What could this be? Would he really have not ordered the rebels to be shot? How could a man like him possibly feel such a desire— "Do not fire"? So, *it* existed. One could ban it, but it would still go on existing in the world, and there was no point in closing one's eyes to this."

The message of the film, alien to Klenk's social nature, could not have produced such an effect if it were a newspaper article. For the power of art is in that it looks for the objective causes of the events it presents in real life. In *Battleship "Potemkin"* the facts of life are selected, interpreted and juxtaposed, i.e., artistically expressed, in such a way that the message becomes quite clear. This is a great message, which cannot be ignored or banned, for it is truth, truth that makes the film artistically perfect.

Goebbels, in his day, envious of the propagandising power of *Battleship "Potemkin"*, ordered his cinema workers to create a film that would have an equally strong effect on the audience. As we know, no such film did materialise, nor could it, on the anti-human basis of fascist ideas.

In this connection it would not be out of place to recall that foreign critics, astonished at the objectivity with which the opposing forces were portrayed in *Chapayev* (the whiteguard officers are shown as cultured and disciplined men, while Chapayev's volunteers are anarchic and, in certain cases, portrayed as pillagers), even asserted that such a film could be made in Hollywood. This is again an absurd idea, for *Chapayev* could only have been made by a socialist realist artist. But this is not the important thing. What is important is that another patently partisan work lays bare the truth of life, which even men of an opposing camp cannot deny. The makers of *Chapayev* do not go straight to the outcome of the struggle, they lead the spectator to it gradually, exploring the complicated and very painful process of the birth of new forces, without embellishing or blackening events or schematising reality. There is no objectivism in the film, but there is the historical objectivity of the appearance of a new world, which is necessary to mankind and cannot be banned or annihilated by any Borozdin, no matter what military training or culture he may command, for these are subservient to something that has already outlived its time. And once again, as in *Battleship "Potemkin"*, the historical truth nourishes the artistic truth, which takes hold of men.

It would be no exaggeration to say that Soviet cinema has perfected itself by becoming deeply tendentious and consistently partisan.

The propaganda films (agitfilms) of the period of the Civil War still treated the revolution and the class struggle in a schematic way, hence their artistic imperfections. As the knowledge of the processes that took place during the revolution grew better, the ground was prepared for the artistic improvement of works dealing with this theme.

This becomes especially clearly visible in a comparison of two films made from the same story, Boris Lavrenyov's

Forty-First, one made as early as 1927 by Yakov Protazanov, and the other in 1956, by Grigory Chukhrai.

Protazanov's picture is considered to have played a positive role in the history of cinema, and rightly so. It played an important part in Protazanov's own ideological evolution after he returned from emigration in 1923 and lent his weight to the new, revolutionary art. It was quite natural that the world of the revolution should have been revealed to the director only in general outline, and this determined the schematic nature of the work. This is particularly visible in the image of Lieutenant Govorukha-Otrok. He is portrayed as a "negative hero" in contradistinction to Maryutka, the "positive heroine", and the director considered it his duty to belittle him. When, after an exhausting march, the detachment hurls itself avidly on its food, Otrok secretly wipes his greasy fingers on the tunic of the Red Army man sitting next to him. The director's intention is clear, but his means of fulfilling it is, in this case, not far removed from those of the agitfilm.

The theme is tackled in a much more complicated way in Chukhrai's film. Here the conflict is not oversimplified. The makers of the film do not deprive Govorukha-Otrok of culture, bravery and sense of duty. At the same time, we are shown the weaknesses and certain limitations of Maryutka, who personifies the positive ideal. The director elevates Maryutka as action develops, he does not intend to anticipate history but tries to catch its direction. The world is not schematised in this film, but revealed in its tragic conflict. So here no attempt is made to lay excess emphasis on the tendentious; it resides in the form of art. And once more this work of art enjoys great success both at home and abroad.

We have recalled the two screen versions of *Forty-First* not in order to reproach the old master and praise the new, for if such were our unworthy aim we should, by so doing, be contravening the concrete historical approach to the assessment of artistic phenomena in the various stages of their development. Our object was to use this as a graphic example to illustrate something else—that partisanship assists in the perfection of works of art. For the young, Communist director, Chukhrai, the ideological pathos and poetic aspirations enrich each other, since they coincide. His stand enables him to see and understand the past in the retrospect and to see things in their complicated historical perspective, not embellishing one fact or blackening another, but going confidently forward without leaving the path of development of reality itself. Partisanship opens the way to freedom of creativity, for it makes it possible to be truthful in depiction of life.

Partisanship also aids the science of art to be truthful, for it helps to reveal the contradictions in the process of the development of art as related to the development of society, and thus to provide a scientific explanation of it.

The history of world cinema embraces thousands of facts of this, the youngest of the arts, which has developed tempestuously and unevenly in our complicated and contradictory twentieth century. Only a materialist understanding of the history of society and the history of art can save one from being lost in a labyrinth of facts and help him catch and reproduce the underlying complicated processes of development of world cinema.

As long as Soviet studies of cinema art were based on a mechanistic conception of "traditionalists" and "innovators", scholars of the cinema could not logically reveal the processes of the development of the cinema in relation to the development of Soviet reality. Cinema studies made a step forward by representing the history of Soviet cinema as one of the appearance and consolidation of socialist realism in cinema art. This approach was genuinely scientific, because it was partisan and historical, it suggested an examination of the ideological struggle and creative evolution in connection with the internal and international situation of the country that is building socialism.

The problem now is to proceed further, both vertically and horizontally, from the positions already occupied in the history of cinema, to deepen our understanding of a number of phenomena that are especially complicated and contradictory.

One of these phenomena is FEX ("The Factory of the Eccentric Actor")[1] about which there is still controversy, and not without reason. The works of the FEX in the earlier period were either subjected to undiscriminating criticism or, to spite the "traditionalists", were as indis-

---

[1] Founded in 1921, it included Kozintsev, Trauberg, Yutkevich and Moskvin.—*Tr.*

205

criminately acclaimed as "innovation". Both extremes hinder examination of the evolution of the FEX, i.e., an explanation of how it came about that directors who began in the twenties as formalists could, only one decade later, create the trilogy about Maxim,[1] an outstanding work of socialist realism.

Before they made their trilogy, the directors—Kozintsev and Trauberg, who had by now stopped calling themselves members of FEX—made the film *Alone* (1931), which is legitimately considered a transitional stage of their work, since here they first took up a firm realist position.

Of course, the Soviet student of cinema cannot fail to approve the realist tendencies in the work or condemn preoccupation with stylistic form, divorced from clear-cut problems of real life. But it is naturally most convenient for us to break the work of the FEX into the "formalist" period, which we reject, and the "realist" period, which we accept, beginning with *Alone*.

Does the cinema expert hold an ideological position in this? Yes, he does. At the same time, this ideological position is the same as that of the first agitfilms, where the positive and negative features of the new, revolutionary reality were shown in an oversimplified and schematised manner. We do not deny the role of agitfilms of the Civil War period. On the contrary, it is quite obvious that they served as early preparation for our achievements in the twenties. For instance, *Strike* (1934), which was still in many ways an agitfilm, was a sort of trial of strength for Eisenstein before he made *Battleship "Potemkin"*. But Soviet cinema could not remain for long on the level of the agitfilm. Soviet reality placed increasingly more complicated problems before the cinema, demanding that it show not only two worlds in opposition, but the process of birth of the new world, a complicated and contradictory process, but one that must be known if we are to exercise any influence on it.

Study of the cinema also strives to reveal the evolution of an artist, no matter how complicated and contradictory it may be. Our purpose is not only to take the side of *Alone* and the trilogy about Maxim and support this line in the work of the former members of FEX, Kozintsev and

---

[1] *The Youth of Maxim* (1935), *The Return of Maxim* (1937), *The Vyborg Side* (1939).—*Tr.*

Trauberg, but also to show the evolution of these two major film-makers.

But if we do not make the customary a priori judgements, but conduct a painstaking analysis of cinematic technique, then we find that *Alone* and the trilogy about Maxim did not appear overnight.

There is a shot in the trilogy in which Maxim begins to dig out cobblestones with a crowbar to make a barricade. This is a magnificent shot, photographed by the cameraman Moskvin. The "preparation" for this scene was not in *Alone* but in an earlier film, *The New Babylon* (1929), where there is one composition that is exactly the same. In a similar situation, when the insurgents are beginning to build a barricade, a young Communard strikes a firm blow with his crowbar and digs a cobblestone out of the road. Here we have not only the same artistic aims, but the same ideological aims, laying bare the strength of the fighter, for whom even the cobblestone is a weapon in the fight for a new world.

This link exists not only in the similarity of individual shots; it is more basic than this. Let us recall the image of Louisa, created by Yelena Kuzmina. The actress subtly portrayed Louisa's gradual transformation in the course of the insurrection. At first her heroine is downtrodden, depressed and deprived of any "self". When Louisa eats a sandwich, her modest breakfast, she shields herself with the palm of her other hand. The girl feels herself to be an outlaw in capitalist society, where the right to life belongs to the owner of the "New Babylon" shop and his like. The revolution drew the girl into its mainstream. Louisa goes to her death staunch, irreconcilable, aware of her kinship with her class and transformed from a downtrodden creature into a human being.

Of course, this film, in which the task of stylisation of material often becomes an end in itself, did not as a whole reveal the historical significance of the Communards' struggle. But the image of Louisa is an artistic achievement, in which the theme is triumphant. In many ways this image is a forerunner of that of Maxim, the working lad in whom the revolution aroused the fighter and whom it placed in the vanguard of the people.

We must overcome the inertia that prevents a detailed and fresh look at the stuff of a work of art, which frequently describes the artist's evolution more objectively than even the artist thinks.

This reproach for inertia, the author of this article directs at himself, too, since in his monograph *The Art of the Film Director*—his first study of cinema, dedicated to the work of Sergei Gerasimov—there is also a mechanical division of the work of the FEX (from which Gerasimov came) into "pre-realist" and "realist" periods, though it was not noticed that the style of Gerasimov's *Masquerade* (1941) was in many ways prepared by *SVD*. In *SVD* the Decembrist revolt of 1825 in Russia was even more poorly presented than the Paris Commune in *The New Babylon*. But the stylistic searchings in *SVD*, connected with recourse to the traditions of romantic painting, were obviously not in vain, apart from the attempt at a screen portrayal of important historical events.

Thus it is naive to think that socialist realism suddenly arose one day in the works of Kozintsev and Trauberg. This process, which requires close study, was perhaps unusually contradictory in this instance. But its final victory was consequently all the more significant. This is not just an artistic victory, but an ideological one that is even more important, since the questing and vacillations in the realm of form were also ideological vacillations, searches for their own identity. The members of FEX approached Maxim via a mastery of realism, and this means a mastery of contemporary life. Their evolution reflected the struggle for socialism and the struggle in art for a new type of artist.

Both mechanical juxtaposition of two periods of the FEX, and neglect of the differences of principle between them result equally in a failure to reveal the process of establishment of socialist realism in the work of the two outstanding artists.

Either approach creates an unhealthy atmosphere in cinema criticism. The artist under criticism frequently finds a lot of defenders simply because he had been picked to pieces by way of "criticism", sometimes with the threat of "official conclusions" hanging over him. But a discussion in which one side tars an artist and the other whitewashes him cannot be very fruitful. In both cases the criticism departs from scientific objectivity. Science is interested only in an atmosphere in which aesthetic criticism is of use to the artist, for it helps him to understand art. Devotion to Party principles enables the critics and cinema scholars to take the right stand. Unsurpassable examples of this are Lenin's articles about Tolstoi; for the first time we have such a precise analysis of Tolstoi's weaknesses and their historical roots, and a revelation of the greatness of the writer whom Lenin called "the mirror of the Russian revolution".

Inertia in assessment of artistic phenomena sometimes prevents a true understanding of the period of the artist's work when he has not yet set out on the path of socialist realism (as was the case with FEX); on the other hand, by anticipating the artist's victory on that path, we sometimes think that his further progress can be taken for granted....

1957

* * *

Socialist realism did not appear out of nowhere "ready-made". Even its links with contemporary world cinema are complicated and shifting. It continues to enrich itself by the experience of other progressive trends in the cinema, and it also exerts an effect on them.

In one way or another, it is the fate of man threatened by nuclear war that is the major theme of contemporary cinema. The world as a combination of contradictions has become the basic subject of art.

Andrei Tarkovsky's *Childhood of Ivan* and Alain Resnais' *Hiroshima, mon amour* (1959) are shot through with the same alarm, and they discuss the fate of their heroes in the same language. In each of them an audio-visual system has become the basis of imagery. In *Hiroshima* the counterpoint of shapes and sounds creates a unity of the small and personal with the great and social. In the *Childhood of Ivan* the same effect is created by the real world of cruel war and the little boy's dreams of a childhood he never knew.

However, though we draw attention to these similarities, we cannot speak of a unified, universal style. Artistic means of expression and the language of art do not yet comprise a style. It is the style itself that affects the means of expression and even the technology of art.

Rich food for thought on this subject is provided by the work of the outstanding Italian director, Federico Fellini. In his film *La Dolce Vita* (1959), the plot is not held together by one dramatic line, and the portrayal of character is not subservient to the plot, i.e., it is not the means of creating the action—it is the action. To understand this film and its point one must sense its cinematic imagery and the variety of its subject. Essentially it is just one person, the journalist Marcello, who links the film from beginning to end. The film consists of a number of episodes, each of which is detailed and elaborate with its own local conflict and closed system of images. Though not linked by external means, these episodes have their own internal regularity and a united, internal dramatic action. The point of each episode emerges before it actually begins to develop, and it is solved long after the action has been completely exhausted. For instance, the episode concerning Steiner's suicide would be totally incomprehensible and senseless if it were seen only within the context of the development of the plot. A lover of philosophy and music, and a happy family man, as we have just seen him, suddenly puts a violent end to his own life and that of his children. We should not have understood the reason for this cruel act if we had not already seen the decadent world surrounding Steiner's household, though he has not himself been shown to us in that world. In the drama of this episode the preceding scenes "participate" in which Steiner's guests listen to tape recordings of the fantastic voices of nature, separated from real life and therefore having a mystic effect on us; or the following, final scene, when on the morning after a senseless orgy Steiner and his guests go down to the sea, which hurls on to the shore a frightful one-eyed monster that creates a feeling that human life on earth has returned to its primitive stage. We then comprehend the Steiner episode not in "isolation", but as a culminating point in the depiction of the world's decay. By his cruel action Steiner prevents his children from entering this world of suffering and himself quits it without waiting for the inevitable dénouement.

Fellini's plot is polyphonic.

Polyphony of action on the screen is not an achievement of our day alone. Eisenstein aspired to it and already revealed the world of cinematic imagery in *Battleship "Potemkin"*. At that time he wrote:

"A completed film is an incomparable combination of the most varied means of expression and effects.

"The historical conception of the theme, the scenic situation and general dramatic development, the life of the image portrayed and the performance of the real actor, the rhythm of the montage and the plasticity of the composition; music, sounds and loud noises; the *mise en scène* and the mutual play of different textures; the combination of light and shadow, etc.

"In a successful work all these are merged into one.

"And everything is governed by one law. The apparent chaos of different incompatible planes and dimensions is combined into one logical whole."[1]

It might seem that these words characterise the unity of the widely differing *Battleship* and *Dolce Vita*. But such a superficial judgement would only give rise to a rash conclusion concerning the unity of contemporary style—a conclusion resulting from analysis only of form, and not its links with content and the method of investigation of that content.

Polyphony may be subject to various laws.

The law of Fellini's polyphony is in accord with the meaning of the reality being described and its philosophy.

What is this meaning? Lev Tolstoi wrote:

"According to the Bible, the condition of the first man before his fall was one of an absence of labour, idleness. Love of idleness remains in fallen man, too, but the curse still weighs down on him, not simply because he has to earn his daily bread by the sweat of his brow, but because his moral make-up does not allow him to be at ease in idleness. A secret voice prompts us to feel guilty if we are idle. If man could achieve the condition in which he could be idle and yet feel himself to be useful and fulfilling his duty, he would have achieved one aspect of primitive bliss. Yet an entire social class constantly takes advantage of such a state of obligatory and irreproachable idleness...."[2]

Fellini portrayed the finale of the life of this class, guilty because of its idleness, unacquainted with labour, taking all but giving nothing and hence becoming impoverished. The poverty of Fellini's heroes is their spiritual emptiness. Complete sensibility to the world around them, relationship with it, the joy of the discovery of harmonious love, which

---

[1] *Mosfilm*, a collection, Part 1, Moscow, Iskusstvo Publishers, 1959, p. 207 (Russ. ed.).

[2] Lev Tolstoi, *Collected Works in 14 Volumes*, Vol. 3, Moscow, Goslitizdat, p. 93 (Russ. ed.).

was once felt by mankind on breaking away from feudalism and the Church—all this is now a thing of the past. In place of sensibility has come sensuality; man has returned to his primitive state, since he has become the slave of the bodily emotions which now rule him. With cruel veracity and courage Fellini showed the "dehumanisation" of his characters.

Fellini has shown the end of bourgeois civilisation.

Eisenstein showed the beginning of the new, socialist civilisation.

A desire to show the universality of these processes engendered the complicated composition of the works of each of them.

The basic difference between them is that in one case the drama is applied to a depiction of universal decadence—the rift between man and nature, and between man and man—and in the other case the whole apparatus of drama is a means of analysing the origin of human solidarity.

Of course, one film does not exhaust an artist's method. In the film $8^{1}/_{2}$[1] we can recognise the maker of *Dolce Vita* in every scene, but in the new work the artist has opened up new horizons, even though he has returned to a portrayal of the same circle of people. The difference is that as distinct from the journalist Marcello, who surrendered to the languors of the irresolution and indolence of the élite and perished in their midst, the artist Guido Anselmi tries to break out of this circle and to protest against the loss of freedom of the personality in art, love and faith. The idea of the film $8^{1}/_{2}$ is based on the experience and torment of the artist and all contemporary Italian society.

But let us return to *Dolce Vita*. Its artistic peculiarities are determined, in the final analysis, not by the material that the artist portrays, but by his attitude to that material.

This attitude is easily seen in the finale, which we have already mentioned and which is described in the scenario in the following way:

"Marcello cannot stop staring at the monster's eye. It might be supposed that in this eye he sees some sort of symbol. The meaning of his stare can only be guessed. This is some secret message, received at the end of yet another

[1] *Otto e mezzo* (1963).

212

empty, wasted night or, perhaps, at the end of the world...."[1]

The fate of one class is portrayed by Fellini as the fate of mankind. This fact determines the extreme tragedy of the film, but at the same time limits its horizon, since an event is not seen from aside as an incident in a general, historical progression.

From such a point of departure Fellini could not, despite his talent, rise to the scale of contemporary realism in *La Dolce Vita*.

We repeat, the thing is not that the main characters' outlook on the world is immaterial, and that he believes that the world has come to an end (it is, incidentally, perfectly logical, that Marcello begins by spying on the world of the aristocracy, then shares its way of life, and lastly absorbs its philosophy). The point is that Fellini's own outlook in the film is no broader than that of any of his characters.

In *Forty-First,* which we have already discussed, Lieutenant Govorukha-Otrok hears Maryutka's shot as the "crack of doom". Govorukha's death is shown as a tragedy, but it is also seen through the eyes of Maryutka, so that the event is framed, as it were, in an immeasurably wider historical context. Nevertheless, Lavrenyov and then Chukhrai did not restrict their own viewpoints to Maryutka's. She is herself shown in her historical contradictoriness and concreteness. She is herself a tragic heroine. The artist carries us through catharsis to the source of the truth of the historical process.

Contemporary realist cinema art forms the drama of inner dynamics and power. This is witnessed by the quests of another branch of contemporary Italian cinema, neo-realism.

The neo-realists have broken down the barrier between art and life and let the people on to the screen. Progressive Italian artists have not only shown the people but have looked at life through the eyes of the working people, indignant at their poverty. The common sense of simple people has become the basis of realism for progressive Italian cinematographers. Bourgeois reality has displayed bitter opposition to neo-realism, restricting its energy, confin-

---

[1] F. Fellini, E. Flaiano, T. Pichelli, *La Dolce Vita*, extracts from the scenario, translated from Italian, published in the magazine *Iskusstvo kino* (Cinema Art), 1961, No. 7, p. 146.

ing its scope and splintering its forces. Its scope has often been so narrow that the artist has sometimes had to step outside it. Roberto Rosselini, for instance, who made *Rome, Open City*[1] and *Paisa* (1946), which brought great success to neo-realism, suddenly produced theological films, notably *Francesco, Minstrel of God*.[2] And Pietro Germi, after a film so packed with social content as *The Engine Driver*,[3] made a film purely for entertainment—*The Straw Man*[4]—dealing chiefly with an eternal triangle, which always comes in handy when an artist has little real-life material at his disposal.

Criticism of the limitations of neo-realism must first be directed at the reality, which is inauspicious for art, and restricts its energy.

But there is more to this. Even the ideologists of neo-realism do not simply blame reality. They introduce basic corrections, both in their aesthetic programme and in their understanding of art of the people, for the people and by the people.

An artist who sympathises with the people begins to look at men and things through the eyes of the people and to evaluate the world through its eyes, too.

However, the people itself changes throughout history, as does its understanding of its own essence and role.

The greatest Italian director, Visconti, made his film about Sicilian fishermen, *The Earth Trembles*,[5] under the direct influence of the realist writer Varga, and especially of his novel *The Malavoglia Family*.[6] The pictures of popular life are tragic in both novel and film. However, a study of the material of life itself compelled Visconti to emphasise protest, reduce the stress on sympathy with insurmountable suffering and tone down the fatalistic nuances.

When Visconti considers the reasons for the enslavement of the peasants and ways of reviving backward Sicily, he goes even further away from Varga.

This is what he writes in connection with the film *Rocco*

---

[1] *Roma, città aperta* (1945).
[2] *Francesco, giullare di Dio* (1949).
[3] *Il ferroviere* (1956).
[4] *L'uomo di paglia* (1957).
[5] *La terra trema* (1948).
[6] *I Malavoglia* by Giovanni Varga (1840-1922).

and His Brothers,[1] in which he tells the tragic story of an impoverished peasant family that has gone to Milan to settle.

"There are various ways of treating the theme of the individual who becomes a victim of society. There is an anti-social way which is purely aestheticising. And there is the careful analysis of the social conditions which have led to this defeat.

"Varga stopped short of this end. . . .

"My film, in spite of being concerned with psychological and human values, arrived at social, even political, conclusions. . . .

"The ending of *Rocco* is symbolic, in a sense, of my convictions on the subject of Southern Italy. Ciro speaks to the youngest of the brothers about the future of their homeland, which is in truth that prospected by Antonio Gramsci."[2]

In their attempts to explain the modern world, the Left wing of the neo-realists inevitably comes to Marxism.

The evolution of the aesthetic views of the ideologist of Italian neo-realism and its leading dramatist, Cesare Zavattini, is typical. Discussing his visit to Cuba and work on a scenario about the Cuban revolution, he says:

"In Cuba neo-realist art must be excelled, because the revolution took place after the fall of fascism. In other words, the Cuban revolutionaries must have a clear picture of the vital moments in the development of contemporary mankind, and this must help them to pass quickly through the stage of 'describing' phenomena and penetrate into their very essence."[3]

This is in no way contradictory to what Zavattini proclaimed earlier in his article "Some Thoughts about the Cinema",[4] which was a sort of aesthetic programme of neo-realism. In this he wrote:

". . .The perspectives of neo-realism are much broader than they might seem today; namely, to compel the cinema to carry out the task of analysing the enquiries into the reality that surrounds us." Elsewhere he states: "We mean a situation in which man's life, every minute of his existence, should be given the significance of an historic event."

---

[1] *Rocco e i suoi fratelli* (1960).
[2] *Films and Filming*, January 1961, p. 11.
[3] *Inostrannaya literatura* (Foreign Literature), 1960, No. 8, p. 227.
[4] *Iskusstvo kino* (Cinema Art), 1957, No. 7, pp. 111-15.

What used to be expressed as a wish or intention has now become a practical necessity, when the artist finds himself in a revolutionary situation. The new programme relates to its predecessor as socialist realism relates to critical realism.

* * *

Socialist realism is under fierce attack from the bourgeois camp. These attacks have become stronger in recent years, when socialist realism has begun to develop everywhere as an historical necessity of contemporary culture. In one way or another the criticism has been directed at the tendentiousness of progressive art and its open link with the communist ideal. It is typical that criticism of socialist realism grows into rejection of realism in general. In this respect we cannot cede an inch. But it is precisely such a cession that has been made by certain writers and critics who suggested to replace the concept of "socialist realism" by a broader concept of "socialist art". It might seem that there was some sense in this, in that such a concept would unite contemporary realist art into a world-wide stream.

But such a substitution would be a cardinal error.

First, as regards Soviet art and its practice, this would mean returning to the point of departure, at which in the early days, the new content was clothed in old, traditional forms. It would mean renouncing what has already been achieved in the creation of new forms that correspond to the new content.

Secondly, as far as the broadening of the world front of realism is concerned, such a retreat from socialist realism would, in fact, result in a narrowing and weakening of the front, and a strengthening of the anti-social, aestheticising art, which could be overcome in our era by the old realism only if it assimilated the materialist aesthetics that explain the actual organisation of the world. The evolution of such an outstanding contemporary artist as Brecht gives clear evidence of this. And whole schools in art, especially in the cinema, provide further proof. In an article on the work of Pudovkin, the late Italian critic, Umberto Barbaro, who translated the Soviet director's literary works into Italian, wrote that in them the Italian cinematographers saw:

"The great point of departure for a review of the general

aesthetics and a way out of the crisis in which romantic and idealistic aesthetics now find themselves."

Our method was laid down and continues to develop in a struggle with dogmatism and its understanding of the method and nature of art.

The ethical force of the best works of cinema art lies in their very artistry. This is how it was, beginning with *Battleship "Potemkin"* and *Chapayev*, and how it still is with the best contemporary films.

Let us recall the scene in Chukhrai's *Ballad of a Soldier* when Shura is reminiscing about her last meeting with Alyosha. Scenes appear on the screen that we have already been shown, but they are not just repetitions of what we have seen earlier; they portray new moments that Shura recalls to mind as especially dear. Contemporary cinema tries more and more to go beyond mere pictorial representations of real-life situations and to investigate them by poetic means.

A poor example in this respect is the film *Scarlet Sails*.[1] Its makers fail to see that poetry cannot be expressed by pretty coloured pictures; the film would have possibly gained if it were made in black and white, with just one colour sequence introduced to show the appearance of the scarlet sails on the horizon. But there is also the major error: the maker of the film does not put his trust in artistry. In the novel, Alexander Grin elevates the poetry of life—love and human endurance—above its prose—self-interest and narrowness of vision. At the end of the film comes the "dénouement", explaining the idea of the film, when the heroine marries and thus achieves a secure existence, but this results in bringing the prose to the forefront. The poetry falls down to earth; the director does not put his trust in the ethical power of the artistic quality itself, and together with the artistry he loses the ethical principle.

Dogmatism nourishes such art, for it displays just such a lack of trust in artistry, seeing it only as a subordinate means for illustrating definite ideas. Dogmatism is excellent at producing formulas, but in practice it does not distinguish genuine art from imitation.

Let us take another example: in the collection *Problems of Marxist-Leninist Aesthetics* there are two articles by

---

[1] From the novel of the same name by Alexander Grin (1924).—*Tr.*

P. Trofimov. One of them, called "Socialist Realism—the Creative Method of Soviet Art", contains a true comment that "realism presents the broadest possibilities for the multiform manifestation of the individual characteristics of the artist's style".[1]

But in the other article—"The Beautiful and the Lofty"— in the section that deals with the "lofty", he denounces the "inclination towards false pathos, outward grandeur and stilted imagery" found in art, and as an example of lack of verisimilitude he quotes the following episode from the scenario of Dovzhenko's *Arsenal*:

"...The machine gun would not fire. Timosh, infuriated, kicks and strikes the machine gun. He straightens up.

He hurls a stone at the advancing enemy.

Haidamaks run up to Timosh.

'Stop! Friend or foe?'

Timosh stands by the machine gun.

'A Ukrainian worker. Shoot!'

The Cossacks fire at Timosh.

Timosh stands like a man of iron.

They fire again and again.

They cry out in horror:

'Fall! Fall. . . . Are you wearing armour, or what?'

Timosh, the Ukrainian worker, is still standing."

The author of the article comments as follows:

"The idea of the spiritual immortality of the fighter for the good of the people is unconvincingly expressed. It is impossible to believe that a human being can be impervious to enemy bullets fired at him point blank."

Dogmatism facilitates the divorce of theory from practice, since it does not feel and, therefore, does not believe in the power of artistry. Dogmatism is earthbound; it collates art and life by means of a mirror, forgetting that art has no need to be taken for reality.

In its merciless struggle on two fronts, our art is developing its method, for this alone can ensure harmony between contemporary philosophy and artistic practice, thus facilitating progress towards the "great communist art" (Lenin) by working out artistic forms corresponding to the new content.

---

[1] *Problems of Marxist-Leninist Aesthetics,* Moscow, Gospolitizdat, 1956, p. 278 (Russ. ed.).

This is a complicated process, experiencing difficulties and steep changes of direction, but its chief line is where the screen reveals the link with the life of the people.

The life of the people—this is History. By comprehending this, the cinema comprehends itself and thereby achieves historical significance.

1964

Alexander Ivashchenko

THE MOST IMPORTANT DEVELOPMENT
OF CONTEMPORARY ART

Life has dispelled our ideological enemies' legends that socialist realism is the result of bureaucratic invention, introduced mechanically into the living process of creativity as a foreign body, alien to its organism. Underlying the terminology used to designate the various artistic trends of our times there may be seen to be something more than just a battle between various ideological-aesthetic principles. Such well-known terms as "avant-garde" and "abstract" art are thought by their proponents to express some sort of "style of the epoch" and to represent the essence of contemporary artistic culture. This pretention towards universality is quite remarkable: the modern reformers of art are putting forward a sort of artistic programme for an entire historical period!

Of course, such avant-gardist claims are patently absurd. But the attempts to define the leading artistic tendencies of the times naturally merit serious attention. For the history of art has never been a chaotic interplay of forces or an equilibrium of different streams. The supremacy of certain creative principles has left an imprint on the artistic development of mankind in the various periods of its existence.

Socialist realism is the outstanding achievement of contemporary art. In what may we see the source of the ideological innovatory character of the progressive art of our times? This was defined with exhaustive clarity by Lenin:

"It will be a free literature, enriching the last word in the revolutionary thought of mankind with the experience and living work of the socialist proletariat, bringing about permanent interaction between the experience of the past (scientific socialism, the completion of the development of socialism from its primitive, utopian forms) and the experience of the present (the present struggle of the worker comrades)."[1]

The new artistic method arose logically from a synthesis of progressive revolutionary thought and the experience and practical activities of the socialist proletariat. This synthesis of theory and practice of the liberation movement constitutes the most important feature of our contemporary life. This is why socialist realism, not being a platform for some definite tendency, is the completely natural creation of a progressive society and the aesthetic experience of mankind. It is the product of a new culture. Being "*part* of the common cause of the proletariat" (Lenin), it thereby assumes aesthetic universality and is far removed by its nature from the narrowness and exclusiveness of any one formal "manner".

Attempts by certain representatives of the creative intelligentsia to see the contemporary, progressive style only in laconism and expressiveness are contradictory to the very essence of the new method of realism. Socialist culture cannot be built without a critical survey and the assimilation of the colossal experience accumulated by world art. New aspects of reality and new relations between men cannot be revealed without a striving towards multiformity and innovation in means of artistic expression.

In striving for variety of form and style, representatives of socialist realism in foreign literatures do not, of course, in consequence defend "omnivorousness" and arbitrary, indiscriminate choice of means. In their search for new forms, innovation and variety of content are basic points of departure, as is the demand for generalised and total reflection of reality. "Above all the artist must seek a broad, *poetic* explanation of the world around him; ... this law of art has not died and will never die, for in it lies the difference between art and other fields of human creativity."[2]

No matter what literature, Soviet or foreign, the expert may study, he must proceed from certain general facts deserving serious attention. What are these facts?

Recent years have made obvious the unusual bitterness of the ideological battles taking place around the idea of social-

---

[1] Lenin, *On Literature and Art*, pp. 26-27.
[2] V. Pudovkin, *Selected Articles*, Moscow, 1955, p. 306 (Russ. ed.).

ist realism and, even more widely, around the basic principles of the Marxist-Leninist ideology. The furious attacks of our enemies have been provoked not by any kind of crisis of these principles, but by their growing power. After the Second World War, the situation in the world shifted in favour of the world system of socialism, and these changes cannot but have an effect on the development and prospects of world literature in our times. Can literature and art remain indifferent to the fact that the ideas of peace and social progress, and the struggle for national liberation, embracing entire continents, are becoming an invincible material force?

Obviously, the student of any national literature nowadays cannot get by without a basic and guiding principle in his work, without, that is, an understanding of the *international significance* of the principles of socialist realism. The task of the science of literature is now to study the tremendous pace at which the new artistic method has been gaining ground.

There is no doubt that we are now quite naturally concerned with analysis of socialist realism in its clearly developed form. But we should also distinguish the transitional stages and forms of the general movement of progressive world literature towards the new method. After all, even the critical realism of our day is not quite the same as it was in the last century.

In critical realism there is now a detectable strengthening of the theme of the hero's personal responsibility for the fate of his society and his people; a sharpening of the problem of the social identity of the individual and his choice of means for achieving it; the need to change the state of things in the world grows more imperative. And the very function of exposing faults, so characteristic of critical realism, cannot but feel the effect of the historical experience of the masses and the deepening crisis of capitalism.

The gigantic task of forming an integrated conception of the development of literature and art in the twentieth century is yet to be fulfilled. But even now there is no doubt that a leading place in this conception will be occupied by the new type of realism, which, as necessity increases, will become the universal form of contemporary art.

What place in the art of our epoch will be filled by the various non-realist trends like decadence or modernism? It must be emphasised that in very many cases the modernists' innovation has a purely negative character, that is, it leads to the total destruction of literary and artistic traditions. Examples of this are the so-called poetry of the hermetists, or the avant-garde school of the "new novel" in France (Robbe-Grillet, Nathalie Sarraute), or the proponents of abstraction in painting, sculpture and music. The atonal system in music, denial or typification and logic of subject in literature, and modern painting without a subject are apparently supposed to give the artist a "total vision of the world". French film director René Clair rightly commented on the Western art of the early twenties: "By that time poetry, music and the plastic arts had become closed fields. . . . Literature for the littérateurs, music for the musicians, painting for the painters; the public seemed to be excluded from the game, whose rules were revealed only to the professionals. And art turned off into such a blind alley that its very existence seemed pointless."[1] Since that time modernist art has significantly "matured", becoming ever more deeply embedded in the morass of arbitrary subjectivity.

Innovation in socialist art is inextricably bound up with the traditions of a realistic vision of the world.

It is important to define in principle our attitude to the past and present of world literature, and to the artistic experience accumulated in the course of its development. We must repeat this again and again: the lofty social mission of socialist realist art determines its breadth and freedom in approaching the problem of form. The deep ideological content demands from the progressive writer a rich and flexible system of imagery. Moreover, eclecticism in the field of form is incompatible with a clear and genuinely humane view of man and society, which is basic to socialist realism. Recourse to multiform means of expression is completely compatible with rejection of many of the pseudo-innovatory artifices of contemporary avant-gardists and modernists, who discard the basic principles of artistic comprehension of reality.

There is no contradiction in the assertion that breadth and variety in the realm of form does not mean eclecticism. The more ideologically significant and talented the writer, the more manifest will be the law of the unity of form and con-

---

[1] *Sovietskaya kultura* (Soviet Culture), March 19, 1959.

tent in his work. The more significant the thought, the richer and more flexible must be the system of means of expression.

The new creative method enables the writer to give the fullest and genuinely multifaceted reflection of life. The Polish theoretician Stefan Zulkiewski, defending socialist realist art in polemics with the revisionists, stressed that the point at issue was a new method and the system of stylistic means associated with it. He cited Sholokhov and Brecht. Zulkiewski's opponents reproached him for his apparently too wide range of arguments: could such widely different phenomena be grouped within the framework of one single method?

This is an example of obvious misunderstanding: a method, quite plainly, is not a sum of formal-stylistic techniques or a prescription to use certain means of artistic expression to the exclusion of others. The socialist realist method, being the basic means of typification of reality, opens up opportunities for the broadest generalisations, the discovery of ever new sides of life, and this would of course be impossible without variety of forms of artistic expression. The defenders of capitalism, however, are not in a position to rise to an integrated view of reality or to a reflection of "historical phenomena being presented in objective interconnection and interdependencies and treated as a whole".[1] The reactionary, empty and anti-humane nature of content is inextricably connected with degradation of form and with desperate attempts to conceal emptiness of content under various formal experiments.

* * *

A close examination of the actual process of development of foreign literature and art brings the investigator to the conclusion that realism is often interwoven with more or less obvious formal elements characteristic of modernism. A sharply grotesque shift in actual proportions of reality, the use of elaborately complex associations, simultaneousness of portrayal, expressive density of form, etc. Is this good for realism, or bad?

A simple "yes" or "no" would not do here. First of all, there can be no doubt that realism cannot have anything in common with the principles of absence of subject, abstrac-

---

[1] Lenin, *Collected Works*, Vol. 23, pp. 272-73.

tion, atonality and so on, which belong, strictly speaking, outside the sphere of aesthetics. Such formal elements as those mentioned above, which are found in the work of the modernists, do not stand up to criticism, since with the representatives of non-realist movements they claim the role of universal artistic principles operating independently of content and image. Laconism and expressiveness may be of various sorts. There is the sort of laconism that led to such models of "contemporary style" as *The Black Square* or the chaos of smudges of the tachists. "The laconism of Daumier or Serov is of a totally different order. In the complicated and varied picture of the modern world they tried to distinguish the major social forces and their basic traits, to give them the clearest and most precise evaluation and, for this purpose, to find a definite, effective and convincing idiom. Such laconism results from profound analysis and understanding of the subject; it is laconism of synthesis and generalisation, achieved at the cost of many years of observation and exacting labour. Such laconism cannot be imitated, and only the experience of the artist's life produces it."[1]

The practice of many contemporary realists shows that, without by any means appearing as a general artistic principle, associative artistic thinking and the so-called stream of consciousness are subordinated in their works to the content, are internally justified by it and linked with artistic images. This internal dependence of form on content is that which distinguishes realism from the formal experiments of the modernists. Of course, the link between realist works and the techniques of modernist art is not always artistically justified or convincing. An example of this may be seen in the story *Das Brot der frühen Jahre* by Heinrich Böll.[2]

Clarity of ideological content is a not unimportant condition for clarity and integrity of artistic form, too. Common ideological views and consistency in their defence are in full accord with a variety of means of expression employed.

All more or less noteworthy realist writers who hold aloof from the principles of socialist art, experience a growing

---

[1] A. Kantor, "On the Contemporary in Art", *Iskusstvo* (Art), 1960, No. 4.

[2] A good illustration, for example, is the end of Böll's story: "I had never before realised that I was immortal and at the same time so mortal," and further on to the end.

necessity for integral artistic thinking. More than thirty years ago Stefan Zweig wrote to Gorky:

"I don't know if we are in a position to create another entire world, as Balzac or Dostoyevsky did. Perhaps our epoch is moving too fast for us to embrace it at one glance. But it is possible that the works of individual writers will give the next generation an integral conception of the state of our hearts."[1]

In our times the Italian prose-writer Italo Calvino has already come to the conclusion that the form of novel does not correspond to the impetuous rhythm of contemporary life.

The accelerated tempo of social development which is typical of our times not only does not remove the necessity for an integral view of reality, it makes it more acute. And, of course, it is only devotion to the Party, to the ideals of socialist reshaping of the world and an understanding of the historical perspectives that can open to the writer a reliable path to artistic synthesis and to generalised images of the constantly changing reality.

The great historical changes that have resulted from the existence of the socialist camp, its ideology and culture have indicated a clear path for the future development of contemporary literature.

In this connection I should like to recall a passage in a letter by Ibsen. This is what he wrote as long ago as 1890:

"Having taken as my life's work the task of portraying the character and fate of men, I came—in the process of working out certain problems—quite unconsciously and unintentionally to precisely the same conclusions as social-democratic moralist philosophers had reached by scientific research."[2]

Here it would not be out of place to recall also Zola's confession that the study of life had led him spontaneously to the ideas of socialism. And we could supplement this with Jack London's narration of the paths by which he also came to socialist beliefs. . . .

Such examples from the past could easily be multiplied. They make more comprehensible the profound accuracy of

---

[1] Letter to Gorky, December 19, 1926. From the archives of A. M. Gorky in the Institute of World Literature.

[2] Henrik Ibsen, *Collected Works*, Vol. 4, Moscow, 1958, p. 727 (Russian translation).

the concept of "unconscious tendency towards socialism" that Marx attributed to certain cultural figures of his day.

In our age the interrelationship between writer and reality is undergoing a radical change. The historical perspectives of social development have become clear; the ideas of communism have become palpable, material force. And what limitless opportunities are now open to those writers who have joined their fate with socialist realism. It is not an unconscious tendency towards socialism, but a consciousness of history and the artistic transformation of partisanship that guide the work of the greatest contemporary writers. The logic of history and the logic of creative endeavours will undoubtedly lead more and more new writers to the standpoint of socialist realism.

From the fact of the universal significance of the principles of socialist realism many basic consequences result.

The nature of the attack on socialist realism has noticeably changed. Some thirty years ago our ideological enemies condescendingly acknowledged the existence of Soviet literature and even admitted that it had certain merits. However, there was always that fatal "but...", which meant in effect that the creative principles of Soviet literature apparently had no relevance to the art of the "civilised West". This, of course, was an obvious lie.

Nowadays even our enemies cannot deny that socialist realism exists as an international phenomenon. But now they put forward a new argument: yes, they say, it does exist, but as a factor outside art, something that lies outside its parameters. We may now observe stubborn attempts to ignore the most important achievements of contemporary literature and art, to ignore the new artistic method and by various means to discredit the experience of socialist realism.

Bourgeois ideologists are attempting to restrict the scale of application of the method of realism, claiming that it operates only within the framework of one genre—the novel, but is powerless in lyricism. In other words, the new method is too crude an instrument (being "sociological") to be applied to such delicate (psychological) material as the genre of the lyric. It is hardly even worthwhile stressing the point that this idea will not stand up to the slightest criticism.

To what ingenious devices will our ideological enemies not fly in their struggle against the growing influence of the method of socialist realism! In bourgeois literature one meets with such conceptions—if that is the right word—as, for instance: actual reality has many facets and many planes. Each literary tendency is orientated on the artistic assimilation of one definite aspect of reality. Hence but a slight effort is needed to make the conclusion that both contemporary realism and modernism may peacefully coexist, since each of them deals with its own aspect of reality. Needless to say, we reject such a theory of the equality of rights of realism and decadent tendencies hostile to it.

All attacks on art of socialist realism have something in common. This is an attempt to neglect the basic innovatory quality of socialist realism and the universal character of the new method.

The Soviet literary critics are faced with an absolutely clear task: they must follow the demands of the further development of art of socialist realism and firmly oppose any manifestations of reactionary bourgeois ideology and revisionism in literature and art.

Socialist realism has its own principles of generalisation and typification which took shape on the basis of progressive social experience and socialist ideals.

Our first task is to investigate the aesthetic pithiness of the principles of socialist realism. First and foremost this concerns the partisanship of art, a fundamental principle of socialist realist art. This principle is extremely rich in content; the depiction of reality in its revolutionary development, having as its aim the education of the people in the spirit of socialist ideals, harmoniously combines ethics, aesthetics and politics. Moreover, the concept of partisanship is strictly in accord with the demands of historical objectivity.

To take partisanship out of the sphere of aesthetics, as our opponents would have us do, means to ignore the actual basis on which the writer's philosophy and practice are united. At the 14th Congress of the Communist Party of France, Maurice Thorez stressed that:

"By placing the artist and writer face to face with true perspectives and actual problems, Marxism-Leninism broadens their horizons, enabling them to rise higher, penetrate deeper and create significant works."[1]

As Maurice Thorez's speech makes clear, it is obviously not a question of an author literally translating or illustrat-

---

[1] *L'Humanité*, July 19, 1956.

ing Party directives in his work. The principle of parti-sanship as understood, for example, by György Lukács, who relegates it to the sphere of publicism only, has nothing in common with the treatment of this principle in Marxist aesthetics. For the socialist realist the principle of partisan-ship stands out as the objective quality of what he creates.

Another task of unusual and, one might say, vital impor-tance is the study and generalisation of the artistic experi-ence and riches accumulated by world-wide socialist realism. This constantly growing experience demands detailed in-vestigation.

One feels that we have now reached a new stage in our science of the study of literature. In past years we spent quite a lot of our time proclaiming and defending our theo-retical principles in their most general form, and summaris-ing the manifestations of socialist realism in other coun-tries. This, of course, was important and necessary at that time. Our science has accumulated many valuable conclu-sions and acute and interesting observations, but this is no longer sufficient. It is now acutely essential to carry out *profound* study of the artistic experience of contemporary liter-ature.

We are now faced with the enormous but fascinating task of systematising and making widely known the riches and colossal experience amassed by socialist realism, studying the concrete forms of the new aesthetics and investigating the innovatory essence of socialist realism, which is mani-fested in the wealth and variety of artistic forms. Such a scientific treatment of artistic experience corresponds to the demands of socialist realism itself and stands out as an im-portant condition for the further development of realism.

Detailed and differentiated study of artistic experience, especially of the problems of the appearance and develop-ment of socialist realism in capitalist countries and People's Democracies, is of great significance. Writers living in the conditions of both capitalist and socialist systems are united on the platform of one single method, but the most interest-ing question of the differences in their approach to certain creative problems still remains unanswered.

We are faced with many very important questions: the mutual relationship between the writer's individual exper-ience and one single method of realism; the national pecul-iarities of artistic form, etc. And finally, it should be stressed over and over again that there is the insistent need for research into the aesthetic nature of the principle of partisanship. If we now have a general idea of the way in which the principle of partisanship influences the structure of, say, a positive image in art, then an analysis of the influence of the principle of partisanship on the structure of a negative image would be similarly important, as would a clarification of the innovatory quality of socialist realism as compared with contemporary critical realism. This presents the researcher with a mass of interesting opportunities.

Our foreign friends say, with complete justification, that a new reality demands new means of expression.

In this connection it ought to be stated that sometimes the customary terminology does not embrace or express the novelty and complexity of the artistic forms that have come into being during the development of socialist realism. What happens, surely, is that on the one hand, we proclaim the multiformity of our art, and on the other hand, we often apply the standard evaluations and definitions to all of them, involuntarily impoverishing the genuine wealth of artistic forms engendered by socialist realist art.

We are not talking about artificial creation of incredible "isms". But the study of literature and criticism must not lead to a mere reflection of what has been reflected. Like literature, the science of literature has as its foundation a living, changing reality. This truism must have its concrete expression in the concepts on which the science of literature rests—concepts that are sufficiently flexible and mobile to catch the artistically interpreted truth of life. In his *Philosophical Notebooks*, Lenin wrote:

"Concepts are not immobile, but—in and for themselves, by their nature—transition."[1] The movement of concepts reflects the movement of the objective world.

But ideally, for the new means of depicting reality there must be a corresponding new aesthetic system of analysis and evaluation to reveal the artistic richness of socialist realism. Thus Pablo Neruda's *'Universal Song'*, which is magnificent in its ideological scale and most varied in its means of poetic depiction, necessitates, by the very fact of its existence and its effect on the mass of readers, an urgent, innovatory

---

[1] Lenin, *Collected Works*, Vol. 38, p. 225.

search for new means of analysis and theoretical generalisation.

It seems obvious that in the course of the development of our literary science we shall also create a new system of analysis and criteria of artistry, capable of more sensitive appreciation of the growing and increasingly more profound experience of the world's progressive literatures.

To this we must add one further consideration. Our literary science fulfils its function when it takes active part in the formation not only of a man's civic qualities, but of the multiformity of his aesthetic tastes, too.

Our literary science can and must facilitate breadth and variety of aesthetic tastes. Serious and thoughtful research into the multiformity of socialist realism is directly related to the artistic-educative function of literary study and criticism.

1960

Vladimir Shcherbina,
Nikolai Gei, Vladimir Piskunov

SOCIALIST REALISM AND THE ARTISTIC DEVELOPMENT OF MANKIND

Profound examination of the problems of socialist realism is possible only on the basis of a concept of the artistic development of mankind in a wide historico-literary perspective, embracing all the artistic riches accumulated throughout the centuries and created by contemporary artists. Incidentally, the opinion is still expressed that socialist realism is a special, isolated phenomenon, a separate branch of world artistic development. Foreign critics of socialist realist art allege that it avoids fundamental questions of contemporary man and his life, has nothing in common with the problems of the rest of literature, is alien to the problems of personal life, happiness, humanism and the tragic contradictions of the modern world, and that doubts, inquiry and artistic experiment are unknown to it.

Solution of the most complicated and major problems of the epoch, the problems of the revolutionary transformation of the world and the education of free man, enables socialist realist writers to put forward a new artistic concept of the world and to occupy a leading position in the contemporary literary process. This was magnificently expressed by Becher, who asserted in his *Experiments* that his task as artist and thinker was the creation of the image of the new man, who is building a new world and who is prepared to defend it against the threat of the atomic bomb.

At the time when other artistic movements sometimes restrict themselves to individual aspects of reality and thus claim for their own experience the status of universal truth and the meaning of life, or refrain from any conclusions at

232

all, socialist realism strives to create an integral conception of human character.

The modern period of the history of world literature is distinguished by the intensity of the struggle between ideological-aesthetic viewpoints. There are various tendencies and schools, views and nuances, each of which claims a monopoly in art and casts aspersions on all other unacceptable principles, including such a basic principle as humanism.

Socialist realist writers are working out the problem of profound analysis of social life without, at the same time, introducing any dogma about human individuality. They put the highest value on its unique quality, and see their chief and ultimate aim in guaranteeing the opportunity for "the free and original development" of each individual (Marx). Lenin emphasised that in art, as distinct from science and publicism, "the whole *essence is in the individual* circumstances, the analysis of the *characters* and psychology of *particular* types".[1]

Socialist realist aesthetics refuses to make any a priori definitions of the essence of the human personality and sets unlimited value on the originality of every man. It is concerned not only with the unique individual, but with the integral spiritual life of all people and the psychology of the nation.

Genuine socialist realist artists do not prescribe any predetermined schemes for life. They strive, in an unquestionably correct manner, to reflect the objective internal development of life, whose pivotal moment is its movement towards communism.

Socialist realism was born of reality, embodies the revolutionary passion of our epoch and penetrates boldly into its dramatic conflicts, investigating the complexity of life. By ignoring the works of the greatest masters of socialist realist art and placing the best achievements of Gorky, Sholokhov, Mayakovsky, Eluard, Nezval and Brecht outside socialist realism, the opponents of the new creative method try to compromise it by citing the poor artistic quality of some works.

Controversy over the new method is fruitless without a deep inquiry into its artistic foundation and a scientific as-

---

[1] Lenin, *Collected Works*, Vol. 35, p. 184.

similation of the more than half a century of experience of world-wide socialist realist literature.

The first attempts to portray reality in its revolutionary development and the introduction of proletarian humanism are visible in works of literature from the early years of the revolution. The new literature spoke up loudly through Gorky and Mayakovsky.

Gorky's humanism is inextricably linked with the new voice in which the writer spoke and which was sensed by such a delicate artist as Blok, who said: "If there really is such a concept as 'Russia' or, still better, 'Rus' ...then to an enormous extent we must consider it expressed by Gorky".[1] To appreciate the full significance of this declaration it should be remembered that Blok most certainly did not share Gorky's general aesthetic views at that period. The article quoted served for Andrei Bely as the pretext for an attack on Blok.

Nevertheless, with the honesty typical of him, Blok confessed that it was precisely the socialist writer, Gorky, and not, let us say, Sologub, Bely, Merezhkovsky, Ivanov, Andreyev or Bunin who could give the fullest and most profound expression to the Russia of that time.

On March 4, 1912, Blok wrote in his diary: "Thanks to Gorky.... After aestheticism, futurism, apollonism and the bibliophiles I feel the smell of reality."[2] This direct opposition of Gorky's position to that of the various other trends is highly significant.

In the spring of 1919, Blok said: "Fate has laid a heavy burden on Maxim Gorky, the greatest artist of our times. It has made him the mediator between the people and the intelligentsia...."[3] One might question the wording of this formulation, but its spirit is true.

Gorky's works provide an original and profound embodiment of the integrity and elemental nature of Russian life and an inexhaustibly varied and multicoloured artistic world.

Of course, the question of the definitive nature of Gorky's work for the Russian literature of his time requires fundamental research. But the very proposition that Gorky embodied the basic artistic problems of twentieth century Rus-

---

[1] Alexander Blok, *Collected Works in 8 Volumes*, Vol. 5, Moscow-Leningrad, Goslitizdat, 1962, p. 103 (Russ. ed.).

[2] Ibid., Vol. 7, p. 131.

[3] Ibid., Vol. 6, p. 92.

sia earlier, fuller and more profoundly than anyone else cannot be doubted.

Socialist realist literature is a stage in the artistic development of mankind, logical, essential and proportionate with earlier stages of artistic thought. The creative experience of the Renaissance and the Enlightenment, romanticism and realism makes it possible to interpret the new method from a position of historical generalisation and to see how deeply it is rooted in history. At the same time, the artistic discoveries made by socialist realism render it possible to look afresh at the logic of literary development.

All stages in the development of artistic thought make a unique contribution to the general treasury of culture and have an intransient significance. Further development and artistic discoveries reveal new aspects and facets of the classical heritage and illuminate it with a special light. Thus it may be said that not only do Tolstoi and Chekhov aid us to explain Gorky's discoveries, but the work of the founder of socialist realism also opens up new aspects of what was done by his brilliant predecessors. The work of many contemporary poets stems from sources in romanticism which seemed to have dried up until their inexhaustibility was suddenly revealed. Julian Tuwim's poetry will remain a sealed book to anyone who passes by the artistic discoveries of Mickiewicz and Słowacki. The traditions of Lesya Ukrainka and Ivan Franko have had a fruitful effect on Soviet Ukrainian poetry. The passion of the young Gorky evoked the bold striving and high tension of the revolutionary romanticists.

The romantic hero aims to represent the true society, not separate classes or social groups. Maximalism does not permit him to be content with little things or with half-measures and demands that he be "the man of all men".

The historical service of active romanticism is in that it points a sharp and definite contrast between the world of the ideal and bourgeois reality. These contrasts embody the uncompromising nature of romantic poetry. Byron's Don Juan defies the conventional moral standards, and Childe Harold would not be reconciled with man-made laws, while Cain even raised his hand against the laws of the Universe.

Having perceived and demonstrated the doom of the illusions of the Enlightenment and laid bare the hitherto concealed layers of social contradictions, the romantics themselves became creators of new illusions. They revealed the unfettered character of man and turned their attention to his inner world, but they set the romantic personality above real people.

Romanticism suffered tragically from the incompatibility of the ideal and reality. Literature was faced with the task of finding a basis for the ideals in true life and pondering their motivation and actual feasibility.

Realism reaffirmed the ideal on the much more stable basis of a real knowledge of the relationship between character and milieu, circumstances and man. As distinct from romanticism, realism not only postulates the ideal, conditioned by life, and speaks of the reality of the ideal; it also gives it an artistic embodiment, which puts the question of the necessity to turn the ideal into the real, relying on the progressive movement of reality itself. Socialist realist writers have pondered the historical truth of life and the necessity of changing its apparently most immovable foundations.

The theoreticians of contemporary modernism deny the significance of realism for the twentieth century, saying that it is an insufficiently fine and efficient instrument for the revelation of "all the complexity of the processes of life". They consider Stendhal, Balzac and Tolstoi as artists who have outlived their time. The world of things loses its empirical time-space shell of existence and becomes an enigmatic hieroglyphic of inner experience, in the light of which, they believe, the works of Goethe, Balzac and Tolstoi are "houses buried in dust", and Rembrandt's pictures are "trivial combinations of platitudinous melodies and hackneyed chords".

As a living tradition, they oppose realism with a myth, which they proclaim as the universal, general seedbed of art.

Realism is opposed by a whole system of philosophico-aesthetic arguments. One of the foremost American philosophers, John Dewey, categorically denies the correspondence between art and the objective content of life. According to Dewey, the criteria of the value of art do not rest on reality but on the constantly shifting concepts, notions, moral norms and desires of men. And André Malraux, in his *Psychologie de l'Art*, asserts that artistic creativity breaks the link between man and the world. Art, in his opinion, means engrossment in the world of illusion, which develops according to immanent laws. Thus the purpose of artistic creativity is to draw man away from life and to create illusions.

However, as the experience of world art has shown, realism is not only unexhausted, but has been developing fruitfully in the works of such major writers as Shaw, Rolland, Martin du Gard, Stefan Zweig, the Mann brothers, Hemingway, Čapek and Galsworthy.

October 1917 changed the world literary climate and opened new paths to art. Of course, this process could not be a "smooth" one; it took place amidst struggles and sharp conflicts, and was notable for its drama and tension. But these were the growing pains of literature due to its complicated approximation to the revolutionary life of the people and the historical achievement of the epoch.

The development of socialist ideas has become a mighty factor in the establishment of socialist realism throughout the world. The upsurge of revolutionary literature in the countries of the West during the twenties and thirties was indicative of the crisis of capitalism and the growing scope of the world revolutionary movement. This may be sensed in the revolutionary poetry of the beginning of the twenties, in Hašek's novels, the activities of a whole pleiad of Hungarian poets and writers who took part in the Hungarian revolution of 1919; in the confidence with which Henri Barbusse supports the ideas of socialist art, and in Romain Rolland's approximation to the aesthetics of socialist realism which was noticeable in the thirties.

Socialist realist artists reveal the motive forces of history, penetrate into the essence of the phenomena of life and aim to discover the logical regularities, processes and perspectives that lie beyond the surface of that movement. They aspire to grasp the logic of the process of world history and the objective meaning of what is portrayed, and to convey the truth of life broadly and profoundly. The innovatory nature of socialist realism has its sources in the artistic revelations of the increasing activity of the masses and their historical role.

Socialist realism has enlarged the field of vision of art to an amazing extent, illuminating reality with a new light and revealing the sources of the beautiful.

Gorky expressed belief in man and human nature, and affirmed the idea of the change of the personality and awakening of its latent capabilities, the best that is dormant within it, during the process of the revolutionary transformation of life. He showed the growth of the historical forces that were destined to achieve the revolutionary transformation of the country and put into effect the noble dream about Russia, which as he said in his novel *Mother* would become "the brightest democracy on earth".

Reactionary literature ignores the masses and portrays the ordinary people and the man of humble origin, as downcast and unenlightened. It cultivates the image of the people as a faceless, uniform crowd, spiritually empoverished and having no future. This highly negligent attitude to the masses leads to a contrasting of the outstanding personality with the run-of-the-mill individual. In the opinion of that extoller of the personality, Mounier, for example, the "free creative personalities", the "human élite" is distinguished from the characterless "simple individuals" who comprise the grey masses.

Soviet literature, while denying levelling and attaching great value to giftedness and variety of character and talent, does not tolerate the abasement of ordinary people or the denial of the creative forces present in the masses. The appeal of Gorky's characters is in the force of talent and giftedness, in their unbounded energy. The legendary Vasily Buslayev, as Gorky described him, wanted to melt the snows, cultivate and adorn the whole planet, making the life of mankind beautiful and happy.

The liberation of the creative energies of the masses is one of Gorky's leading artistic ideas. His hero does not heap all the blame on circumstances or seek to justify all his shortcomings, but considers himself personally responsible for what is happening.

Referring to the experience of socialist realist literature, the English student of the novel, Ralph Fox, asserts: "Epic man is man in whom no division any longer occurs between himself and his sphere of practical activity. He lives and changes life. Man creats himself."[1]

Searches for the new method have followed various paths.

In the autobiographical cycle, the plays about Bulychov and Dostigayev and the chronicle of the age, *The Life of Klim Samgin*, we find a basically new approach to reality, in which the future is a revelation of the potential possibilities of the present and a comprehension of the genuinely revolutionary activity of the masses.

In an attempt to reflect the progress of history and man's role in it, Alexei Tolstoi turns to monumental realism, a de-

---

[1] Ralph Fox, *The Novel and the People*, New York, 1945, p. 87.

piction of the epoch as the collective fate of men. The message of such art is the happiness of all mankind and its aim is "the creation, amidst passions and grandiose tensions, of a type of Man."[1]

In his search for new forms of revolutionary poetry, Mayakovsky broke beyond the traditional bounds of the poetic and made the whole world the subject of lyrical experience. His works combine confession and sermon, intimate and universal. The lyrical revelation by the poet of his own self became a confirmation of the transformatory force of the revolution.

It is also no accident that the profound historical contradictions revealed by the First World War were fully reflected in the work of another socialist realist writer, Henri Barbusse, especially in his novel *Le Feu*. This novel, which appeared in 1916,[2] is often considered by Western critics to be the first work in the so-called literature of the lost generation. To some extent this is what it really is. Barbusse anticipated Hemingway, Remarque, Céline and Oldington, and first raised the most contemporary of problems, that of the individual and war, human individuality and total anti-humanity. It must be confessed that Hemingway later analysed the problem of "the individual and war" with greater artistic depth and expression, but Barbusse also raised another question, that of "the people and war", "war and revolution".

The integrated series of problems embodied in the work of the socialist artist has, as it were, disintegrated in the literature of other directions. The "school" of the lost generation, which is a kind of offshoot of critical realism, deals only with the problem of "the individual and war", and in the avant-garde drama of the expressionist trend the question of the faceless mass in war and revolution is isolated from all others.

The war compelled many artists to become unusually acutely aware of the senselessness and degeneracy of the very foundations of the social and state structure of the old world. This was the subject of the work of Jaroslav Hašek, an artist with a socialist feeling for the world. He wrote one of the

---

[1] Alexei Tolstoi, *Collected Works in 15 Volumes*, Vol. 13, Moscow, 1949, p. 286.
[2] Awarded the Prix Goncourt in 1917.—*Tr.*

most outstanding books of the age, in which the absurdity of a world in which a senseless and long war could break out is depicted in a unique combination of the grotesque and the epic. In the broad narrative Hašek created a whole gallery of human individuals who are oppressed and devastated by the general absurdity. And he presented the immortal figure of Schweik, a unique personification of the national character who can withstand the world-wide absurdity, sliding into total chaos and oblivion.

At the same time as Hašek, artists of other directions, like Kafka and later Breton, Beckett, Ionesco and others also took up the theme of absurdity, but they left the human individual alone in the all-embracing absurdity of the capitalist world, in which the individual is inevitably defeated and disintegrates, itself becoming a focal point of absurdity and chaos.

We are faced with the same historical situation: the socialist writer gives an integrated and unique artistic solution of the problem of the attitude of the individual to the world, but writers of other directions deal with one aspect only.

This certainly does not mean that in the literary situation of the twentieth century the "first word" inevitably belongs to the socialist artist. Every genuine artist reveals something new. The supremacy of socialist artists lies in the fact that they give an integrated solution of human problems which in modernist literature are illuminated only in a narrow or distorted way.

The search for the new art took place in documentary genres. Their creators—John Reed, Williams Rhys, Egon Erwin Kisch, Mikhail Koltsov and Julius Fučik—did not work within glossy dust-jackets but on the coarse pages of the newspapers. It was precisely in such essays that the publicistic and political-activist elements emerged as an independent component of the works. Publicism was ahead of all other genres in assimilating developing reality and making a conscious emphasis on the new artistic principles. The achievements of revolutionary publicism played a serious role in the development of the epic genres of socialist realist literature, especially the novel.

The history of socialist realism is the history of the working out of artistic forms most adequate to genuine freedom of creativity. In these searches for form, no help could be afforded by the idea of "unbounded realism", for the problem is the creation of the most fruitful artistic forms, that is, the definition of the "bounds" within which art may develop freely and strongly.

Lunacharsky wrote that the common feature of the new literature was "its definite turn to social realism".[1] And five years later Fadeyev was to say: "The genuine revolutionary artistic method is first of all a true depiction of reality in the process of development, in its basic tendencies and its living wealth."[2]

The new term "socialist realism", which arose as a result of the inquiries and experiments of writers, poets and critics, emphasised their concern with the life of the people and reality in its revolutionary development. It was directed against oversimplified illustrativeness as laid down in the RAPP (Russian Association of Proletarian Writers) formula for "dialectical materialism in art".

Attempts to characterise socialist realism were made by foreign writers in the thirties. In his book *The Novel and the People*, Ralph Fox discusses the new horizons of artistic creativity, the capacity for embracing life and the conceptual breadth offered by socialist realist art. In the works of the English Marxists, Christopher Caudwell, who perished prematurely in Spain, and A. West, socialist literature is contrasted with bourgeois art. Becher's articles are an attempt to outline new possibilities of progressive poetry.

Socialist realist art is the sum total of the lengthy development of literature and the practical, ideological and artistic experience of all generations of revolutionary writers.

The problem of the development and enrichment of socialist realist art is still by no means fully researched. It is only in the last few years that we have begun to publish books dedicated to a historical survey of the development of socialist realist literature in the countries of the capitalist world and in socialist countries. But as yet there are no works that generalise the regularities of this development; or make a study of collective artistic experience within the framework of the specific circumstances of an individual nation; of the historical stages in the progression of socialist

---

[1] *Na literaturnom postu* (On the Literary Watch), 1927, Nos. 22-23, p. 20.

[2] Alexander Fadeyev, *Thirty Years On*, Moscow, 1957, p. 89 (Russ. ed.).

art; or of the new features that have arisen in given historical conditions in different countries, and of the interrelationships of the artistic discoveries of various national cultures.

Every epoch confronts literature with new tasks, which inevitably combine with the more general regularities of the development of art.

The unity of revolutionary struggle and patriotic traditions, the closing of the popular ranks around the democratic ideals of socialism, and the affirmation of political activity and collective responsibility produced the literature of the Resistance, linked with the names of Julius Fučik, Nikola Vaptsarov, Johannes Becher, Bertold Brecht, Anna Seghers and Paul Eluard.

Within the socialist world system, the development of socialist realism has entered a new stage and embraced a number of countries. The growth of revolutionary independence of the popular masses and the hectic tempo of scientific and technological progress has all given unheard-of acuteness to the question of the present and future of mankind, the place of man in real life and his responsibility for everything that takes place in the world now divided into two social systems. All this finds reflection in socialist realism, the rapidly burgeoning revolutionary art that is in a constant state of movement, struggle, inquiry and discovery.

The formation of socialist realism is closely linked with a concrete national-historical process. What is new in literature is an organic national phenomenon with its roots in the life of the people and continuing the traditions of democratic culture.

National literatures may be young and old, the paths by which they came towards socialist realism and the level of their development may vastly differ; all this demands utmost attention to their concrete historical peculiarities.

For example, students of Ukrainian literature speak of the prime significance of the revolutionary-romantic traditions of Shevchenko, Franko and Lesya Ukrainka for the development of socialist Ukrainian literature. Rylsky, Dovzhenko, Yanovsky and, similarly, contemporary prose-writers like Gonchar and Stelmakh are attracted to romantic poetics and have eager recourse to unbounded lyrical poetry and lofty pathos.

The literature of the Soviet Central Asian republics was

formed and has thriven on the same national soil and literary traditions; behind them is the centuries-old experience of ornamental poetry, educative genres, play upon words and love of jesting which embody the wisdom of the people. This has set an unmistakable imprint on the work of Aini, Ibragimov and Auezov.

The work of the writers of the Baltic republics is remarkable for its tendency towards realistic poetics and epic circumstance, as in Upit, for example, or analytical fixation of milieu and customs, as in Vilde, or bold emotionally excited colours, as in Čiurlionis or the romantic flights of Rainis.

Every people contributes its own part to the common multicoloured spectrum of the multilingual and multinational Soviet literature that is united by the inner proximity of socialist cultures.

Bourgeois ideology seeks to impose a certain uniformity upon art. For this, a theoretical basis has been devised: quite definite national peculiarity is acknowledged to be a feature of only small or peripheral literatures that apparently have not yet risen to questions of universal human significance or torn themselves away from their national roots and ethnographically narrow descriptiveness. It is absence of national peculiarity, and cosmopolitan "sweep", with irrelevance of form to any content, that are proclaimed as the criterion of modern art. And the hero of such literature is the personality in general, the "integrated man".

It is typical that until recently bourgeois literary studies in Western Europe and the United States paid hardly any attention to questions of the national peculiarities of art, since these were considered old-fashioned in the age of the atomic bomb and cybernetics.

During the past half-century there has been a denationalisation of modernist art. An average "West European-American" type of art has evolved, in which the national specific qualities of French, English, German and American (US) culture have dissolved. The literary ranks have been joined by such writers as the Anglo-American Eliot and Pound, and the Franco-British Beckett, for whom there seems to be no basic difference between the national cultures of the peoples of the USA, Britain and France.

Meanwhile, socialist realist writers—Sholokhov, Brecht, Hašek, Eluard—give a profound and powerful embodiment of the wealth of national character, and this embodiment, far from contradicting the internationalist spirit of their art, is an essential condition of it.

The emergence and consolidation of socialist realism linked with the specific forms of the struggle for liberation, characteristic of each given people, have expressed a profound national need. It is for this precise reason that the formation of the new creative method has taken place in different ways in different countries.

The art of Martin Andersen Nexö springs from the experience of the Scandinavian workers' movement and the especially sharp social line of development in Scandinavian literature at the end of the nineteenth century.

Barbusse's novel *Le Feu* arose out of the holocaust of the First World War and contained all the might of the critical and humanitarian traditions of French realism.

John Reed's *Ten Days that Shook the World* was created directly after the events of the Great October Revolution and under their decisive influence. But the creative method employed by John Reed, a socialist realist writer, was formed on his own national soil. John Reed came to Russia having gone through the school of the workers' movement in the USA and been involved in the Mexican revolution, to which he dedicated his splendid book, *Insurgent Mexico* (1914).

The gospel of national nihilism is directed against the cultural heritage of the peoples and, in the first place, against realism, which is, allegedly, hopelessly out of touch with contemporary life and therefore continues to typify reality in the old fashion, on the basis of its concrete national forms.

The denial of the national character of a literature also leads to a levelling down of artistic discoveries, so that writers are condemned to endless repetition of long familiar truths.

National reality assists writers to solve general creative problems, and artistic discoveries acquire a wide and varied existence in the general process of development of national literatures.

An artistic discovery made in one national literature is also an artistic discovery for other national literatures; these do not simply transfer it on to their own soil, but in the light of their own national specific circumstances they reveal new facets and aspects of it, enriching themselves from what has

244

been done, and in their turn enriching others and making their contribution to the treasure store of socialist realism. It is only in the sum total of all these various aspects and relationships that genuine revelation of truth, in all its wealth, multisidedness and complexity can be achieved. Without this collective experience it is impossible to envisage the contemporary state of socialist realist art.

In the establishment of socialist realist art, a major significance is attached to international cultural relations and, in particular, to literary relations. The new nature of such links became apparent at an earlier stage in the establishment of socialist literature. Proletarian literature attracted the attention of Marx and Engels, who stressed the need for acquainting the readers with the achievements of the socialist literature of various countries. Within such achievements they included, for example, the poetry of the Chartists and the verses of the revolutionary poets, Freiligrath, Weerth, Johnson and Dupont. Marx and Engels several times stressed the fruitfulness of making use of the artistic experience of all peoples for developing the socialist tendency in national literatures.

In 1918, during the period of proletarian revolutions, Lenin wrote: "The workers of the whole world are building up their own, internationalist culture, which the champions of freedom and the enemies of oppression have for long been preparing."[1] The establishment and development of socialist realism is a process with an international sense, and a process that must be studied as a new stage in the development of artistic awareness.

In the post-war years there has been a constant development of new and closer forms of interrelationship between the literatures of the countries following the path to socialism. These have been conditioned by the historical community of the tasks and problems of the building of socialism and, at the same time, have made possible a much more intensive literary exchange.

A socialist perspective facilitates very profound changes in the basic direction of literary creativity. This has been comprehended by many Western literary masters and theoreticians in their assessment of the changed literary situation.

---

[1] Lenin, *Collected Works*, Vol. 19, p. 92.

In every national literature, socialist realism provides a solution of the specifically national problems facing it, and at the same time it takes its place on equal terms among the common-problem-areas that go outside national frameworks.

* * *

Those features of the development of socialist realism mentioned above also determine the specific nature of research into the socialist literatures of our day. The primary task is working out the theory of socialist realism, which can be feasible only when complemented with research into the past and present experience of world artistic development and the creative practice of socialist literatures and their specifics.

Discovery of the complicated dialectics of content and form is the problem with which socialist realist theory is now faced, for until it is solved there is a danger of the identification of literature with all other forms of social awareness or the appearance of literary works which, in the final analysis, will be fruitlessly formalistic and divorced from real life.

Prime importance in socialist realist theory is given to its methodological foundations in Marxist-Leninist theory, which is common to all the humanitarian sciences and vital for correct understanding of the development of society under socialism and the historic destinies of the revolutionary proletariat, the Russian people, and man in a socialist revolution.

In Lenin's works we see the fate of man who suffers and thinks, stands erect and grows, brought up by the Party and transforming himself, finding the road to socialism and becoming the architect of a new society.

Lenin's heritage is a profound source of understanding of that man who has become the hero of socialist realist literature, and of his place in history.

The Leninist understanding of man and his destiny in the socialist revolution makes it possible to clarify the basic aspects of literary works. An important task of socialist realist theory is to show how Lenin's heritage makes it possible to formulate the question of the upbringing and formation of the new man and, by this process, to reveal the content and message of many outstanding literary works in a quite new way.

Such a cardinal and much analysed problem as devotion to Party and people cannot be studied sufficiently deeply without putting the question as to how the given work of art depicts the fate of man in the socialist revolution and in the building of socialism. The Leninist criterion of the political maturity of a man in the struggle for socialism is the most reliable here.

In his classic work *The State and Revolution*, written in August-September 1917, Lenin explained: "...How infinitely mendacious is the ordinary bourgeois conception of socialism as something lifeless, rigid, fixed once and for all, whereas in reality *only* socialism will be the beginning of a rapid, genuine, truly mass forward movement, embracing first the *majority* and then the whole of the population, in all spheres of public and private life."[1]

This proposition has enormous significance for the revelation and deepening of the concept of the revolutionary development of life, which has become one of the fundamental elements in the definition of socialist realism.

Lenin believed that it is in the struggle for socialism that the talents of the men of the people manifest themselves. For Lenin, the growth of the masses and the growth of the individual, the rise of the masses and the discovery of individual talents are indivisibly linked.

In his words, "at moments of great upsurge and the exertion of all human capacities, revolutions are made by the class-consciousness, will, passion and imagination of tens of millions, spurred on by a most acute struggle of classes."[2]

Such a mighty upsurge naturally presupposes also the discovery and development of "all human capacities" and the talents of each individual man taking part in the revolution and building socialism. On the other hand, these words speak of the extreme tension and complicated nature of the spiritual life of the people in a revolutionary epoch.

In the words of Lenin, "capitalism stifled, suppressed and killed a wealth of talent among the workers and working peasants. These talents perished under the oppression of want, poverty and the outrage of human dignity. It is our duty now to bring out these talents and put them to work."[3]

---

[1] Lenin, *Collected Works*, Vol. 25, p. 472.
[2] Ibid., Vol. 31, pp. 95-96.
[3] Ibid., Vol. 30, p. 73.

Lenin constantly refuted the slanderous bourgeois allegation that socialism levels down the people, depriving them of individuality. "The hangers-on and spongers on the bourgeoisie," he wrote in the article "How to Organise Competition", "described socialism as a uniform, routine, monotonous and drab barrack system." In actual fact, it is precisely socialism that creates the possibility of "drawing the majority of working people into a field of labour in which they can display their abilities, develop the capacities, and reveal those talents so abundant among the people whom capitalism crushed, suppressed and strangled in thousands and millions".[1]

In a socialist society a man's individual worth is revealed, supplemented and enriched. Collective experience and competition provide new stimuli. On the other hand, the growth of the powers and talents of each individual enriches the collective and multiplies its strength.

It is quite obvious that the problem of the people and the individual, the collective and the single personality is one of the most central and topical from the point of view of the real-life and philosophical content of literature. It contains many contradictions of both an objective and a subjective nature: as an example it is sufficient to cite Mayakovsky, who put this question in a number of his works. And it is his approach to the question, in the context of the Leninist heritage, that enables literary science to reveal the contribution made by Soviet literature to the solution of this problem in world literature.

The Leninist heritage gives us the most reliable criteria for defining the falsity both of the dogmatic conceptions that tend to dissolve and level down the personality within the collective, and of the bourgeois and revisionist attitudes that deny the mass character of man's spiritual growth and, either overtly or covertly, intentionally or involuntarily, extoll the individual as an expression of the spiritual make-up of the intellectual élite. In actual fact the growth of the individual and the growth of the collective are interdependent.

In this connection, Nadezhda Krupskaya's letter to Gorky of September 30, 1932, is of great interest. "People must grow in mind and heart. And on the basis of this growth of every individual within our conditions a new type of mighty

---

[1] Lenin, *Collected Works*, Vol. 26, p. 404.

socialist collective will finally take shape, in which 'I' and 'We' will merge into one indivisible whole. Such a collective may arise only on the basis of a profound ideological unity and an equally deep emotional proximity and mutual understanding.

"In this, art, especially literature, can play a quite exclusive role."[1]

The Leninist heritage indicates the surest paths of approach to socialist realist literature from the point of view of its role in training "a generation that is fully capable of building communism",[2] and in the education of the new man.

The theory of socialist realism, like the theory of literature and literary studies in general, must occupy an important position in the social sciences and solve the general problems by its own methods and on the basis of the material peculiar only to itself, thus enriching the study of the laws of the building of communism.

The theory of socialist realism has not yet given sufficient attention to the study of man in a socialist society, of the process of his historical change, and of all the difficulties and contradictions of his growth.

Socialist realist theory is yet to study the educative and transformatory role of artistic literature. And it is precisely in our day that the role of literature has acquired especial significance.

In realist art, and especially in art of socialist realism, comprehension of the world is inextricably bound up with its transformation. In reflecting reality and the life of the people the realist artist creates the sort of image that expresses the richness of reality together with a desire to improve it still more.

"The ideal of every epoch is that epoch purged of fortuity—a transformed vision of the present."[3] Herzen's words assist us to understand the indissoluble link between knowledge of reality and its transformation in art.

Russian revolutionary-democratic aesthetics, which played such an enormous role in the development of materialist aesthetic thought, could not yet fully work out this aspect of the problem of realist art. The problem of the active role of

---

[1] *Oktyabr*, 1941, No. 6, p. 25.
[2] Lenin, *Collected Works*, Vol. 29, p. 111.
[3] A. I. Herzen, *Collected Works in 30 Volumes*, Vol. 3, Academy of Sciences of the USSR, Moscow, 1954, p. 87 (Russ. ed.).

progressive art, indivisible from the principles of partisanship, was raised only by Marxist-Leninist aesthetics, and demands further creative development.

In this connection the following aphorism by Becher is noteworthy: "When justice, wisdom and peace achieve power, then the power of poetry will also increase." The poet elucidates further: "Poetry wielded power in the past, but in the new relationships, when the entire people has the opportunity to know its beauty and depth of thought, poetry in such a State is not only possessed of equal rights and useful to society, but will itself become the most important factor in the upbringing of man and will exert an influence on the formation of the State."[1]

1966

[1] *Inostrannaya literatura* (Foreign Literature), 1964, No. 5, p. 206.

Recent Progress Publications

ZELINSKY K. *Soviet Literature. Problems and People*

Korneli Zelinsky, a noted literary critic, was the personal friend of such outstanding Russian writers as Mayakovsky, Yesenin, Fedin, Paustovsky, Ehrenburg, Leonov, Fadeyev, A. Tolstoi, Serafimovich, Ostrovsky, Makarenko and Pasternak. He also spent much time with Maxim Gorky. During the Civil War (1918-22) K. Zelinsky was a war correspondent; in the thirties he became one of the leading theoreticians of the constructivists, a literary group; he attended all writers' congresses.

This book discusses the major stages in the development of Soviet literature and the problems it has faced. There is also a wealth of personal recollections about the various poets and writers, their views and impressions.

Cloth 13×20 cm 276 pp. Illustrated.

Lenin Prize Winners. Soviet Stars. Stage and Screen (Collection)

The whole world is familiar with these names: Alexander Dovzhenko, Roman Karmen, Sergei Bondarchuk, Grigory Chukhrai, Georgy Tovstonogov, Yuri Zavadsky, Grigory Kozintsev, Innokenty Smoktunovsky, Galina Ulanova and Maya Plisetskaya.

The recollections, articles and stories collected in this volume will further the readers' acquaintance with these celebrities, and tell them about the work on the films *Land, The Ballad of a Soldier, War and Peace, Hamlet*, and the stage productions of *The Masquerade* and *The Optimistic Tragedy*. Actors Maxim Shtraukh and Boris Smirnov, who have most successfully rendered the image of Lenin on the stage and the screen, speak of their work.

The book is illustrated with black-and-white and colour photographs.

Cloth 14×17 cm 372 pp.

Lenin Prize Winners. Soviet Stars. Soviet Fine Arts. (Collection)

The book will give the reader an idea of the development of Soviet sculpture and painting. The creative careers of such well-known artists as V. Favorsky, A. Deineka, P. Korin, B. Prorokov and others are traced. Meetings with Sergei Konenkov and Martiros Saryan are described by Ilya Ehrenburg, Marietta Shaginyan and Natalya Konchalovskaya.

Readers will find it interesting to learn all about the monuments to Pushkin in Leningrad (sculptor M. Anikushin), to Karl Marx (sculptor L. Kerbel) and Vladimir Mayakovsky (sculptor A. Kibalnikov) in Moscow, and the monument to the victims of nazism in the Lithuanian village of Pirciupis (sculptor G. Jokubonis).

The book is lavishly illustrated.

Cloth 14×17 cm 264 pp.